PROHIBITED IMMIGRANT

PROHIBITED IMMIGRANT

John Stonehouse
M.P.

50477

THE BODLEY HEAD

LONDON

To
young Africans, of all races,
and the hope of co-operation among them

© John Stonehouse 1960
Printed and bound in Great Britain for
THE BODLEY HEAD LTD
10 Earlham Street, London w.c.2
by C. Tinling & Company Ltd, Prescot
Set in Monotype Fournier
First published 1960

Preface

PART ONE of this book describes two years spent in Uganda and also my experiences in neighbouring Kenya during the Mau Mau period. Part Two relates to a visit to Africa I made as a Member of Parliament in February and March of 1959 when, in order to finance the trip, I also undertook to write articles and to prepare a report.

The countries of East and Central Africa are fascinating because they have been thrust, suddenly, into the twentieth century, with the tremendous pace of development that that implies; and also because it is there that Britain faces her biggest challenge, for she holds in trust the future of nearly 30,000,000 people—black, brown and white—who live in those territories.

I have been most grateful for early encouragement given to me by Fenner Brockway MP, and by W. P. Watkins of the International Co-operative Alliance, and by Ignatius Musazi of Uganda.

For my most recent journey to Africa I must express thanks to Canon John Collins and to Christian Action, who sponsored the trip to obtain the report on the position in Rhodesia and Nyasaland, and to *Reynolds News* who published my articles. I apologise to them both that I was unable to fulfil all my assignments and that the Nyasaland part of my itinerary had to be struck out.

To those who assisted me on my many journeys, who are too numerous to mention here but who appear in the text, I also express my sincere thanks. I am grateful to my publishers, The Bodley Head, who have been most helpful throughout.

Finally, my warmest thanks go to my wife Barbara for her unceasing encouragement and her work on the book itself; without her help it would never have been written.

John Stonehouse

Canonbury, London,
1st January, 1960

5

Permission to quote from the following books
is gratefully acknowledged:

H. Maclear Bate's *Report from the Rhodesias*
(Jarrolds); Jomo Kenyatta's *Facing Mount Kenya*
(Secker & Warburg); Sir Andrew Cohen's *Changing
Policy in British Africa* (Routledge & Kegan Paul);
C. T. Stoneham's *Out of Barbarism* (Museum
Press).

Contents

7

Illustrations

11. (*above*) An aerial view of Kariba Dam, nearing completion in   144
    June 1959
   (*below*) African workers at Kariba Dam
12. The author with his wife after arrival at London Airport from   145
    the Rhodesias, March 1959

Permission to use photographs is gratefully acknowledged to the following: Dr John McFie, Federal Information Department, Kenya Public Relations Office, Rhodesian Selection Trust, *The Times*, and Uganda Information Department

Glossary

Baganda—Uganda tribe from Buganda Province.

Banyoro—Uganda tribe from Bunyoro Province.

Batonka—tribe living on Southern Rhodesian side of the Zambezi.

Buganda—Province of Uganda.

Bunyoro—Province in North-West Uganda.

chai—tea.

duka—shop.

fundi—builder or carpenter.

Kiganda—descriptive of the Baganda.

Kwashiorkor—a severe form of malnutrition.

Luganda—vernacular of the Baganda.

Lukiko—local assembly of Buganda.

Mashona—tribe in Southern Rhodesia.

Matabele—tribe in Southern Rhodesia.

matoki—green bananas.

Muganda—a member of the Baganda tribe.

Munyoro—a member of the Banyoro tribe.

Sindebele—vernacular of the Matabele.

Sishona—vernacular of the Mashona.

Uhuru—"freedom" in Swahili

Valley Tonga—tribe living on Northern Rhodesian side of the Zambezi.

PART ONE

Africa at the LSE

In those days the wide Kingsway was dominated by the Royal Air Force and the Stoll Theatre. Now the great ugly Stoll is no more and the RAF has moved to bigger offices in Whitehall. Gone are the pretty recruiting posters we read on our way from the Holborn tube—'Join the RAF for adventure and see the world', 'Learn a trade', or 'An exciting career in the WAAF'. To those of us who had just been demobilised these appeals were a particular pleasure; they were a daily reminder of the life from which we had recently escaped.

My own war years in the RAF had been spent partly in Manchester's Heaton Park, waiting for posting; partly picking potatoes at Padmore; but mostly in the United States, learning to fly. When the atom bombs dropped on Japan and hostilities ceased pilot training continued only for those signing on for regular service. So, I transferred to Educational and Vocational Training (EVT for short) as a Flight Sergeant. It was an interesting job and gave me a chance to improve my own education.

There was a lot of catching up to be done. At school I had not been a success. But, when I left school at sixteen, my job in the Southampton Probation Department had given me a new outlook on life. For three years I helped to cope with the social problems of a dock town in wartime. As all the Probation Officers had been called up except for the Senior Officer, a kindly man called Mr Thurtle, I had to do my stint of interviewing estranged married couples and dealing with delinquents. The misery of some people's lives made me feel that social service was not enough; the wider environment needed to be changed by political action. Politics became real for me, and on visits to London I went to the House of Commons to breathe in the atmosphere.

Then came the RAF and, after pilot training, a correspondence course in economics. This helped to get me an ex-serviceman's grant to finish the degree. When I put on my demob suit and took the train for London a new chapter opened up for me.

Behind Kingsway is the little thoroughfare of Houghton Street, the home of the London School of Economics and Political Science; a meeting place for students from all over the globe. In those days they came in hundreds to sit at the feet of Professor Harold Laski or to pull at the sleeve of Professor Lionel Robbins. They came from America— many were ex-servicemen like ourselves—they came from Asia and from Africa. We could learn as much from the students as from the lecturers.

Harry Nkumbula, thickset, very forceful even in his undergraduate days, I met in the crowded hallway of LSE. He was one of the very few to come from Northern Rhodesia in the post-war years and he cut short his studies to return home to build the African National Congress. I met Babu Modi from Kenya, the son of a prosperous Indian business man. So often did he take the African point of view that eventually his father cut him off and he was left to finance his studies by betting on horses, for which he developed a true talent. David Lubogo's father was a cotton farmer in Busoga, Uganda, and was paying for him to take his bar examinations. Later David became a Member of the Legislative Council and leader of the United Congress Party.

Through the International Union of Socialist Youth I arranged groups to visit schools, conferences and camps in Europe. International politics fascinated me and in Hamburg we made the first post-war contact with German Social Democratic students. They were recovering from the ravages of war and were hungry spiritually as well as physically. During our long discussions they drank in the advice from Britain and Scandinavia. The Africans were amazed to find that the Germans were not in the least concerned with African problems, so wrapped up were they with their own. The Africans wanted colonialism to go; the Germans wanted bread and respectability. Both suffered from excessive obsession with their own problems and could not easily break out of the mould of self interest. They were a sharp contrast to the British and Scandinavians, most of whom were intensely interested in social and economic problems outside their own country and anxious to help.

To the Africans there was not much example of the value of civilisation in the mountains of rubble which represented Hamburg. That rubble was a monument to the crass stupidity of the educated Europeans, who spent more on destroying each other than on civilising Africa. Those meetings in Hamburg were held at a time of dramatic change in the two continents. Soon after that the German currency reform ushered in the period of the economic miracle and the beginning of Germany's climb back to a position of a major power.

And Africa? What of Africa? In those days the colonial students' psychology was based on a feeling of resentment and agitation against the white oppressor. Now that outlook is gradually dying. The Ghanaians, with their independence, have developed in its place a bouncing self-confidence; Nigerians too. But the transition is full of dangers. Those discussions in Hamburg and elsewhere convinced us that the peaceful future of mankind is dependent on constructive relationships between the advanced nations and the underprivileged. But could such relationships be established in the face of past history? Could something new and hopeful be built on old bitterness?

The Communists were very active among African students, as they knew the importance of Africa and wanted the new order in Africa to be based on their tenets. It was necessary for democratic socialists to find an alternative to colonialism which did not mean dictatorship and the suppression of the human personality. The violent actions which were advocated by Communists would bring no real lasting benefit. The Africans needed a positive share in a democratic society and not merely the substitution of one form of domination for another.

To socialists the problem of Africa was not only a question of conscience. The feeling that Britain and the colonial powers had ignored the Africans in the 'scramble for Africa' was certainly there. But tied up with the emotional reaction against this sort of imperialism was a constructive urge to harness the immense economic potentiality of Africa with socialist techniques of economic planning and to help lift living standards in the world generally. Here was a continent which was evolving out of feudalism and where it could be possible to avoid the worst excesses of capitalism. Perhaps the form of social democracy which has taken a century to develop in Britain and western Europe could be developed more quickly in Africa.

At LSE itself there were scores of meetings and discussions on these problems. One remains vividly in my mind. The speaker was Semukulu Mulumba, self-styled Emissary for Uganda who had been accused of organising the 1948 riots there. His speech was an attack on repressive British colonialism and also included bitter remarks about the young Kabaka of Buganda. The Communists present were pleased. He was their pet. He had appealed to the United Nations through Mr Andrei Gromyko, the Soviet representative, to discuss Uganda. This was the kind of contact man they wanted. But Semukulu was not without his attackers. Up jumped a very smartly dressed bespectacled African whom I had not previously seen. He was Sejjengo Josuah Zake, son of a

Chief whose home had been burned during the 1948 riots. He challenged some of Mulumba's statements and the rest of the meeting was broken up by an open verbal quarrel between them. This was an example of just how divided Africans can be among themselves.

The idea that the African problem is a simple question of black against white is shattered by such an experience. I learnt that within the African society itself there are constant manoeuvrings to protect one section or to limit the power of another, and I found later that this is particularly true of Uganda. As the cementing force of tribalism crumbles under the impact of outside influences, the conflict between different African interests can become intense. The African landlord class remains very powerful but other elements want to take over. The problem for the imperial power in Africa is not only to transfer responsibility to Africans—that is relatively easy—but to transfer power in such a way that the new system of government has the respect and consent of the governed and the capacity of lasting. It is then that the tremendous political energies of Africans can be harnessed to the task of conquering the more complex enemies of ignorance, poverty and disease. They cannot be easily defeated if independence results in successive violent political upheavals as different groups jockey for power. A democratic structure of one man one vote is most likely to have lasting success providing that through democratic institutions Africans can learn to protect themselves against black autocrats. What can we do to establish democracy before we leave Africa?

The problem intrigued me. I discussed it often with students who were the potential leaders. With Mohamed Yassein, now a top official in the Sudan Foreign Service; with Charles Njonjo of Kenya, Nkumbula of Rhodesia and Godfrey Binaisa, now with the United Congress Party, of Uganda. Most of them said, 'We want our independence first, we will worry about such problems after.'

All these distractions from purely academic work increased when I was elected Chairman of the LSE Labour Society. I was in close touch with Harold Laski, the Society's President, and he recommended the Twickenham Labour Party to adopt his twenty-three-year-old student as prospective parliamentary candidate. I suppose he thought that practical experience would be good for a political philosophy undergraduate. It was a severe shock when soon after the 1950 General Election Harold Laski died. The students loved him as a friend just as much as a teacher. He had a remarkable knack of stimulating the best in others. Many students left his seminars with a glow of purpose besides an academic training. Later some of those students became

Ministers in newly independent countries. It was said that every Government in the Commonwealth had its Laski scholar.

One day when I was reading Locke in the Library an American friend, George Shepherd, tapped me on the shoulder, obviously in a state of suppressed excitement. His parents had been missionaries in China and he had the diffident manner of a clergyman, perhaps inherited from them. He had a chance, he said, to do economic missionary work for the farmers' co-operatives in Uganda. Would I join him?

We went to the House of Commons to discuss the project with Fenner Brockway, newly elected MP for Eton & Slough and a specialist on Africa. It was agreed that as the Burton constituency had only recently adopted me as prospective candidate George Shepherd should go to Uganda alone and keep us in touch with developments.

Within a few months Mr Attlee had called another General Election, but this time he did not return to 10 Downing Street. The Conservatives won twenty-three seats, and at Burton, where their majority was halved, I missed a seat in the Commons by 733 votes.

After the election Burton invited me to remain candidate. It was a tempting offer, with the promise of a political career. I could also follow the example of fellow graduates and take up one or other of the professions. But every week I was receiving enthusiastic letters postmarked 'Kampala, Uganda'. My wife Barbara and I discussed the dilemma. In Uganda we could do a useful job at low pay; if we stayed in Britain our financial prospects would be healthy at last, after years of subsisting on students' grants and part-time work. In the end, however, we succumbed. The call of Africa was too great.

I

The Maiden Voyage

WE decided to go to Africa because expressing pious sympathy with the plight of Africans was not enough. To help them escape from conditions of poverty they needed deeds, not words. Deeds meant not only political speeches in Britian and the passing of resolutions, or even the voting of colonial welfare and development funds. Deeds meant working with Africans and giving an example on the spot. My main interest was still in a political career in Britain, but as I was reasonably young I could afford to give up two years and return to it later.

The invitation from Ignatius Musazi to assist the Federation of Uganda African Farmers seemed to be the opportunity I wanted, for it was an organisation of peasant people built up by their own efforts and undertaking a practical job. It was bringing the various tribes in Uganda together, and taking an interest in wider social objectives than purely commercial activities. It could be the basis for developing a positively successful and democratic Co-operative Movement.

After cables to Sir Andrew Cohen, the Governor, from Fenner Brockway, and a letter from the International Co-operative Alliance, we were eventually given permission to travel about twelve hours before the ship left.

The maiden voyage of the s.s. *Uganda* was the beginning of the adventure. Ahead lay Africa. Barbara and I queued, waiting our turn on the gangplank, drenched by a steady downpour of rain, and each carrying a baby daughter. Our luggage sat in puddles on the quay side, whilst the dockers went off for lunch. Incongruous in its enormous wooden case, stood the harp. The Shepherds had rushed off to Africa and in their haste had left much of their baggage behind. In a rash moment we had agreed to take it with us. Shirley Shepherd was a harpist and had an ambition to introduce this bit of culture into darkest Africa. It was our job to deliver the harp, her washing machine and sundry other American appliances. These gradually disappeared into the hold, 'Not wanted on Voyage', but the harp had not gone unnoticed. Strange as it may seem, another was in the hold. A passenger for Beira was emigrating harp-wise to Rhodesia and the thought of another harpist on the same ship excited her enthusiasm. Every day during the voyage Barbara was pursued by this woman, whose only conversation was harping!

Besides the red-headed musician there were many others on board with missions in Africa. Some missions were more reputable than others. The Church of England parson who had officiated in the diocese of the remote West Nile district of Uganda talked with fervour of returning home to his Africa. Emotionally and spiritually his life was bound up with Africans. The veterinarian, leaving rural Britain for the first time, was on his way to Tanganyika for a Government appointment; his mission, to save cattle from incipient disease. The beasts, he had been told, were being ruined by overstocking and the tsetse fly. A graduate in forestry was on his way to Mount Kenya, eager to apply his theoretical training. For him the problem of Africa was soil erosion. 'The desert of northern Kenya is steadily encroaching towards the south,' he said. 'Only the forests and the judicious planting of more trees can stop the process.' He had a misssion, and he believed in it.

The Personnel Officer of a tea company, no less than the others, thought he had a mission as well. His was to keep the Africans in their place, subservient to the Europeans. He used every opportunity to boast about it. Giving a course in Swahili for the newcomers to East Africa gave him a chance to indoctrinate fellow-passengers with his ideas. His opening gambit was:

'Don't hit an African yourself, always get another African to do it.'

Then he proceeded to give a little of the anthropological background of these people. 'After all,' he said, 'you must remember, these beggars have only been down from the trees for ten years.'

The one non-European in the class soon left after this. He was a mild-mannered Sikh, a builder from Nairobi. 'The Europeans had ideas of superiority in India once,' he said, 'and don't imagine that you can hold the Africans down. They won't be treated as inferior beings.'

There were, in fact, no Africans travelling on the ship, but relationships between the Europeans and the few Indians gradually worsened on the voyage. In the Bay of Biscay and the Mediterranean all was friendliness, but nearer Kenya colour prejudice was blatant.

At Port Said I made a quick visit ashore to set first foot in Africa. It was not very impressive; the bazaar was squalid, the beggars miserable, and the pimps nauseating. In every shop was a photograph of General

Neguib (few then knew Nasser). The 'gulli-gulli' man who came on board won universal admiration. He was a brilliant illusionist and combined his skill with flamboyant showmanship. Our small daughters stood enthralled as he produced day-old chicks out of his mouth, eggs from his ears, and made pound notes, wrapped round stones, disappear overboard, only to reappear seconds later in his right hand pocket. The passengers checked the numbers of the notes, found no flaws, and stood open-mouthed in amazement.

Then began the journey south through the Canal. British troops waved to us from the banks; the sun was hot and unbearable. The swimming pool was always crowded, and so was the bar where steaming fat men threw back their whiskies and gin-and-limes. The two ladies from Glasgow on a 'round Africa' cruise went on implacably playing bridge. Nothing could destroy their ardour for the game, not even the heat, and partners once caught were not released. Only the meal gong would allow them to escape.

Through the Red Sea it became even hotter. When the cool night came, the moon threw a soft light over the vessel purring through the still waters between Arabia and Africa. A Goanese band played on the deck. The experience is recommended for tired souls.

The next port was Aden. It is an incongruous place. A port of call set down in the middle of nowhere and yet a meeting place of worlds. We went ashore in a tender and discovered another reason for Aden's existence—business. The duty-free shops were crammed with hardware from Sheffield, knick-knacks from Birmingham, dolls and ceramics from Germany, carvings from India, carpets from Baghdad, silk ties from Italy, and cheap textiles from Hong Kong. Shopping needed skill and perseverance. The bargaining with the shopkeeper was recognised as part of the fun. The profusion of goods was impressive, but one wondered whether the trade justified the big stocks. Few of our fellow travellers were prosperous.

We were glad to get out of Aden; it was a smelly, untidy and inhospitable place. No rain ever fell, and that was a pity. It needed freshening up. In the back streets were hovels and the streets were strewn with wooden beds; some of them carried snoring Arabs and others ugly-looking goats, sitting in comfort. Chickens galore were running around screeching and scratching the hard sun-baked earth. Even the children were unable to endear Aden to us or convey a touch of the glamour which we had supposed to exist in the Middle East. With their grey half hidden little faces they looked pathetic and we could only think of their empty bellies and their miserable homes. Darkness fell as we left by the tender. In front of us the ship was resting in the water like an illuminated swan. We looked behind and saw the twinkling lights of Aden, and beyond, the ominous mysterious blackness of the Arabian peninsula.

We cast off during the still night, with only stars breaking the deep blackness. It was an eerie light. As the ship churned her way steadily southwards towards the Equator, I stood at the stern, looking at the wake thrown up by the propellers, alone with my thoughts. This was a much-travelled route. Vessels had passed this way hundreds of years before, carrying the trinkets of Arabia, and returning with slaves for the harems. Before that the Chinese too had taken this route, edging the coast of West Asia from the East. Traces of Chinese civilisation are still seen on the coast of Kenya. The Portuguese too had been this way, returning to Europe from their outposts in India. They had established forts and ports as stations on their route to the East. They never ventured far into the interior of what is now Kenya; it was too inhospitable. Further south they occupied Mozambique, nearly took over Nyasaland and had ambitions to occupy Central Africa between Mozambique and Angola. But in Kenya they built only Mombasa. It was towards Mombasa we were steaming. The sea was not so calm as the placid waters of the Red Sea. The number of passengers at meals became less and less. Only the children seemed to be immune. Geoffrey Lester, the parson, and I were left attending to five children under five between us as both our wives spent most of the remainder of the voyage in their bunks.

Barbara did get up on India Day. The European passengers were invited by the Indians to join them for a drink to celebrate India's independence. It was rather ironic to drink alcohol for a prohibition India, although that was not the reason that we were the only Europeans to turn up. We went up on deck to join in the ship's dance. It was so obvious that the attitude of the Europeans towards the darker-skinned passengers had appreciably worsened. The bonhomie of the Mediterranean had been replaced by cold indifference. One of the Indians asked Barbara to dance and she accepted. Within minutes I had a fresh-faced, smart middle-aged Englishman by my side.

'Is this your first trip to Africa?' he said genially.

'Yes,' I replied.

'Well, old boy, take my advice. Don't let your wife dance with a coloured chap. It's not the done thing in Africa.'

I was beginning to realise that prejudice is the accepted social code of whites in Africa.

During the last two days of the trip the passengers for Uganda and Kenya were full of animated anticipation. For those returning, Africa had an almost mystical fascination. They loved its primitiveness and its vast beauty. Or perhaps what attracted them was the escape from the prim orderliness and daily routine of Britain. To others, power attracted. The mastery over Africans, the sense of superiority, the automatic acceptance into a higher society and the feeling of having 'arrived' socially were all factors in the attractions of a country where 99 per cent of the population are automatically considered as 'inferiors' because of their colour.

There were the do-gooders and the well-wishers who had an ideal. For them the sense of purpose was greater than in the home country because the canvas was larger and the colours stark and real. The immensity of Africa is the challenge to such people and not only the vast distances of mile upon mile of scrub or jungle, but also the gap between tribal primitiveness and western technology, which cries out to be bridged. The yawning chasm is one of conscience as well as science and the link must be of culture as well as techniques.

There were the adventurers or the settlers. These see Africa as a challenge not so much of conscience or bridging the gap between black backwardness and white progress, but as a challenge to themselves, and a chance to carve out a personal career of achievement. They escape from what they consider to be a form-filling, molly-coddling Welfare State. They want to be a someone in an environment which allows a certain amount of swashbuckling pretence. The pioneer spirit appeals, but so does the feeling of an innate superiority over the millions around them, whom they consider inferior.

The civil servants, new and old, were mostly a kindly lot. These are men with a sense of vocation who see the colonial service both as a service and a career. Most of them are graduates with second or first class degrees, who could certainly do much better for themselves in commerce or industry. They are worth all the praise they get. It is a pity that some become tainted from contact with the settlers who have the false ideas of superiority and vested interests.

We arrived at Kilindini Harbour, Mombasa. Sprawled before us was an untidy mess of warehouses and cranes and railway lines criss-crossing the roads, along which were stacked old crates. Further away, near the warehouses, were bales of cotton and sisal, the wealth of the coastal plantations and of the deep interior. And below us were hundreds of black steaming bodies, pushing, dragging, lifting, yelling and whistling as they worked; some were lazing, even sleeping, amid all this cacophony of sound and activity. The jarring noises and the thick smell of sisal and coffee had a pungency for us after weeks at sea. Barbara and I watched as the harp arrived in Africa. The crane lifted it high above the ship and the dock. To our dismay the crate bumped to earth, splitting its sides. African dockers ran up to release the ropes of the crane, and knock the sides of the crate together with a few nails. They were naked except for tattered shorts. I turned to a passenger who lived in Kenya:

'How much do they earn?' I asked.

'About fifty shillings a month,' he said.

2

Nairobi on a Tightrope

No one meeting Mbiyu Koinange would imagine for one moment that this happy, hearty, tubby fellow could be described as the second-in-command of Mau Mau. The Kenya Government believe that he was and refused to allow him to return to Kenya from London where he has lived, in exile, for eight years. Although a graduate of Columbia University (before that he studied at the Ohio Wesleyan College) he does not have the manner of an intellectual. Nor does he have false pride although he is a leader of the Kikuyu and the son of an ex-Senior Chief. When he realised that he had to live in England he did not beg charity, nor did he seek a sinecure with some sympathiser. On his own initiative he took a job as a dairy hand with the London Co-operative Society at the Willesden depot. His fellow-workers elected him as their shop steward; and he was described as a model worker by the management. Few, if any, of his associates at work knew of his standing in Kenya.

I first met Mbiyu when he came to London in 1951 with his Luo friend and colleague Achieng Oneko, then General Secretary of the Kenya Africa Union. Their mission was to put before the British people the problem of land hunger among Africans in Kenya and to ask for the opening up of the White Highlands to African agriculture. I helped in their campaign and in another for the right of Seretse Khama to return to Bechuanaland. I was regularly cutting my lectures to speak at one meeting or another.

Seretse had been banished as Chief of the Bamangwato because he married a London typist, Ruth Williams—a marriage which made apartheid-minded whites in the Union of South Africa livid with rage.

Seretse was head and shoulders above Mbiyu in public performance, although he did not have the same academic background and was still struggling to get through his bar examinations. Mbiyu was a flabby and disjointed speaker, whilst Seretse, impressive in stature, had a brilliant faculty for interpretation and expression.

One night we took the train to Basingstoke, an ideal provincial town for evening meetings. (It is usually possible to guarantee a crowded town hall and a good lively audience and also to get a convenient train back to London.) Seretse was in fine form that night. His analysis of democracy and politics was as good as any political philosopher could muster. The audience was fascinated and entranced. When it came to my turn to make the appeal for the Seretse Khama Defence Fund the pound notes and cheques came up in healthy profusion, including a very generous donation from the local Tories.

The one thing common to both men was a warmth of personality and generosity of feeling. None of us who were associated with these campaigns knew them to express any bitterness against Europeans as such, although there had been much indignity and humiliation to provoke them. Mbiyu's chuckling and buoyant manner was sometimes a severe embarrassment. Once on the tube to Hounslow West, where I lived, he questioned me closely about flying in the RAF. He wanted all the technical aspects to be explained to him. I did my best with explanations about air pressure and curvature of the wings, with little diagrams on the backs of envelopes—but this was not enough for Mbiyu. He got up from his seat and to the consternation of the staid and solid nine-to-fivers of suburbia, he jumped up and down demonstrating what happened when an aircraft took off. I was glad when we got off the train.

At home the children were delighted when Mbiyu took his tea from Jane's dolls' tea-set. Another time Achieng Oneko was there too and Barbara gave him a long lecture about the rights of women. Achieng, who had spent months campaigning for political rights, did not agree with this aspect of equality because he thought women were meant to be servants. He was rather flabbergasted when asked to help with the washing up, but resigning himself to the British Way of Life, he found his way into the kitchen and with an apron tied round his waist he helped with the dishes and also learned how to make tea. Mbiyu was delighted.

When we decided to go out to Africa Mbiyu and Achieng were enthusiastic. Seretse, however, had his doubts. I met him in the cafeteria of the House of Commons one night when he was in a particularly dejected mood. He was quite disparaging when I told him about my prospective mission.

'They will either buy you out or ban you, if you haven't already given up in frustration.'

'They', of course, meant the Colonial Government or the settlers.

Achieng went back to Kenya, leaving Mbiyu in Britain to follow up the land campaign. I arranged to meet Achieng in Nairobi and Mbiyu gave me an introduction to his father, the ex-Senior Chief of the Kikuyu, who is known as Koinange Mbiyu.

* * * *

When we arrived in Nairobi after the hot overnight train journey from the coast, with two lively children, we did not know what or who to expect. Our contacts in the colony had only post-box addresses in Nairobi and the old Chief lived somewhere out in the Kikuyu Reserve. But they were more efficient than we had feared. The old Chief had contacted J. M. Desai, a stalwart of inter-racial co-operation, who was waiting at the station and whisked us off to the home of the Indian Commissioner. Apa Pant, an aristocrat turned democrat, was cutting his diplomatic teeth on the grisly bone of the Indian problem in East Africa.

At breakfast, whilst our two families sat at a long table eating corn flakes, we discussed the difficult problems of integrating the immigrant Indians into East African society. Apa Pant's job was of great importance to the Commonwealth, but the problem was not new. Lord Delamere, one of the first white settlers, had made a strong attack on Indian immigration fifty years earlier.

'What is the next stage in the history of a country which has once allowed Asiatic immigration to get a foothold?' he wrote. 'The small man having been pretty well squeezed out, planters and farmers employ Indian labour, and then comes the stage that Natal has reached today when the Asiatics are as numerous as the white colonists and when they own large areas of land and business all over the country. White colonists will not go to a country which is filled with Asiatics, and the Asiatics go on increasing.

'This shows again that it lies with the Imperial Government today to say whether Africa is to become a white daughter colony or an Asiatic granddaughter colony, to use an expression of Mr Winston Churchill's.'

Apa Pant was a tall, extremely handsome man in his early forties and had a charm and grace which soothed all those who came into contact with him. He was the same to all men, not changing his manner for Africans, nor, indeed, for those white settlers who were so nastily anti-Indian. There was a mystical, poetic air about him; speaking about an inter-racial school or any of his other plans, the words were quite beautiful in themselves.

He turned out to be as practical as he was poetic and quickly found us a house to borrow during the few days we were to spend in Nairobi.

Now we could look around and feel the pulse of the city. Four hundred miles from the coast and chosen as a capital not for any outstanding attributes but merely because it was a convenient rail head, Nairobi joins the plains to the hills. The city builders in 1901 had wallowed in mud along Government Road whenever the rains came, and the frogs in the nearby swamps kept the newcomers awake for days before they could get used to the hideous noise, and the lions prowled everywhere.

Half a century later the city had modern roads criss-crossing the town, fine hotels and shops (mostly Indian), and on the pavements a motley collection of humanity. There were the farmers from the Highlands with their bush hats and swagger; the prim housewives from the Nairobi suburbs looking hot and flustered in their smart frocks; a few Kikuyu women dressed in skins shuffling along and carrying loads on their backs; the Indian women in exotic saris, and the African ayahs in their cotton frocks. For their part the African men wore an assortment of European clothing, ranging from the smartest of suits to shabby khaki shorts and shirts. Many were bare-footed but we noticed that some wore home-made sandals cut from the rubber of discarded motor tyres.

We met Achieng again and went on a tour of the Burma Market, so named by the returning soldiers in 1945, where many of them had set up business with their gratuities. The stench, the dirt, the squalor, and the sheer gruesomeness of it was an affront to all the senses. Achieng said,

'We want you to see the worst, as well as the best.'

And, indeed, we saw the worst that day. A shack for a butcher's shop, where the meat was covered with thousands of gluttonous flies, making it look black instead of red. Then a bakery, where an assortment of insects made up a large part of the bread's ingredients. The buildings, if such they could be called, were made up of pieces of corrugated iron, old tin cans, cardboard packing cases, bits of old wood, and kept together by wooden supports and heavy stones on the roofing. In all it presented a picture of grotesque misery and ugliness; muck and filth abounded everywhere. Yet the market was crowded, packed with Africans, their black bodies sweating in the midday heat. Achieng shepherded us through the squalid slum which, he said, was the outward sign of his people's poverty and despair.

The Africans stared intently at us; we did not look like Government officers and they wondered why we were walking with their own leaders. Achieng was determined that something should be done about the Burma Market; he wanted the whole area to be rebuilt and the

African shop-keepers given proper tenancies. Unfortunately he has never been able to see what improvements have taken place. Within a few weeks of that day he had been arrested and soon after the Burma Market was burned down. Only the Mau Mau gunmen who lost ammunition in the fire regretted its passing.

I went to a meeting addressed by a visiting American negro and Mr Eliud Mathu, a very able African politician who lately, however, has got the reputation of being a stooge for the Government. This is a pity because his contribution has been a considerable one. The American was as cautious as he possibly could be, diplomatic and suave, but beneath it all was a bitterness of the black man who has suffered discrimination and senses a common bond with the Kenya blacks.

Apa Pant, in the chair, needed all his ingenuity to guide or deflect the questions of the eager voices in the audience. How those Africans needed an outlet! It was obvious that under the fuzzy black bobbing heads of the hundreds who had thronged this meeting there lay a passionate desire for emancipation. It was inchoate, but powerful.

It was dark inside the hall and when I walked into the street with a stream of excited, intense and eager Africans the sunlight blinded me. The stark reality of Kenya was very different from the hopes and aspirations expressed inside the hall.

This was only too evident when I took some African friends to meet the forestry officer I had known as a student at Queen Mary College and had met again on the ship. He was staying at the New Stanley Hotel waiting to move to the Forest Reserve on Mount Kenya. We had talked during the journey, and as he was interested in people beside trees we both thought it would be a good idea for him to meet some Nairobi Africans before travelling out to the back of beyond. I took my friends, all of them well dressed and quietly behaved, into the foyer of the New Stanley and asked the receptionist politely if she would ring through to the room of the forestry officer. She looked at me in horror.

'Are those men with you?' she said. 'They can't possibly come in here, they must leave immediately or I shall call the Manager.'

So, to avoid provoking a scene, we all left.

One of the few places where Africans and Europeans could meet was in the house of J. M. Desai. It was, and is, a centre of inter-racial friendship. As many influential discussions on the future of Kenya have taken place there as in the Legislative Council itself. At practically every mealtime in the Desai house there were visitors. If one of his friends expressed a wish to Desai to meet one of Kenya's personalities, rest assured he or she would be produced the next day at breakfast, lunch, tea or dinner.

Desai, with his clean-cut features and energetic, forceful manner, has established himself as a Kenya politician although the idea of office itself has never appealed to him. He is an inveterate talker and has been known to take visiting Members of Parliament to the Nairobi Game Park where, instead of letting them see the animals, he has kept talking for two hours at a stretch. But it is all to good effect, if you have the staying power. I must admit that around one o'clock in the morning, after a day of discussions, I have been guilty of nodding off. Not so Desai, who could keep going for another two hours if necessary and still be up bright as a lark next morning with yet more guests for breakfast. The whole family plays a part in the constant entertaining. Movie films taken by Desai and his sons are the favourite diversions, along with dancing by a beautiful and talented daughter. J. M. Desai is a businessman in Nairobi and has sacrificed a lot in his efforts to bridge the gap between the races. Many of his European business associates have made it difficult for him because of their prejudices.

Barbara, the children and I went out to the Kikuyu Reserve to meet the grand old man of Kikuyu politics, Koinange Mbiyu, then eighty-four years of age. The ex-Senior Chief had been a member of a deputation of the Kikuyu in the 1920s which visited Westminster. Later he helped to found the Kikuyu Central Association, which later gave birth to the Kenya African Union. His standing among the tribe has always been high, but his greatest success perhaps was when, in defiance of the authorities, he insisted on growing coffee, then reserved exclusively as a white farmers' crop.

African peasants were not allowed to grow it because the white settlers thought it would lead to disease from the African shambas spreading to their coffee estates. They also said that widespread stealing would result, and that the white farmers would find it difficult to get labour at cheap rates for picking the European crop. The white farmers also assumed that the quality of the African coffee would be low and that this would affect the good name of Kenya coffee in the world market. The old Chief said 'fiddlesticks' in Kikuyu and defied them all. His campaign was so successful that the regulations had to be changed and now thousands of Africans grow coffee in Kenya with yields as high as the European and the quality as good.

At eighty-four, the ex-Senior Chief was still an active politician. Shortly before we arrived he addressed a meeting of 30,000 people, including a few Europeans, at Gethunguri, and said:

'I can remember when the first Europeans came to Kenya. I worked alongside your father (pointing to a European) and you are my son. In the first World War you asked our young men to go to fight with the British against the Germans and many were killed. In the second World War you came again and asked us to fight against the Germans and the Italians and our young people were again ready to go.

'Now there are Italians and Germans in Kenya and they can live and own land in the Highlands from which we are barred, because they are white and we are black. What are we to think? I have known this country for eighty-four years. I have worked on it. I have never been able to find a piece of white land.'

We left Nairobi on the way to the Kikuyu Reserve, passing the neat houses of the Nairobi Europeans, pleasant little villas with pretty gardens where, with coaxing, anything would grow; with a nameplate at each entrance an illusion was given that everyone was a someone. Then, within minutes we were in the countryside, the tarmac road had become murram and the car was throwing up a trail of red dust. Some of the trees by the roadside looked more red than green, covered as they were by a permanent film of the pervasive dust. We were driven by John Koinange in a big comfortable Ford; on the way we passed Kikuyu girls hobbling along, carrying heavy loads of wood on their backs, water in debby cans on their heads, and sometimes a baby suckling at the breast as they went along. John Koinange told us that his people often had to walk miles in order to get water.

Barbara soon found herself in another argument about the rights of women. She protested that the men, sometimes smartly dressed, followed behind their over-burdened women carrying nothing but a walking stick, and she asked John Koinange how much Kikuyu politicians concerned themselves with the plight of these unfortunate women. Her concern startled John. By tribal custom the Kikuyu women are inferior and are regarded by many men as beasts of burden and labourers on the land. It was obvious that the Kikuyu politicians did not concern themselves much with the plight of their womenfolk.

The road along which we were travelling divided the Native Reserve from the White Highlands. On one side were neatly painted fences and a coffee plantation with trees properly pruned and standing to attention in rows of well ordered lines; on the other side of the road, patchy cultivation and land which looked overworked and was eroded in many places. We were gradually climbing up into the hills when we passed an incongruous sign dangling from a tree at the entrance to a European farm. It proclaimed that it was an 'Hotel for Dogs'. On the other side of the road were the Kikuyu scratching out a living from the soil, probably getting less out of life than the cosseted, pampered dogs across the road. But those dog kennels were something of a symbol to the settlers, a sign of bourgeois Surrey normality which they wanted to carve out for themselves in the middle of Africa.

We turned off towards the Koinange house and, narrowly missing several goats and a dozen screaming chickens, drew up outside it. The house was well built and white-washed with a tiled roof, but the windows were bare with iron bars and wooden shutters. Scattered around the compound were the mud huts, topped by their thatched roofs, where each of the old man's six wives had her own establishment. Smoke trickled through the roofs and goats and chickens chased in and out of the huts with naked toddlers; the women stood at their doors and studied us closely when we stepped out of the car. They seemed particularly interested to see our two blonde children.

The old man came out to meet us. He was a small wizened figure with keen, piercing eyes, his ears enormous, cut and extended according to the Kikuyu custom, reaching almost to his shoulders. He was dressed in a light-weight brown striped suit and wore a big smile. Through John, who acted as interpreter, he gave us a warm welcome and we responded, passing on the greetings of his son in Britain.

Lunch had been prepared by Koinange's youngest wife, assisted by an older wife's daughter who had been doing a domestic science course. We sat down to roast beef and Yorkshire pudding—everything possible had been done to make us feel at home! Then we put the children to bed in a small back room which had been specially prepared for them with sparkling white sheets and mosquito nets and sat and talked to Koinange and the Kikuyu leaders he had brought in for the afternoon. By tea-time we had a fairly good idea of what the Kenya African Union was trying to do.

Their main grievance was shortage of land, the first love of all peasants. Koinange took us out to see his farm. Here was none of the orderliness of an English farm; everything seemed to be growing in mixed abandon. We saw the famous coffee trees and Koinange's face lit up with a smile of triumph as he pointed them out to us. His expression changed as he looked a bit further afield and pointed out across the valley the land of the nearest white settler. We saw a solitary tree in the middle of a field, and shaking his fly switch he said:

'That land was Kikuyu. It was wrong of the settlers to say they never took the land from us; that very tree was well known as a tribal meeting place before the Europeans came.'

1. (*above*) The author with Uganda farmers, 1952

(*below*) The author's children on the balcony of Kitemerike House, Uganda, 1953

2. (*above*) Uganda: a family group

(*below*) A Baganda tea party

The tea was as English as the lunch, all specially prepared in our honour. Cream cakes from the Nairobi tea shops, milk for the children and cups of tea for us, poured from a large china tea pot. While we were having it the sounds of jazz drifted through the compound. Charles, another son of this ancient begetter of sons, had arrived in his own little house and was playing records of Benny Goodman and Fats Waller. To this day, 'My very good friend, the milkman says' always reminds me of the Koinange compound.

We said goodbye to the old man and, holding our hands in his leathery grasp, he said, 'Go well, friends.'

Down the winding road we were shown one of the Independent schools established by the KAU because there were too few mission schools for primary education, and also because there was a resentment against the dictates of the missionaries. The Kikuyu wanted their children to have the benefit of education but had tribal objections to doing away with the customs engrained by age-old tradition. One of these customs affected the status of women and the suggestion that it should be abandoned aroused bitter resentment among the menfolk. Very rightly the missions had made a stand on the practice of clitero-dectomy. One of the effects of the operation, so it is said, is that sexual intercourse for women is painful and that therefore they have no desire to have adulterous affairs outside of marriage. In his book, *Facing Mount Kenya*, Jomo Kenyatta describes the custom and defends it.

'The Gikuyu name for this custom of *rite de passage* from childhood to adulthood is *irua*, i.e. circumcision, or trimming the genital organs of both sexes. The dances and songs connected with the initiation ceremony are called *mambura*, i.e. rituals or divine services. It is important to note that the moral code of the tribe is bound up with this custom and that it symbolises the unification of the whole tribal organisation. This is the principal reason why *irua* plays such an important part in the life of the Gikuyu people.

'For years there has been much criticism and agitation against *irua* of girls by certain misinformed missionary societies in East Africa, who see only the surgical side of the *irua*, and, without investigating the psychological importance attached to this custom by the Gikuyu, these missionaries draw their conclusions that the *irua* of girls is nothing but a barbarous practice and, as such, should be abolished by law.

'On the other hand, the Gikuyu look upon these religious fanatics with great suspicion. The overwhelming majority of them believe that it is the secret aim of those who attack this centuries-old custom to

C

disintegrate their social order and thereby hasten their Europeanisation. The abolition of *irua* will destroy the tribal symbol which identifies the age-groups, and prevent the Gikuyu from perpetuating that spirit of collectivism and national solidarity which they have been able to maintain from time immemorial.'

By Mbiyu Koinange the Kikuyu people were given a choice between the mission schools which taught opposition to the practice of cliterodectomy and the independent schools which Mbiyu set up after his return from the United States and his graduation there, and which followed the teaching of Jomo Kenyatta. Some have said he set them up because when he returned from America he was offered a post in a Government school at half the rate paid to the previous teacher who was a European. I think he did it because he is a nationalist first and a teacher second.

On the way back to Nairobi we made a detour to call on Chief Njonjo, father of Charles, a student friend of mine in London. Although they were not expecting us, his charming wife and daughters, dressed in cool cotton print frocks, prepared an excellent salad supper in a summer house in the garden. Their house had a typical English style gate and fencing, unlike other African dwellings. As we ate they told us of their farming problems. The difficulty of finding water, for instance, when the bore-hole dried up, and the overcrowding on the land.

We sped back to Nairobi where Desai had gathered a large party to meet us. We saw films of his expeditions to the game parks and in between had earnest conversations with Indian businessmen and lawyers, an African barrister who had married an Irish nurse only a few weeks before, and some English commercial representatives who knew nothing about Kenya politics but tried hard to be in the swim. Peter Wright, however, was different. He was brilliant, and a sincere believer in democracy for Africans. In his spare time from his job as a master at a Nairobi school he advised the KAU on the lay-out of its policy documents. This greatly upset Jomo Kenyatta who did not like having a white man around, however sympathetic. He was not the only one to dislike Wright's activities. Within a few weeks Wright lost his job. He was politically unreliable in the eyes of the Kenya Government, who sacked and prohibited him. Wright then found his way to India where he became a college principal.

The next morning I went to see the secretary of the Kenya Indian Congress, Pio Pinto, who was always bubbling over with energy, ideas and comments flowing from him in an enthusiastic spate. His task, as he saw it, was to guide the Kenya Indian Congress towards a closer relationship with the Africans. It was not always an easy one as many of the Indian businessmen thought they would do better as pro-British. Pio was sympathetic to the African cause and felt that the future of Indians in East Africa could only be effective if they threw in their lot with the black masses.

'The white settlers have always tried to play us off against the blacks,' he said; 'they want to build up enmity between us so that they can keep the effective political power. We are not anti-white but we do feel that power and opportunity should be shared among all the races in this country.'

Pio had arranged a meeting with about twenty-five Africans, so that I could describe the growth of trade unions in Britain and suggest ways in which trade unions could possibly be developed in Kenya. I met them in the room of the Kenya Indian Congress, sitting around a committee table. I sat at one end with Pio and talked for about half an hour and then answered questions. There was great interest in the building up of trade unions on the western democratic pattern, but their chief concern was the difficulty of organising workers, who invariably had one foot in the town and one foot in the Reserves. The number of Africans who were really urbanised, in that they had their roots in the town, could be counted only in hundreds.

Easiest to organise were the transport workers, but by far the greatest need was among those who worked on plantations, where conditions of labour were appalling. Labourers on the European farms in the White Highlands also needed help but it was next to impossible to maintain contact with them. Their wages were as low as 20s. a month. These prospective trade union organisers thought that Kenya had many parallels with Britain in the 1840s, but their own situation was bedevilled by the fact that the strongest commercial class was of another race. The British working class did not have to struggle against racial discrimination.

A few months later I heard that almost all the men at that meeting had been detained under the Emergency Regulations as being members of Mau Mau. After a year Pio Pinto was also detained without trial, the only Asian in Kenya to be imprisoned for political activities during the Mau Mau period. The only one, to my knowledge, who was not arrested was Joseph Murumbi, who later became the General Secretary of the Kenya African Union and eventually turned up in Britain as an official at the Moroccan Embassy.

Although I had been in Africa for less than a week I had become deeply aware of a pervading sense of bitterness. The tension between the races was building up in Kenya, but nobody knew how it would be released. There were rumours of an underground organisation called Mau Mau, but no one would admit any knowledge of it. Some said that Mau Mau was a figment of the European imagination and that rumours were spread in order to undermine the growing strength of the Kenya African Union. It was an ugly atmosphere and we were glad we were stopping only a few days.

We had been told on the ship, 'They are soft with the natives in Uganda.' We hoped it meant tolerance and better relations between the races than in Kenya, where the cauldron was about to boil over.

3

Uganda and the Peasants' Rebellion

THAT part of Uganda which lies around the north and western side of the lake Victoria-Nyanza has been blessed by nature. Four thousand feet above sea level and cooled by the breezes blowing across the great lake, the climate is far from oppressive. The rainfall is plentiful, sometimes descending with a terrifying force, beating the ground into a quagmire in a matter of minutes. There is thick, lush green vegetation everywhere. It is in striking contrast to the arid plains of Kenya or the grassy slopes of the Highlands.

This richest part of Uganda has known a system of government for many generations. In 1862 when John Hanning Speke arrived he found an effective administration presided over by a king who was the thirty-fourth ruler in the royal line. Kabaka Mutesa I was a despot who ruled over his subjects with a cruel justice which many a German prince in the Middle Ages would have envied. He was proud of his forefathers and told the story with great relish of how the line was founded. One of his ancestors who was a great hunter from a distant land arrived in Buganda and promptly won the heart of the leading lady of the land by his prowess. She forthwith poisoned her husband to make way for this fine man and he was accepted by the people as their new king.

A more likely story is that a powerful tribe from the Horn of Africa invaded the rich lands by the lake, conquered the locals, intermarrying with them to increase the size and influence of the tribe. However it happened, the Baganda became the largest and most intelligent tribe in East Africa. A century ago the number owing allegiance to Mutesa I was over three million people.

Speke was impressed by the roads winding over the hills, the thatched mud houses and by the appearance of the people, standing erect and proud and clothed in bark cloth and skins. H. M. Stanley, the journalist explorer, called Mutesa an Emperor, recording that he could read and write in Arabic and could mobilise an army 150,000 strong.

After Stanley's famous appeal for missionaries in the *Daily Tele-*

graph in 1875 the churches began to take an interest. The result was a series of religious wars between the Africans supporting Protestants or Catholics or the Muslims, who had been the first to be converted by the Arabs trading with them long before the British arrived. The animosity between Protestants and Catholics continued for seventy years. Only recently have Africans of different churches found it possible to co-operate. But the atmosphere in places where there is a majority of Catholics or of Protestants is rather like Ireland. To this day the three senior Ministers of the Buganda Parliament (the Lukiko) have to be allocated according to religion, which means in effect that two are Protestant and one is Catholic. Recently the Catholics have chafed under this restriction and have organised a political party of their own, but that is another story, and must await another chapter.

Thanks to the efforts of an adventurer called Karl Peters Uganda nearly became a German colony, but Britain ceded Heligoland to placate the Germans. It was a fair exchange. About this time the British East Africa Company sent Captain Lugard to Buganda and he set about con-solidating Company rule. Britain became involved in paying a Grant-in-Aid for administering the territory. In 1898 this jumped from £89,000 to £339,000 and politicians in Britain became very worried about the expensive luxury of the colony. Sir Harry Johnston was sent out as a Special Commissioner with orders to economise and make Uganda pay for itself, look into the possibility of merging Uganda with the East African Protectorate (later called Kenya), and to put down the slave trade. A tall order for any man.

Through his negotiations an Agreement was signed in 1900 with Buganda, making it part of the British Protectorate and recognising the Kabaka as His Highness. Fifty-three years later quarrels over the inter-pretation of this Agreement caused a major political crisis.

Sir Harry not only made a political settlement with the Baganda, he also created a land system which established a landed aristocracy whose influence is still very considerable. Nearly half the land in Buganda was allocated as freehold plots to various Chiefs. In one way it was an astute move because it broke the power of the Kabaka, in whom the land had previously been vested, but it has made it vastly more difficult to create a democratic system half a century after. The Colonial Secre-tary today is still plagued by the vested interests of the land-owning class who use the Kabaka and the feudal court as a means of protecting their own economic privilege.

The quick-witted Baganda were used as administrators for other parts of Uganda and became the allies of the British in conquering

Bunyoro and places further north. That role has not been forgotten by the Baganda, nor by the other tribes. On the one hand the Baganda people believe that they are entitled to a special position within the country, whilst the others are deeply suspicious that, given the chance, Buganda would dominate them and in fact be worse colonists than the British. It is an understandable fear. The Baganda are a proud, conceited people and some of them would dearly love to set themselves up as dictators. Fortunately this is not true of all of them. Many have imbibed the ideas of equality and want to knit Uganda into a united country on a democratic basis, in which case the Baganda would be in a minority. They are only a fifth of the total population, but one of the obstacles to political progress is the fact that too many Baganda have illusions of grandeur and have been fed on so many stories of the might of the Kabakas that they believe they have a divine right to rule the rest of Uganda.

Those Baganda who have realised that the fragmentation of the country into tribal units would be a disaster have tried to douse the flames of tribalism by setting up nation-wide organisations to which anyone can belong. One of the first of these was the Uganda Farmers Union, which saw in co-operative marketing one of the ways to help African advancement.

Cotton, like mosquitoes in West Africa, saved Uganda from white settlers. It enabled the Protectorate to carry on without a Grant-in-Aid. There would have been a move to introduce settlers into Uganda if it had not shown signs of becoming self-supporting. Since the early 1900s the peasants have grown cotton as a cash crop; coffee followed in the 1920s. Coffee exports are now worth £20,000,000 and cotton £18,000,000 a year, and provide most of the money for capital development. Almost all of these crops are grown on small peasant plots; a perfect answer to those Jeremiahs who say that Africans will not work. By comparison Kenya exports only half that value of coffee and fifty times less cotton.

Although so important at the primary producing end the Africans had virtually no part in marketing the crop, or in processing it, until recently. The Indians were the middle men and they were not averse to petty swindling of the African peasant to add to their margins, and build up a fortune to be sent to India. Early attempts before the war to set up African farmers' co-operatives were not successful and Government officers gave no encouragement. They feared that if the farmers learned to co-operate it would not be long before they would be thinking in terms of taking political action as well.

After the war the returning soldiers, who had learnt a lot in the Abyssinia and Burma campaigns, were encouraged to form co-operative societies by the Labour Colonial Secretary. Many Africans, however, thought that these societies were merely tools of the Government and the smart European Co-operative Officers coming round to the villages in Land Rovers were looked upon as Government agents, rather like District Commissioners though perhaps not quite so important.

The model rules for Co-operative Societies seemed to be repressive to Africans, for they could not make decisions without the approval of the European officer. He had the power of veto. When the Uganda Farmers Union was set up as an independent African-organised body it won much support from Africans who saw the advantages of co-operation but did not want the strings which were attached to the Government scheme.

The founder and President of the organisation was the impressive, softly spoken ex-theological student, Ignatius Musazi. His ambition was to set up a Uganda-wide string of African co-operatives which would market crops, by-pass the Indian and European traders and give the Africans a stake in the development of their own country. He strongly resented the relegation of his fellow Africans to inferior status and believed that through the growth of co-operatives Africans would not only obtain a bigger say in the economic activities of the country but also acquire a stronger base from which to demand political advance.

Ignatius collected around him a body of supporters, most of them idealists like himself, but some were self-seeking adventurers, or squalid moneymakers, wanting to use the simple peasants' aspirations as a means of lining their own pockets. The inability of Ignatius to sum up his fellow Africans and his weakness for adulation were big pitfalls and he had no frank advisers to warn him against the hangers-on.

In 1949 the situation in Buganda became desperate. The African resentment against the Government become so powerful that the peasants responded to a call for a cotton boycott. Instead of selling their cotton they stored it up in their huts. Africans had long objected to the lack of African participation in the ginning industry and the ostentatious show of wealth on the part of the Indians who controlled it. When one of the Government officers tried to enforce the selling of the cotton —it was essential to Uganda's economy that it should be shipped overseas as it provided the main source of taxation and export income— tempers rose on both sides.

'To the Kabaka' was the call by the Africans. Their young king, who had recently returned from Cambridge University, would be the one to pass on their grievances to the Europeans. They collected in thousands outside the Kabaka's palace, known as the Lubiri, which is surrounded by a stockade of long woven reeds. Before 6 a.m. 500 people were already there and within an hour or so the numbers had grown to 4,000. The Kabaka refused to see a large group but agreed to see a delegation of eight. The crowd was then quite good-humoured and sent off the delegation with clapping and shouts of 'Bu', which is a nationalist cry. The delegates took with them a flag on which had been written the words 'Uganda asks for independence'. It bore the picture of a man dressed in bark cloth who had a rope tied round his throat. Another flag showed a picture of two women standing side by side with the words 'Kabaka give us liberty—our cotton may be ginned.'

The delegates took a petition headed 'Long Live the Kabaka. We ask for Freedom'. They wanted to gin their own cotton and to sell their own produce in foreign countries. The Kabaka gave only evasive replies to the delegation. They were not satisfied when he said that the question of representatives had been dealt with in the 1900 Agreement and that 'with regard to the ginning of cotton and selling of your produce direct I will go into the matter after having received the advice of my advisers'.

When the delegates returned to the people outside with this news the crowd became angry, but eventually they dispersed to their homes. On the next day, however, they congregated again and were harangued by one of the farmers' leaders. The police received instructions from the Governor to clear the crowd. They fought them with batons for nearly an hour before clearing them from the hill. Riots then took place around Kampala. Houses were burned, cars were overturned, mobs roamed the streets calling slogans. What had been a peaceful, contented country became wild and disorderly. The police and the military forces swept down on the rioters, 1,100 arrests were made and the two organisations alleged to be responsible for the riots and the arson were banned. These were the Uganda Farmers Union and the Bataka Party, a Buganda nationalist body.

All this time Ignatius Musazi, who was the President of the Farmers Union, was in England making political contacts. When he returned by air to Uganda he was immediately arrested and sent to a remote area of the country for detention. He was accused of being in league with Semukulu Mulumba, the one who had presented a petition to the United Nations through Mr Gromyko. The evidence that Mr Musazi was involved in the riots was not very convincing. Eventually, after appeals from Fenner Brockway MP and others, he was released from detention and allowed to resume his leadership of the farmers.

One of his first steps, after changing the name to the Federation of Uganda African Farmers (FUAF), was to send the invitation to London for someone to go out to Uganda to help organise the farmers' co-operatives. George Shepherd accepted and he had been in Uganda for nearly a year when I left to join him. After reading an impressive list of achievements and a 'Five-Year Plan For Progress' I was all set to join a thriving movement, so the disappointment with what I found was all the more intense.

*   *   *   *

The train pulled its way through the 6,000 and 7,000 feet Highlands of Kenya and descended to the swamps and fields of Uganda; it skirted the northern shores of Victoria-Nyanza, passed through Tororo and reached Jinja, the first big town after the 400-mile haul from Nairobi. This was our first view of the country where we were to spend two years. The people were different from the Kenyans, happier, better dressed, whole families of them crowding along the platform. Beggars were there too, but not so many as we had seen on the wayside stations through Kenya. Our companion on this part of the journey was Ecriver Kigundu, a tall handsome dome-headed Muganda we had known in London. He was a teacher on his way back to take up a post with the Education Department and his good humour kept us amused through the tedious hours when the train seemed intolerably slow and it became oppressively hot. We had a good chance too to learn our first Luganda. We practised the words, rolling them over our tongues until Kigundu could not stop himself laughing. But at least when we arrived in Kampala we were able to greet the welcoming party in their own language. When the train steamed out of Jinja we had a magnificent view of the Nile at the Ripon Falls, majestically starting its long journey to the Mediterranean.

Over the Nile we were on the last sixty-mile lap of our journey to Kampala; we travelled through sugar plantations, tea plantations, and then past mile upon mile of banana trees. Nestled among the banana shambas we could see the little mud huts, mostly with their thatched roofs, but some boasting corrugated iron. At the tiny stations crowds of children would appear as from nowhere, running up and down the length of the train shouting their greetings and holding out their hands to catch the pennies and sweets thrown from the windows.

Suddenly we were at Kampala station and, like most stations, it was on the dirtier side of the town in the so-called Industrial Area. The train came to a halt with a shudder and the engine let out a baleful noise, which sounded like a sigh of relief. On the platform to greet us was Ignatius Musazi, dressed in a loose-fitting bush jacket, slacks and suede shoes. He looked awfully smart against the other members of the reception committee. Peter Mary Joseph Sonko, a small, lean, hawk-eyed figure in a tattered brown pin-striped suit and battered old trilby was there. Eriza Bwete, a lanky awkward fellow, was also in European clothes, but several of the others were dressed in long white kanzus, embroidered around the neck rather in the Russian peasant fashion, and one wore a red fez. They all helped to shift the luggage, including the harp, into a blue Chevrolet truck. George Shepherd directed the operations. He was now a Doctor of Philosophy as his thesis had been accepted, but he looked a typical American on safari. His coloured nylon shirt was practical but his khaki topi helmet was unusual; it had long been abandoned by white men, though some Africans wore it as a symbol of authority.

We climbed into a green Ford Prefect and drove through the centre of the town, past an African shack suburb on the fringe, and up the hill towards the Lubiri, the scene of the riots three years before. Then we saw what was to be our home for twelve months. It was a double storied mud house with a massive corrugated iron roof, and looked from the distance rather like a mansion out of the American Deep South. It had an air of dignity, with its tree-lined drive, well-kept lawns and flower beds, and mauve and orange bougainvillaea around the door. Once inside, however, we found that the house was built on the simplest principles imaginable. Instead of the usual staircase and bannister, we had to climb steep wooden planks set into the wall to reach our flat on the top floor.

Its amenities were almost non-existent, although just before we arrived the Shepherds had succeeded in getting an electricity system installed—sufficient to run the lights. There was no water and no sanitation. For water we would have to rely on the rainfall caught in the gutters and collected in two great tubs. Later, in a period of drought, we had to pay the shamba-boy anything up to two shillings a debby can for filthy water drawn from a stream half a mile away which was used by the surrounding villagers to wash their babies and their clothes, mend bicycle tyre punctures and wash their cars. When we realised where the water came from we had to beg for it elsewhere.

But although the house lacked amenities it commanded a most magnificent view, situated as it was on top of Mengo, forming a triangle with the Kabaka's palace and his Prime Minister's house. It had been built by a Saza Chief whose widow, an aunt of the Kabaka's, now lived with her daughters in the flat below our own. From our balcony we could see five of the seven hills on which Kampala, like Rome, is built. On three of the hills stand the two Cathedrals (Roman and Protestant) and the Mosque, all perched like watching angels over the sprawling town below. They are a visible reminder of the rivalry of the three religions of Uganda. The shining white mosque, with its beautiful minarets, was by far the most picturesque as seen from the balcony. At night it would stand out in the moonlight like a dream floating in the sky.

As soon as we arrived I was ushered in to a committee meeting which was held in Musazi's flat on the ground floor. This was the first of many long and sometimes tedious meetings which I was to attend in an attempt to untangle the complications of African democracy. This meeting was devoted largely to greetings as each member of the executive took his turn to give a speech of welcome and thanks for my safe arrival.

We settled down happily enough in the bare rooms of our flat; we were not in the least disappointed as we had not expected much. Shirley Shepherd had supervised the cleaning and with a limited budget had it furnished with the simplest essentials.

It was Sunday when we arrived and the next day I went with George to Katwe, which was about three-quarters of a mile down the hill. It was a squalid slum, with shops and houses in a muddled disorder straddled across the main Kampala-Entebbe road. This was the route taken by the Governor when he left Government House at Entebbe to come to the commercial centre of Uganda and it must have shocked his conscience every time he passed through it. That probably explains why, when the Queen was due to make a visit to Kampala, plans were hastened for a fine new by-pass to avoid this smelly, insanitary place. It is rumoured that the Governor's plans for the cleaning up of Katwe by the building of a model village were vetoed by the landlord clique, which is so powerful in Buganda, because of the fantastic profits they were making from the rents received for hovels. We were told that as much as twenty shillings a week was paid for one room in a mud hut. It was a breeding place for vice and crime and it amazed me that it was never overrun by plague. Rubbish, dirty streams and filthy dogs were everywhere.

We reached the office of FUAF, situated right in the middle of Katwe. All around us was a cacophony of noise and a hustling of people. Nearby was a motor car repair works boasting the name of 'Garage', where a brawny man was knocking out the panels of a broken down car. Next to that an ancient was cutting up old tyres to be used for making sandals. Across the road a haggling group of Africans were buying bunches of matoki (green bananas). Next to the office was a tailor, and four of his young assistants were pedalling sewing machines like bicycles on the shop verandah, making shorts by the score and scattering pieces of khaki drill and thread around them. Next to that was an 'Hotel ne Chai' where people congregated to drink thick sweet tea and argue ceaselessly in high-pitched voices.

Within a few yards was the printing works of the vernacular *Uganda Post*, established by one of Uganda's most colourful characters, Joseph Kiwanuka. In 1949 he had been the editor of a newspaper owned by Europeans and was regarded as a dupe of the whites. The crowds had set upon him, beating him and leaving him for dead. When he recovered the Government gave him a certificate of loyalty and a big sum in cash compensation. With that Kiwanuka set up his own printing press and his own newspaper and became one of the most vociferous critics of Government policy.

The three rooms of FUAF were the headquarters of a national organisation which claimed 80,000 members. But they were as unlike offices as the 'Hotel ne Chai' down the road was unlike an hotel, for both were housed in mud huts, no bigger than garden sheds. I had never expected a palatial building, but I was surprised to find George and the directors of FUAF working in such ramshackle quarters. Alas, there was much more than this to appal me. I was soon to discover that the shabby, derelict buildings were more or less a reflection of the sloppy way in which FUAF's affairs were being run. As I walked into the office I noticed a group of about fifteen people, dressed in long white kanzus and obviously in from the country areas, sitting patiently outside. I found out later that they were waiting for the money for their crops which had been collected by FUAF the season before, but not yet paid for.

In one of the offices was Mr Lukabi, the earnest, hard-working treasurer, who was bent over his ledgers diligently making entries for hours every day. In the corner of his little room, lit only by the light coming through the door, was a safe and into that every day went the cash collected for the sale of crops and the money collected in the form of shares. Out of the safe every day came the out-of-pocket expenses of directors, the transport costs, and other payments. FUAF had a bank account but the bank was about two miles away in Kampala and payings-in were the exception rather than the rule. The cheque book was only an occasional device. Several of the directors had their own keys to the safe and were not averse to helping themselves to expenses. Harrassed Lukabi must have been at his wits' end trying to control these transactions.

Notwithstanding his other duties Lukabi was also responsible for paying all the Shepherds' own household expenses. George had thought that it would be rather immoral to take a salary from FUAF and he preferred them to pay for all his family's basic requirements. Shirley, when making a visit to the chemist or anywhere else, would have to collect an itemised receipt and go to the offices to have each item checked by Lukabi for reimbursement. Sometimes there were questions and Shirley was hard put to it to explain the necessity for her purchases. Difficulties were created because Lukabi with his African background could not understand that an American wife and mother, born and brought up in Florida, and with a University degree, had a far longer list of necessities than himself. Two different worlds were brought together in that miserable little office in Katwe and the chasm between them was very difficult to bridge. Apparently, Barbara and I were expected to adjust ourselves to the same system of accountancy.

I had been told that FUAF had 80,000 fully paid up shareholders in all parts of Uganda. But the capital equipment consisted of only three trucks, the dilapidated offices and two or three godowns in the course of construction. There was precious little to show for all the work put into the organisation by the directors, (grandiloquently called 'Directors-at-Large'), and George Shepherd himself. There were the big ledgers in Lukabi's office. There were, indeed, bales of cotton which had been sold and bags of coffee too—but promises were the biggest stock in trade. The members had an incredible faith in those promises although, so far, not much of material value had been achieved. They believed their leaders and thought that the millenium was just around the corner.

4

Safari to Bugerere

WITHIN a short time it became apparent that the fine organisation which I had been led to expect was nothing more than a figment of hope. There was certainly great public support for Musazi and for his semi-political objectives, but it was also clear that every day the Federation went on trading by its inefficient methods it would be running itself further and further into debt to the peasant farmers whose interests it was supposed to be serving.

Most of the operations were plainly uneconomic; farmers' cotton, for instance, was collected over such a wide area that the cost of running trucks more than outweighed the tiny margin earned in disposing of the crops. In some districts agreements had been made with Indian ginnery owners to gin FUAF's cotton. In theory this gave the Africans a share in the processing of their own crop, but in practice they were getting nothing out of it as the costs more than absorbed the profit. It was even doubtful whether the farmers would receive a fair price for their crop at the end of the season.

I faced an agonising decision; whether to leave Uganda and return immediately to Britain, or to stay on to help guide the organisation into effective co-operative work for the benefit of the peasants. My inclinations were towards staying as it seemed so defeatist and wasteful to travel all the way to Uganda at the expense of the Africans and then to leave them in the lurch. But on the other hand, could they afford to support another white family?

Barbara and I discussed the position and decided that she should try to obtain a job as a secretary with one of the European companies so that in the event of our staying I should need only a small salary from FUAF. But in any event we would not have the expenses nonsense with the justifying of every voucher to Mr Lukabi—a quite ludicrous system when compared to the squandering of hundreds of shillings every day on wasteful transport.

When I was invited to Uganda my particular task was supposed to have been assisting the development of genuine co-operatives. FUAF was pressing for a change in Co-operative Law so that Africans could control the policies of their own societies, whilst the auditing and supervising of accounts continued to be done by the Government. Once that legal change came there could be no obstacle to the gradual conversion of FUAF groups into genuine co-operative societies, under proper supervision. There seemed a useful job still to be done; so I stayed.

It was agreed to tighten up the financial operations and to concentrate the marketing activities on profitable ventures. The grandiose schemes for ginning cotton all over the Protectorate, which were beyond the administrative capacity of FUAF and could only lead to its early downfall, were to be dropped. These decisions could not be implemented immediately because ginning contracts had already been signed and other marketing schemes arranged. It was clear that if these schemes were stopped suddenly the directors would be quite capable of attempting to carry them on without advice. To bring the schemes gradually to an end was our wisest course, cutting out, where we could, the waste. An ambitious scheme for curing coffee was also shelved, although Dr Shepherd had set high hopes on it, and the expensive machinery had to be written off as a dead loss.

Dr Shepherd was a likeable enough man although difficult to work with. To him Africans could do no wrong and any action of an African was always judged from the best possible of motives. FUAF members called him 'The Good Shepherd' and I am quite sure that is how he saw his role; he did not realise that among his flock were black sheep, tricksters, and crooks, who came into this mushroom organisation to make a quick penny for themselves. He worked under the assumption that behind a black face there was always an underprivileged human being who by sheer definition could never be dishonest. His early up-bringing by missionary parents in China had given him a philosophical outlook and whenever one tried to tie him down to the practical realities of a situation he had a far-away look in his deep blue eyes. He is one of the most honest and sincere men I have known; he was prepared to sacrifice everything for Africans. I have never known him think in terms of an immoral act, but his very virtue was a trap as he could not see through patent dishonesty. His faith in the Africans could not be dimmed—even when a burglar broke into his flat one night, stealing all his trousers and leaving him the jackets.

The Co-operative Department, staffed by civil servants who knew little about the principles of the Co-operative Movement, was disliked

3. (*above*) The remote Karamojong people

(*below*) A Muganda mother collects milk powder at the clinic

KENYA BEEF
„ MUTTON
„ CHICKENS
SIRLOIN
OX TAIL
SHIN & SOUP MEA
PORK
MEAT FOR BOYS
„ „ DOGS
„ „ CATS
PIG HEADS

4. (*right*) A sign in a meat shop in
Kampala, Uganda

(*below*) A political rally in Uganda

by the farmers. The officious way in which the Department was run made the farmers regard the co-operative societies as mere branches of the Government rather than as democratic organisations which reflected African aspirations. George Shepherd's most useful proposals were those for changes in the law, for they had considerable influence on Sir Andrew Cohen, the Governor, who realised the need for more effective African control and introduced helpful amendments soon after we arrived.

I took on the job of supervising the maize marketing in Bugerere, which had been organised before my arrival. Five godowns had been built in that area, so I was told, and local branches of FUAF were to collect the maize crop at these storage centres for transportation to the markets. The plans seemed satisfactory, but on my first safari from Kampala into Bugerere I soon realised that paper plans were not enough.

I left Kampala early one morning with one of the 'Directors-at-Large'. The first fifty miles were easy, travelling along the tarmac road which led to Jinja. Every few miles were clusters of huts with a duka or two. This was the road to the great Owen Falls Hydro-Electric Scheme and we passed several trucks of the construction companies driven by jaunty Africans. The villages were thronged with people and even away from the villages along this main road there always seemed to be people walking purposefully along; a string of immigrant workers from the Belgian trust territory of Ruanda Urundi, for instance, who had probably walked 200 miles in their search for work in the plantations and the farms of Buganda. Trudging along for the endless miles with their few belongings on their heads, they were sustained by the hope that they would acquire enough money in a few years to walk home again, buy a wife, and settle down on a patch of homeland. During the previous year no fewer than 86,000 of these workers had entered Uganda from the south-west, or nearly 10 per cent of the total population of Buganda.

We passed school children walking to school—sometimes as far as ten miles, barefooted. Most of them were in tattered clothes, although always very clean, their smiling happy faces and bouncing energy disguising the fact that usually they go all day without food. The women were a joy to see—so unlike the unhappy Kikuyu women we had seen on the outskirts of Nairobi. They sauntered regally along the roadside, handsome and erect. If they had a load to carry—a bunch of matoki, a can of water, or a bundle of washing—it would be balanced on the tops of their heads with the aid of a banana leaf crown. The

D

young babies clung to their mothers' backs, supported by brightly coloured slings of cloth, a practice often criticised by doctors as it causes so many babies to have bandy legs.

We passed hundreds of bicyclists, for there are more bicycles in Uganda per head of population than in any other country, except Holland and Denmark. To possess corrugated iron sheets, for a decent roof, and a bicycle, are the chief ambitions of all men. Raleigh is the most popular make because it was first on the scene, but also through a most skilful advertising poster showing a man riding nonchalantly away from a lion. Posters for other makes have simply not made the grade and one of them, showing an elephant riding a bicycle, positively discouraged sales! Customers knew, after all, that an elephant had no chance of riding a bicycle and any one who was silly enough to publish an advertisement like that could not, the Africans concluded, be very good at making bicycles. They laughed their heads off and saved up their money to buy Raleighs at three times the price.

A whole family was balanced on one bicycle, husband riding and holding a toddler on the handlebars, and a buxom wife sitting on the carrier at the back. It was quite a feat for her to balance there at all, but she managed a load on her head as well. With such performance no wonder the Africans looked upon the bicycle as a necessity. During the selling seasons it also became a transport vehicle, carrying sacks of cotton or coffee to market.

Along the main road all was a feast of activity with people working in the fields, children running in and out of their huts, women-folk cooking over open fires outside their homes, or people just walking. When we drove into the Mabira Forest the contrast was as great as if we had gone into a church. People did not wander into the forest along the road which cut between the tall primeval trees like a canyon, nor could they walk between the trees as the undergrowth was inpenetrable. The forest shut out the bright sunlight and the sombre silence was broken only by the occasional screeching of monkeys. Perhaps the drop in temperature made one shudder slightly on entering the forest, or perhaps it was the solemn mystery of the tall trees looming over the tiny lonely vehicle like the arches of some gothic cathedral. It seemed almost sacrilege to tear a tarmac road right through the heart of the Mabira.

Beyond the forest, where the country had been tamed, were miles of sugar plantations on land which had been alienated before the Agreement of 1900. Uganda Africans have every reason to be grateful for the Agreements signed by the native rulers of the early 1900s as they have prevented an influx of European settlers and the concomitant problems of race relations.

After the sugar, the tea. We drove past rolling hillsides of evenly-spaced neat bushes of tea, before turning off on to a dirt track winding its way through a coffee plantation. There we saw the barracks of rondavel aluminium huts put up for the immigrant workers from Ruanda Urundi. When the truck went by them they stood and stared, with arms akimbo. Most were dressed only in sacks and they were the most miserable-looking men I have ever seen, except for prisoners.

Out of the coffee plantation the road wandered into a maze of peasant shambas, each indistinguishable from the next. To the un-initiated the countryside appeared to be only half tamed. Tall elephant grass grew along the roadside to a height of ten feet or more, obscuring vision. But behind, the land was carefully allocated between families with little marker trees which showed the boundaries. Everywhere bananas grew in rich profusion, their green leaves spreading a shade and softening the harsh light. To the Baganda it is the tree of life, providing the staple food and all manner of other uses. Even at death it has its uses. I once saw the funeral of a two-year-old boy whose body was wrapped in the enormous banana leaves and buried beneath a nearby tree.

The track along which we travelled was no more than six feet wide in some places, but it was the only link for the people of a whole county with the towns, the markets and civilisation. This part of the journey took two long hours. My interest in the unfolding scene of banana trees, elephant grass, and an occasional clearing with a thatched hut standing in serene isolation, was interrupted by many a jerk as the truck wheels hit a deep rut in the track. We reached a trading centre which was nothing more than a desultory string of corrugated iron shacks where Indian middlemen sat to weigh and buy coffee beans. Further along were a few tiny shops, selling soap, sugar, salt, candles, piece-goods, and, inevitably, Aspro and Pepsi-Cola. Pepsi-Cola was my best friend; for this warm sickly-sweet liquid was usually the only safe drink in such remote places.

From this village another even narrower track took us to the home of the local farmers' chairman. In his modest little house, standing in a clearing just off the track, I sat at the rough-hewn wooden table. From the back room he brought forth his nervous, smiling, buxom wife who went on her knees and clasped her hands together in greeting before going back to the out-house to make tea. We discussed the maize buying programme and I heard to my horror that the godowns had not yet been fully built, although the sheets for the roof had been delivered and were lying on the sites for a month. This was at the beginning of the maize season and the crop was expected to be a bumper one, but the Indian buyers were known to be in the area ready to snap up the crop at favourable prices.

It was urgent to get at least two godowns completed so that the African farmers could have some share in the marketing. After tea and conversation we went to the godown sites to meet the local farmers. The first building was less than half constructed; the frame of wattle standing bare to the skies like a surrealist's dream, while the mud base only stood a foot high. Already the grass was growing over the heap of corrugated iron sheets meant for the roof. A few farmers had collected on the site, their gleaming white teeth smiling a greeting, each giving a slight bow and proffering moist palms for friendly handshakes. I gave a little speech, as expected, explaining to them the importance of building the godown before any maize could be collected and they agreed to start work the next day.

After another meeting with FUAF members we returned to the local chairman's house just before nightfall. Darkness descends suddenly in Africa and by the middle of the evening everything is black. Then the night noises—a chorus of crickets and other insects—begin. Preparations for the evening meal were already under way; the wife and her sister were preparing chicken and matoki. Whilst we sat in the tiny living-room and talked, the wife brought a bowl of water round with a clean towel for each of us to wash in turn. In the corner of the room was a hissing Tilly lamp, perched on a pedestal, throwing a soft light over us. The walls and floor were plain mud, nailed on one wall was an Indian trader's calendar in English and Gujerati, and on the floor a straw mat.

The food was brought in steaming hot and set in the middle of the table. The women did not join us. I had the luxury of a spoon, but the others plunged their hands into the steaming mould of matoki and put a handful on their plates, covering it with the slightly curried chicken and sauce which they picked up in the same way. My first mouthful of matoki was difficult to swallow, and I made a mental note to avoid it in future. It was like a gluey, sticky mush of mashed swedes, but much harder to chew. It formed a ball in my mouth and I felt like choking. The chicken saved me; it was eatable and very tasty. Slices of ripe pineapple from the garden outside were served next, tasting sweet and refreshing after the matoki. Coffee followed, thick and sweet.

After the meal I wandered outside to breathe the night air, cool and caressing. The stars threw an eerie light on the banana trees surrounding the house. It was a far cry from Europe and the towns for Europeans a hundred miles away. And yet I was not lonely. I felt a comradeship with my African hosts which transcended the different worlds from which we had come. Theirs was the age-old struggle against poverty and ignorance, although only recently had the Africans begun to wage the battle with any enthusiasm. How much better, I thought, that they should win it as self-reliant individuals, able to reap the rewards and help in guiding the course of events. How much better that they should have a share in shaping their own destiny rather than be buffeted by primitive forces or cosseted by western paternalism throughout their lives.

The night air turned a little chilly and I turned inside the house; the padlock on the door was then locked behind me. I felt as though we were in the middle of nowhere, but this rural community was relatively thickly populated and thieves were not unknown. There were bars on the windows as well as shutters.

My little room had a wooden bed, clean white sheets, clean blanket and a mosquito net. I hung my clothes on a long nail knocked in the mud wall and climbed into bed, tucking the mosquito net around me.

I was woken in the morning by the sound of children playing at the back of the house. I opened the shutter and the bright African sun streamed in. A bowl of hot water was placed outside my door and I washed and shaved, balancing it on a small wooden table. Breakfast consisted of slices of white bread and butter, a boiled egg and sweet tea.

We started up the truck and drove down to the warehouse sites where we started the farmers on building the walls of mud. They worked willingly once given direction; it was a genuine communal effort, no one was paid, and the godowns when completed would belong to all. It was vitally necessary to get them built before the maize season began.

According to the arrangements which had already been made by Dr Shepherd, cash advances for the maize brought in by the farmers would be given on delivery at the godowns and at the end of the season a general share-out of surpluses would take place. I discussed these arrangements with the local officials and showed them how to use tally books, and told them gunny bags would be delivered.

The return journey to Kampala gave me ample time and opportunity for thought over this venture. I was far from satisfied that all the details of this maize operation could be controlled, but how else could Africans learn responsibility unless they exercised it? To them it was a lesson in self-help and practical organisation. I fervently hoped it would succeed—so much depended on it.

5

A Fabian in Government House

MANY Europeans in Kampala were suspicious about the activities of Dr George Shepherd and myself. There was an immediate suspicion of any Europeans who deviated from the well-worn path of the English in the tropics. One was expected to fit into a convenient niche—to be a civil servant, living in a Government bungalow, or a businessman representing British firms, with, usually, a wider circle of contacts. For commercial reasons the businessmen must meet and mix with members of the Indian community, as they are the people who keep the wheels of trade turning and no commercial representative could succeed without them. Apart from the missionaries, nearly all Europeans fall into these two categories, and Africans have precious little contact with them.

The exceptional English are at Makerere College, a tower of higher learning on the hill just outside Kampala, where Africans and Europeans mix in a self-conscious, artificial sort of way. I was shocked, however, when I met one of my old associates at LSE who had taken up a job at Makerere as a lecturer. When I asked him whether he ever invited his African students into his house he said:

'Good gracious, man, you can't ask these people into your home.'

'Why not?'

'They aren't civilised. They haven't even reached School Certificate standard.'

'But aren't they supposed to get London University degrees from Makerere?'

'Yes, but don't you know that their marks are up-graded? Some of my so-called University students don't have the education of an ordinary Grammar School boy.' This remark was not, of course, fair to the many students who could more than hold their own at British Universities.

The real oasis on Makerere Hill was the East African Institute of Social Research where anthropologists from America and Britain fore-gathered under the direction of Dr Audrey Richards. Here was a very industrious team with no side, no snobbery, and no colour prejudice. Apart from these few and some teachers and missionaries, there was very little genuine friendship between Europeans and Africans. It was no wonder that the white community regarded those of us in the Kitemerike House as oddities; we not only mixed with Africans, we lived in an African house, with African families.

But the suspicion went deeper even than this, as we were to find out within a few days of our arrival. We were being watched. The Special Branch had instructions to keep an eye on us as it was suspected that only Communists would work for an African organisation. The fact that I had been a Labour candidate in two Parliamentary elections probably added to their suspicions of me; for to be a member of the Labour Party is only next to being a Communist, according to many who should know better. For about three weeks I was followed by plain clothes police.

The Civil Service was also curious about my activities and one official was deputed to make friends with us to find out more about us. He became quite a friend of the family and would pop in for the odd cup of tea or a drink. One day, in conversation, he let slip a remark which revealed the extent to which I had been kept under surveillance. The week before I had spoken to a group of Africans in Katwe at what I thought was a private meeting about the development of trade unions —a very popular subject among Africans, who thought it would solve a lot of their problems if they could have a Trade Union Congress. The official mentioned to Barbara that he had been interested to see the report of my meeting in the newspaper—but, in fact, there had been no report in the newspaper. He had read about my meeting in a Special Branch report and his obvious embarrassment confirmed our suspicions.

The police interest in me ended after a curious incident. Barbara and I set off one night to drive the twenty miles to Entebbe and were followed by the Special Branch. We never at any time attempted to shake off the cars following us as we had nothing whatever to hide. After driving through Entebbe the policeman must have been perplexed as he stopped his car when we turned into the drive of Government House and the sentry at the gateway, obviously expecting us, came to attention and smartly slapped his rifle in salute. We were not followed any more after that.

Before I left England I had been a member of a Children's Committee of the London County Council and a close colleague who was a member of the Council gave me an introduction to Sir Andrew and

Lady Helen Cohen; that evening we were taking up their invitation to dinner. It was the first of many meetings we had with them. They were delightful people. It was a sign of Sir Andrew's liberalism that he had invited us to Government House although we were clearly not in the No. 1 Social Register. Our fellow guests at the dinner were Dr and Mrs Sharp of Sharp's Island, where they ran a leper colony.

The contrast of this dinner with the one I had eaten in the bush in a mud house the week before could hardly have been more dramatic. This time, elegant china under silver candelabra with servants unobtrusively removing dishes; the glow of the highly polished table, and superb food. It was a gracious atmosphere. After the meal we sipped coffee and talked about music and lepers.

Sir Andrew Cohen, then about forty-five, was one of the few who have risen in the Colonial Office to become a Governor without going through all the stages of service in the colonies themselves. He did his service in Whitehall. Many colonial civil servants resented him for this: they also resented his reputed socialism. He might indeed be called a Fabian, but never a socialist. Perhaps he would be best described as a progressive liberal. He gave one the impression of a restless elephant, hardly ever able to sit down in one place for more than ten minutes at a time, so anxious was he to stride up and down the room. Both he and his wife looked handsome, dramatic figures. Sir Andrew did not need the plumed helmet of the Governor and Commander-in-Chief to make him look impressive as his stature and bearing were impressive in themselves.

At the Colonial Office he had been the midwife of Gold Coast independence, and his energy was behind Central African Federation. He is obviously sincere, generous and completely without colour prejudice; but his logical intellectualism can be his undoing. Within a year of his arrival in Uganda it was.

He set about his social reforms for Uganda with such a fervour that he antagonised the plodding paternalistic senior ranks of Colonial administrators. They hated the Fabian in Government House and over their whiskies in the clubs were not afraid to say so. His own closest associates in Entebbe once demonstrated very clearly how they disliked Cohen's liberalism. The number one club in the Government town of Entebbe was reserved for whites only. Cohen in his ceaseless campaign against the colour bar wanted to wipe it out in Entebbe as everywhere else, and he proposed to the club, which was largely composed of Government officers, that the colour bar should go. They turned down the request by an overwhelming majority.

Cohen's biggest handicap was his inability to make contact with the junior officers in the field, many of whom were not tainted by the arrogant paternalism of the older colonial servants and were genuinely sympathetic to the reforms Cohen had in mind. The Governor knew that Uganda was on its way to self-government, that it was only a question of time, and he wanted to establish a framework of Africanisation which would hold the state together after the British protecting power had withdrawn. He wanted local government to become established in the rural areas as well as in the towns; he wanted African traders to have a bigger part in the economy and for commerce to be no longer dominated by an alien race; he wanted the development of co-operatives and realised the necessity for them to be genuinely democratic. In all these things he would have found an interest for these ideals among many of the junior officers, but in between the Governor and the younger men recently recruited from Universities, who still had a sense of mission towards Africa, were the hidebound men of years of service with a vested interest in keeping the status quo, frightened of change and frightened of African advancement. Faced with African demands, their first reaction was to reach for a mental baton. These were the men who were heads of departments, who, under the pyramidal system of colonial government, supervised the men in the field and blocked contact between the 'Fabian' Governor and these younger officials, who could have expressed his ideals in practical terms had they been given half the chance.

In spite of the system, Cohen achieved much, but he was struggling against it all the time. He knew that some of his departmental heads were perfectly hopeless. They were in their late forties or early fifties and had been in the colonial service most of their lives, spending no time in Britain except on leave, and as a result had been cut off from the stream of liberal thought which recognised the emergence of backward nations and the dignity of the human individual, however backward. Some of these men were arrogant snobs; perhaps they were not always aware of it, but they had been created by the system. Cohen once said that before he could get rid of a head of department he had to wait for the man's retirement or find another colony to which he could be promoted. Such posts were not always available, or the other colony would not have the transfer, and the men stayed on, serving their time until they were pensioned off.

There were some notable exceptions. The head of the Commerce Department was a go-ahead official and not afraid of new ideas. The Administrator General too, although he had a difficult task, could never be included in the category of hidebound time-servers. Cohen was engaged in a constant struggle against the prejudices of many of the leading officials; but it was not a head-on campaign. They were able to sabotage many of his efforts by sheer bureaucracy. The most difficult of all of them was the Attorney General who often gave disastrous advice to the Governor, bringing Sir Andrew perilously near to undermining all his own good work.

A new Governor, however energetic, cannot sweep the slate entirely clean. The 'In-betweens' are there when he arrives, and they are there when he leaves. Only an upheaval on the part of the Africans in the colony and pressure from the Secretary of State in London can give a Governor enough leverage to open a way for liberal policies to be implemented. Sir Andrew's tremendous energy, coupled with the unrest in the Protectorate which was so vividly manifested at the 1949 riots, enabled quite a lot to be achieved. Action was also taken in London. Before Labour lost the election in 1951 Mr James Griffiths, the Colonial Secretary, announced that some cotton ginneries in Uganda would be compulsorily acquired and handed over to co-operative societies. When the Tories won the election they did not reverse this policy and Cohen was able to implement it. The first ginnery was handed over in January 1953 to the Uganda Growers Co-operative Union. It opened up a new era for co-operative society participation in the economy of the country.

Before the war the cotton industry had been chaotic. Indian ginnery owners were rushing hundreds of miles around the countryside, criss-crossing their tracks to collect what cotton they could to keep their gins going. During the war the industry was rationalised but the limiting of cotton buying to particular districts gave the ginneries a monopoly value. The system of guaranteed returns protected the profits of the ginnery owners and some very out-of-date plants made fortunes for their owners. When these ginneries were taken over for allocation to co-operative unions the compensation paid was far greater even than the replacement cost. The owners had a capital gain which far exceeded their expectations. The burden on the co-operative societies and their peasant members was correspondingly great. The big cash compensations were a sop to the opponents of African advancement and could have crippled the young Co-operative Unions.

Another experiment in tepid socialism which has proved enormously successful was the setting up of the Uganda Development Corporation. Cohen was particularly pleased with this creation as it primed the pump of economic development. The reputed 'Fabian' at Government House had the co-operation of a genuine fully-paid-up member in the chairmanship of the Uganda Development Corporation (known as the UDC). Mr J. T. Simpson became Chairman in March 1952 and within five months he announced that a great scheme for development of mineral deposits was to be undertaken at Sukulu in Eastern Uganda, which could be the beginning of an iron and steel industry. The project was undertaken in partnership with private companies. Cement in Tororo was another of these ambitious projects which has paid off handsomely—it provided the bulk of cement for the great Owen Falls Dam. The greatest of all has been the copper mines in the Mountains of the Moon at Kilembe, developed in conjunction with a Canadian company, Frobishers. This mining development stimulated the extension of the railway from Kampala almost to the Belgian Congo frontier. The railway track had to be built through hitherto completely untouched country and one of the sidelines of the engineers was big game shooting, but when they hawked the meat in the nearest villages they soon found themselves in trouble as they had no licences.

One of Cohen's proudest moments was the opening of the line, for it added another 2,000,000 pounds sterling a year to Uganda's exports in copper and other goods. A vast area was opened up for economic development and thousands of Africans were given access to markets and a link with the outside world.

The UDC has demonstrated how effective state action can be. It has made a profit. It has provided the initiative and stimulus for the development of Uganda's latent resources. But in a backward economy there are many worthwhile projects which are not profitable in the short term and the UDC has not been able to pursue them. Capital for this sort of development needs to be made available through SUNFED, (Special United Nations Fund for Economic Development) and other world agencies, which should be able to rely on at least one per cent of the national incomes of the industrial countries.

Cohen saw the importance of education and soon after his arrival in Uganda appointed a committee to investigate African education under the chairmanship of Bernard de Bunsen, the tall, devoted principal of Makerere College. He also accepted nearly all its recommendations and allocated £8,000,000 for the development of facilities such as teachers' training and the expansion of secondary school courses. The de Bunsen committee reported that only 320 girls in the whole Protectorate attended senior secondary schools and none in the Northern and Western provinces. They also revealed shocking neglect in the towns. In Kampala, where there were at least 2,300 children of school age, not a single school had been established for African children within the municipal boundaries.

Not much could be done about the religious stumbling blocks in the educational system. Most of the schools are run by missions and the Government cannot afford State schools to be set up in their place. The religious rivalry means that innocent little African children born into a Roman Catholic or Protestant home often have to walk miles to the nearest school of their denomination when there is, metaphorically speaking, another one just around the corner.

It was left to three African members of Mr de Bunsen's committee, in a minority report, to make some bitter comments about the distribution of schools. They said that a young child of six to ten years of age should never be required to walk six to eight miles to school. 'It is physical torture to him and yet most of our schools today serve an area of this size.'

An integrated inter-denominational system of education would be too much to hope for with so much competition for converts, but it would certainly save many sore young feet if children could attend the nearest school. African children are born little Protestants, little Muslims, little Catholics, or little pagans—just as children of an earlier generation were 'little Li-ber-als' in England. But the distinctions are not a little unreal in the context of Africa.

One must not be too hard on the missionaries, however, for they have achieved more for the Africans than any other Europeans. They gave them the first hospitals, schools and the friendly contact with whites which is vastly important if the confident African is to emerge. The Roman Catholic teachers from Italy with their technical skills and hard physical work, shoulder to shoulder with their African pupils, have shown an example which it would be difficult to better.

Sir Andrew's over-riding ambition was to give the Africans a genuine share in central Government as well as control in local affairs. The number of African representatives in the Legislative Council was increased to fourteen, equal numerically to the combined European and Asian representatives of seven in each case. He could not break away from the policy of giving representation to the minority groups, although Uganda was recognised as an African country. The Europeans were not settlers; most of the 6,000 had only a temporary interest in the Protectorate as they were mostly on Colonial Service or commercial short term contracts and had never demanded political rights.

Under the Governor's proposals the African District Councils were responsible for choosing their representatives; but the Buganda Lukiko refused to nominate members of the Legislative Council as they wanted no truck with a centralised Government which did not recognise the demands for Buganda separation. This obstruction to the attempts to knit the country into a unitary state still plagues relationships between the Baganda and the Government and it was one of the reasons for the Kabaka trouble.

Sir Andrew was a man of tremendous energy; he was also very approachable. I had several long talks with him about African advancement in marketing co-operatives and trade. He was desperately anxious to give the Africans a real stake in the country's economy but he realised that this was a difficult job because of the stranglehold of the Indian traders.

Unlike most of his immediate subordinates Cohen wanted to come to terms with the political movements, but he realised that paternal encouragement by a Governor would be the best way of destroying the democratic surge of support for these movements. I often suspected that the heavy hand he used with political leaders was probably employed a little wryly in the sure knowledge that a knock from the Governor would be the best way to boost their prestige and morale. His subtlety was only equalled by that of Twining, the ebullient Governor of Tanganyika.

Everyone who saw Cohen had his stories to tell about him. Two favourites concerned the quantities of biscuits he munched during an interview, striding up and down his room at Government House, and the 'Wimbledon' necks he gave those who attempted to interview him. He saw dozens of reporters who loved his lack of protocol and his frank, blunt manner of speaking. Cohen could not see his junior officers as freely as he liked (the heads of departments saw to that), but he had frequent contacts with members of the research staff of the East African Institute of Social Research. He picked their brains and took account of their ideas in a most unorthodox manner. All most uncolonial service.

He looked really magnificent in the Governor's regalia. I remember him best during the Coronation celebrations at Entebbe when his massive, dominating figure stood out among the many thousands of people thronging the lakeside to watch the canoe races. He paraded in full dress uniform, helmet, sword and all. It was terribly hot that day, but he carried it off brilliantly. Peter Ustinov could not have done better.

6

Through the Colour Bar to Juba

ARRANGEMENTS had already been made for another European to join
our team and although it was far from certain that the organisation
could afford to maintain him it was too late to have him sent back. He
was Dr Roger Cazziol, an Italian graduate in agricultural science who
was anxious to gain practical experience in the tropics as well as express
his idealistic interest in the underprivileged. At least he was a bachelor,
and his needs would not be so great.

During my first few weeks in Uganda we had a frantic message from
Roger who was stranded in the Sudan. He had broken his journey in
Cairo to take a look at cotton developments there and had been unable
to get an aircraft right through to Entebbe, so he did the journey in
stages to Khartoum and then a hop to Juba. But his visa was running
out and the authorities were threatening to send him back to Italy unless
he could get to Uganda within the week. There were no aircraft from
Juba and no other means of transportation unless we could send a car
to pick him up.

Willing to have a shot at anything I set out to rescue him, but the
only car available for the purpose was a 1948 Ford Prefect which was
on its last legs after the hard beating it had taken on Uganda roads. I
took with me on the 350-mile journey one of the FUAF drivers,
Kabega, and we decided to do the trip in two days.

Only a few miles out of Kampala the road towards the north-west
changed from tarmac to a corrugated, rutted, murram track and the
car had a tremendous shaking. It seemed to be worse at thirty miles an
hour than at sixty, so we drove it steadily at the highest speed, rushing
by the tiny shambas and through a number of huge swamps where the
papyrus stretched like a sea on either side of the road.

We were soon out of the green of Buganda and the ground became
drier; in place of the banana tree farms we saw mostly bush and only an
occasional house. The tiny townships we were passing became less
impressive. The most they could boast were one or two Indian-run

dukas, small shops with the proprietor sitting outside on his haunches, chewing betel-nut and waiting for a customer and the beginning of the cotton season. The stock of these Indian shops was remarkably good considering the poor custom they had; a profusion of cloth, shirts, patent medicines, tea, condensed milk, bottles of boiled sweets—and, of course, Pepsi-Cola. In one of these tiny villages one of these shops also had a petrol pump, so we stopped, filled the tank, checked the tyres, topped the radiator with water, drank a Pepsi-Cola each, bought a tin of Kenya cheese and a loaf of bread, and went on, anxious to eat up the miles between us and Lira, where we were intending to spend the night.

Kabega and I got on very well together. He was a jovial fellow, with a wife and four children at home. I taught him a little more English and in exchange he told me Kiganda stories. He had been a driver for the farmers' movement for some years but at heart he was a nationalist working for political freedom for Africans. Considering that he could not read English very well and that the vernacular newspapers were not of a very high standard, he was remarkably well informed. He said he was very angry about what was going on in Kenya and said it was disgraceful that 'those Kikuyu had to suffer from land hunger'.

'Why, look here,' he said, 'there's plenty of room in Uganda,' and he looked over the great expanse of land on either side of the road, covered in places by bush, which could probably be made quite productive with irrigation and bore-holes. 'There's plenty of land in parts of Uganda. There's no reason why some of them should not come here,' he said.

'Wouldn't you Baganda resent it if the Kikuyu came over here and settled on your land?'

'No, why should we, they are our African brothers, and this land is not being used,' he said.

As we drove on through the hot afternoon I wondered how many of Kabega's fellow Baganda would agree with him on this. Probably fewer than he imagined.

We were then in Bunyoro, a strangely desolate country. The Banyoro held out longest against the British and fought against occupation after the Agreements had been signed with the other tribes. They have never quite recovered from their defeat and they hate the Baganda who were the allies of the British in the conquest. They claim that a big slice of Bunyoro land was added to Buganda as a reward for that co-operation with the alien British. Bunyoro is the only county in Uganda where the death rate exceeds the birth rate and as the population steadily dwindles the people themselves become more apathetic. They were not like the happy Baganda we had passed only a few hours before.

Hoima, the quiet capital of Bunyoro, had a number of Indian shops, Government headquarters, and that was all. It was strangely devoid of Africans.

The Banyoro are superstitious people and their pet aversion is fish, although many live near Lake Albert where fish abound. They could certainly have benefited from the protein diet; their listlessness was no doubt due to diet deficiency. One of my Muganda assistants once told me that he was attacked with a stream of abuse by a Munyoro. The gist of it was 'Why don't you go back to Buganda, you damned fish eater?' This was one of the most insulting things a Munyoro could say about another man. To eat fish is worse than adultery to many of them.

The little Prefect was doing well. No punctures so far and that was good going on Uganda roads. This was tsetse-infected area and peasants were not encouraged to settle even if they had wanted to do so. Along this stretch for sixty miles we did not see another vehicle and for half the way the trees and bushes were thick and ominous. On the road we occasionally saw the droppings of elephants and once heard trumpeting nearby. We were not anxious to meet an elephant at close quarters, for that could be quite dangerous. These huge beasts are almost untameable and are much bigger and wilder than their Indian counterparts. An African elephant has been known to crush a car with one blow, and we did not want the feat to be repeated.

At Atura we crossed the Nile which at that point is called the Victoria Nile, flowing as it does from Lake Victoria towards Lake Albert. At Atura it is wide and sluggish, papyrus grows thickly on both sides, and lurking among the reeds are treacherous crocodiles. No one would dare to swim the river here. Crocodiles are generally found in most of the rivers and lakes and because of this most Africans cannot learn to swim. Fifty miles further on the river changes from this sluggish flow to a torrent of cascading water, pressed through a narrow crevice and dropping down fifty feet at the Murchison Falls.

Surprisingly enough the ferry, which was in fact nothing more than a long raft, was full of people. Ours was the only car, but there were many bicycles. Where all the Africans came from I do not know, but they were all going somewhere, carrying bundles of millet or clothing and an occasional hoe. We had long been out of banana country, and there were none of the familiar stacks of matoki to be seen. Most of the men were in the usual shirts and shorts, and the women were mostly

E

bare from the waist up, their long flapping skirts hanging from their waists to their ankles.

On the raft was an old African who had apparently served in the Army as a Sergeant. He wore a suit with holes in the sleeves, a battered trilby hat, brown shoes, and carried a long knobbly stick. When he saw a European he climbed over the ferry towards me and gave me a shattering salute. As he came to attention the ferry literally shuddered. His shoes sparkled, sure evidence that the British Army had had a great impact on one man in Uganda. When we left the ferry I saw him marching off reverently carrying his stick like a rifle, as proud as could be that he had shown due respect for a superior officer!

The other passengers melted away along their different roads and we coaxed the Prefect off the shaky raft, murmuring prayers under our breath that it would not slip back into the murky waters of the Nile. The acceleration of the car could easily shake the ferry away from the river bank. Some of the ferry minders were all too nonchalant about their job and did not bother whether the car went into the water or not.

We stayed that night with Yokasofati Engur, the young leader of the farmers in the Lango district. The Lango people are tall, and Engur is no exception. Nilotics in origin, they are a good-looking tribe. Engur himself is an intelligent, sincere man. We sat up half the night talking about Uganda's problems and I was left under no shadow of doubt that there was more to Uganda than Buganda. The Lango resented the attention given to Buganda which was, after all, only one province of their country. Engur talked not only about political advance, he thought that a great deal could be done in his own area by irrigation and agricultural improvements. 'We will never be able to make much progress while the people are so suspicious of the Government officers', he said. 'Once we have our independence the people will trust the Government.'

Before leaving Engur's little house he told me that I was the first white man to stay with an African family in Lango. Europeans would normally stay in the Rest House or camp out. I thanked him for his hospitality and said I hoped it would not be the last time, for his home was very comfortable, although cramped, and the clean bed and mosquito net were much to be preferred to camping out in the open.

We started early, after a breakfast of porridge which Engur had bought specially. As we drove through Lira the Indian duka-wallas were opening up their shops; on the outskirts we passed a group of children trudging on their way to school. They waved a friendly greeting and we threw them some sweets which they pounced on with shouts and laughter, picking up their treasure and excitedly clapping their hands with glee.

The last town before Juba was Gulu, the chief town of Acholi, where the best soldiers come from. It is here that forces for the Kenya African Rifles were recruited in great numbers. Many of the Acholi also become policemen and askaris all over Uganda. Like the Lango they are very tall.

At an Indian petrol pump we filled up with Shell. We had about 150 miles to go to Juba. We did not have a spare tank, nor even a spare can of petrol, but looking at the map we felt sure there would be another petrol pump at Nimule, just over the border in the Sudan. Nimule is marked on most maps and I have even seen it on globes and certainly BOAC have it on their inter-continental route maps. I had seen its name so often that I felt sure there would be something of a little town there. It was the frontier town and a landing place for the steamers which every few weeks steamed up the Albert Nile from Butiaba, the port on Lake Albert.

Confident with our full tank, we set forth on the last lap of our journey to Juba. Now we were running into really barren country. The houses were very few and far between and we did not see any with corrugated iron sheets. They were the traditional African rondavel type of thatched houses, with a semi-circle of similar but smaller out-buildings. For about ten miles we did not see a single house and the countryside had the emptiness and desolation which I had always imagined Africa to have. For mile after mile the scene remained un-changed. Only one other vehicle was on the road.

Suddenly, as it seemed, we reached the frontier barrier, with a pole across the road and a warning to all vehicles to stop. The Immigration officer, an Indian who was lethargic about his job, confirmed my im-pression that our car was the first to stop there for several days. He usually dealt with about two cars a week. I told him we were going to put up his average as we would be returning the next day. He checked the authorisation in my passport that I was OK to leave Uganda—he had no need to check Kabega as Africans, except for the Kenya Kikuyu, were allowed to wander freely over frontiers in this part of Africa.

The barrier was lifted and we drove the car through into no-man's-land which stretched for another ten miles. The road had at one time been tarmac and although pitted with large holes was a better road than the one on which we had been travelling from Lira. Once it had been in very good condition but for years it had not been repaired. Later I discovered that this stretch of the road had been built during the war to carry East African troops through to the Middle East theatre of campaign.

When we reached the Sudan outpost it took about ten minutes to find the frontier guard, who turned out to be a jovial black-faced soldier with a smart khaki uniform which had been so over-pressed that it glistened in the sun. His badge sparkled, a sure sign of spit and polish, and this was noteworthy, for he probably never saw an officer more often than once a fortnight. He welcomed us to the Sudan and was much friendlier than the Indian ten miles back.

We had about eighty miles to go to Juba and our next stop—or so we thought—would be Nimule. So confident were we that there would be a petrol pump at Nimule that we did not bother to question the soldier about it. We drove on, following a rough sign post towards the port.

The road ended at a landing stage on the Nile, and all we could see there was a corrugated iron godown and two thatched huts; not a single human being was in sight. This was all that existed of a place with an honoured position on the maps of the world. I remembered Evelyn Waugh's novel, *Scoop*, about newspaper correspondents who made up place names to lend distinction to their despatches. Never had I thought that I would be a victim of somebody's caprice in giving a town's name to a landing stage in the middle of Africa.

We had to press on, for although we did not have enough petrol to reach Juba, it was just as far to go back to Gulu. But before setting out we sat by the Nile munching bread and cheese and building up courage. The road, fortunately, was running down a gradual escarpment and in places we were able to free-wheel, conserving the fuel. We were certainly no danger to other road users as we did not see another person for hours. In one place we disturbed a whole family of jabbering baboons who scampered off the roadway at high speed. We had a magnificent view of the surrounding country. To the east, across the Rift Valley, we looked towards Ethiopia. To the west, we could see the forests of the Belgian Congo, and occasionally ahead we could catch glimpses of the White Nile wending its way northwards. In the distance were herds of wild game, too far away to identify. Kabega was as excited as I; he had never seen terrain like this, nor such wild game.

Descending towards the plain of the south Sudan it became hotter than ever, as we were losing the benefit of the plateau of Uganda. The land was desolate, with hardly any vegetation. We had about sixty miles to go and the petrol gauge showed less than half a gallon. I joked with Kabega, but we were both a little apprehensive. It would be none too pleasant to spend the night in this wild country. But a few miles further on we came across the first signs of human life. As if from nowhere a group of boys between six and eight years old were playing a sort of hopscotch in the middle of the road. They were quite naked, very thin, but happily shouting before our car surprised them. The boys stared at us, but it was pointless trying to talk to them because they could never understand us, and even if Kabega or I had been able to speak their vernacular there was probably no word which could convey 'petrol pump' to these wild little boys of the plain.

It was another ten miles before we saw another person—an old woman hobbling along the road with a load of twigs on her back. When she heard the car she rushed into the bush out of sight. It was no good asking her. How much further could we go? There seemed to be a nothingness around us. Obviously somewhere were dwellings but we had seen no sign of them, nor were there any signs of cultivation. The scrub, however, was getting thicker and we had hopes that before long we would reach some signs of habitation and, maybe, even a petrol pump.

There were two villages marked on our map and one of them was called Fagar, which should have been around this spot. But after Nimule we had no confidence left in maps. Just when we were about to give up all hope, with the petrol gauge needle showing well below zero, we saw 200 yards ahead a sight which could well have been a mirage—a truck, standing stationary on the side of the road.

Kabega and I looked at each other questioningly, both hoping that it would not turn out to be derelict. In Buganda we were quite accustomed to passing derelict trucks which had been abandoned by the roadway after an accident. This was the first vehicle we had seen for a hundred miles and we were relieved as we chugged towards it to see three men unloading what appeared to be rolls of wire fencing. Whatever that fencing was needed for in the middle of nowhere I have never been able to understand. The men, obviously from Juba, were not at all surprised to see us and we exchanged greetings. The driver, who had been sleeping in the cabin, looked dreamily at us; it was extremely hot and he could hardly be blamed for sleeping.

Kabega managed to make himself understood, though what variation of East African Swahili or vernacular Sudanese he used I have no idea, and they willingly syphoned off two gallons of petrol from their own tank and fed it into our own. Kabega had been carrying a big bunch of yellow bananas in the boot for the journey and these he handed over in exchange for the petrol. The Sudanese thought they had got the better of the bargain and were highly delighted by this delicacy as bananas are a luxury in the southern Sudan. On the door of the truck was the insignia, 'S.G.', and we realised as we drove off that we had to thank the Sudan Government for the last lap of our journey.

The two places on the map, Duro and Fagar, we never saw, unless the one or two huts we passed had had these names bestowed upon them.

We reached the Nile, where there was another ferry to cross to Juba. We were surrounded by a most fascinating selection of humanity. Where they had come from I do not know, because we had hardly seen any habitation on that side of the river. There were smiling women with their scarves over their heads; some dressed completely in black and others in gaudy coloured clothes printed with Arabic characters. Other black women with bare breasts and bangles galore were not so coy. One woman had a whole armful of bangles and large rings in her ears as well. Most of the men were dressed, but some were completely naked. Kabega was disgusted; he thought it was all rather indecent and said that he thought these people were very primitive.

I tried to draw the smart young Lance-Corporal who was in charge of the ferry into conversation as he could understand English. What better subject to talk about than Sudanese independence, which was coming shortly and would surely be a talking point among the ranks? But when I mentioned independence to him he looked at me with incomprehension written all over his face. I really do believe that nobody had told him that the Sudan would soon be free of the British and in fifteen minutes I did not have time to explain. It was rather surprising to find an African so unconcerned with politics; in Buganda everyone was a politician.

On the other side of the river was a large sign, 'ALL VISITORS ARE TO REPORT TO GOVERNMENT ON ARRIVAL'. It was already about 6 p.m. and night would soon be descending and we thought that it would be sufficient to let our presence be known when the offices opened in the morning, so we went straight to the Juba hotel to find Dr Cazziol.

Driving through the Juba streets speed was kept down to ten miles an hour because of the clouds of dust thrown up by vehicles, but looking hard through the dust we were able to find the hotel fairly easily. Outside it was a group of Dinka visitors to the town, each standing on one leg and, like the men on the ferry, completely naked. Some European ladies going into the hotel ignored them, seeming to regard them as part of the normal surroundings, as indeed they were.

Dr Cazziol was in the hotel and very pleased to see us. He had been given a warning only that afternoon that in twenty-four hours he would have to leave the Sudan. Over a long cool drink in the hotel bar we drank to his future work with the farmers in Uganda. I began to warn him of what he might expect. The atmosphere in that hotel was vastly different from that in the hotels in Kampala. Standing cheek by jowl were white men and Sudanese, ranging from the light skinned Arabs to the large black southerners, drinking at the bar together. The whites were the same sort of men who in a Kenya or Uganda hotel bar would have looked askance at an African if he had dared to enter, but in Juba they did not bat an eyelid.

The argument of those who favour white privilege, that opening the doors to Africans would open the floodgates to a rush of primitive people who would not be able to behave themselves, is really quite ludicrous when considered in the bar of the Juba Hotel. Just outside were the Dinka in a state of complete undress and painted in various shades of ochre, yet they were no more intending to come into the bar of the Juba Hotel for a gin and tonic than the white men were preparing to strip naked and run outside to do a war dance.

After a comfortable night at the hotel (Kabega was given accommodation, with no eyebrows raised), we went to the Government Headquarters to report our presence, and in a rickety building, which looked as though it would collapse under the first storm, we found sweating, harrassed British officers working under the whirling fans in their shirt sleeves. The Senior Officer was very much on edge. He told me sternly that I should have reported the night before.

As we sat and talked a barefooted African clerk wandered in putting papers in the 'In' trays and emptying the 'Out' trays.

'We have a terrible job here,' said the worried Britisher. 'These people have got to take over from us in a few years but we have no one to hand over to.'

Events proved him right. When transfer of power took place the south revolted against the Arab north, and chaos reigned supreme around Juba. Many southerners escaped to Uganda, having more in common with it than with Khartoum.

Making sure of two extra cans of petrol bought from a Greek merchant who ran an all-in grocery-hardware-clothing-petrol shop, we set off. Once over the ferry it was easy going; there was no other traffic. We stopped for lunch at a place climbing up the escarpment where it was possible to see five countries—an awe-inspiring view. Apart from the road there was no evidence of human endeavour for as far as the eye could see. The brown plains stretched towards the shimmering horizon and an absolutely clear blue sky hung like an infinite dome above our heads. There was no protection against the harsh sun and we were glad to get back into the car, although that was an oven inside. The warm air blowing in through the windows as we moved off was some relief from the heat, and as we climbed towards Uganda the landscape became greener. Over the border itself, what had looked like bare scrub the day before was now quite luxuriant to our starved eyes.

We made our first stop at Gulu where there was a Rest House and we called out the African caretaker to ask him for accommodation for the three of us. He said that there was only one room available but that we could all share it and he would put in an extra bed. Then he saw Kabega.

'Sorry, bwana, we don't have drivers stay in the Rest House.'

I was annoyed.

'Do you operate a colour bar in a Government Rest House?'

'Oh, no, bwana,' he said, 'but we cannot let drivers stay.'

'I'm the driver,' I said, 'this is my friend.'

But before we could get Kabega his bed I had to call on the local European Public Works Officer, who quickly gave the necessary instructions. The African caretaker was still very much put out. He was proud of his Rest House and thought it was lowering his own prestige to have to accommodate an African.

On the journey Cazziol talked about the White Fathers he had met at the Juba Hotel. They were on their way back to missionary posts in Uganda after holidaying at home and spoke very freely in Italian about their exploits. Cazziol discovered that business was one way in which the mission work was financed. American cars bought in the Belgian Congo, for instance, always raised a very good price in Uganda or Kenya. Trinkets brought in from Italy, watches from Switzerland, apparently all formed part of their business transactions. Another of their activities was the making of cigars from locally grown tobacco. According to Roger, who was a lapsed Catholic turned Quaker, the Italian missionaries were businessmen first and priests second.

A detour towards Pakwach on the Albert Nile brought us close to some enormous herds of elephant, delighting Kabega, who had never seen an elephant before. The great beasts lumbered across the plain at surprising speed, their big ears flapping, when they heard our car approaching. One great tusker was very curious about us and turned round to smell us out; we made as dignified a retreat as possible. We were in the Murchison Falls Game Park and the elephants are protected. A recent Game Warden's report points out, however, that over eight hundred were shot during the year to protect agricultural and forestry development. In fact this large number of shootings represented no threat to the herds as they are breeding well. Elephants, buffalo and hippopotami are so abundant in Uganda that with the establishment of several National Parks there is now no danger of extermination.

Other animals of the bush are not having such an easy time. Antelope, which make such good eating, are being trapped by local tribes who are using snares made of steel wire cable instead of practising their age-old craft of spear hunting. The Game Wardens are concerned about this because it is an unselective killing and often means that females and young animals which are badly needed to maintain stocks are being destroyed. It can also be extremely dangerous, for buffalo and elephant have been known to get caught in the snares, break themselves free and attack and sometimes kill the first person they come across out of sheer pain and fury.

7

African Enterprise—Straight and Crooked

THERE was an appalling ignorance about co-operative principles among the very people who were supposed to be implementing them. With the agreement of the FUAF directors I started a course of six sessions in Co-operative Practice and Principles which was thrown open to members of the public as we wanted to get a wider appreciation of the social objectives of Co-operation.

When I arrived at the hall on the first night of the course I found that our advertising had not been good enough for only six people had turned up. The number in itself did not discourage me but the reasons for their attendance were definitely disturbing! One, a European, was a Co-operative Officer who had been sent along by the Department to make a report on what I was saying. Another European was a policeman from the Special Branch. He had understood that I was going to talk about Communism! Three of the four Africans were spies from various Government departments, and only one was a genuine student. We chatted amiably, and I invited them all to come back the following week. Fortunately by then we had attracted a further twenty students, including, strangely enough, two Indian shopkeepers.

I described how the Co-operative Movement in Britain had built itself up from small beginnings on the basis of one vote for each shareholder, and membership open to all. There could be no private profit in a co-operative society as the surpluses were either ploughed back for the benefit of all or distributed to members according to the extent that they themselves traded with it. As it gives the widest possible democratic participation it is eminently suitable for Africans emerging from tribalism; it is simple to understand and fair in practice.

The Co-operative Officer was still with us when the course ended and astonished me by proposing a vote of thanks, saying that in the six weeks he had learnt more about the ideals behind Co-operation than he had ever heard before. The two Indian shopkeepers went off intending to convert their shop to a Co-op, and two of the African students who were clerks in Kampala wanted to start up a Co-op restaurant. They said that meals served for African workers in the town, although consisting of only one course of matoki and a dash of meat sauce, were costing as much as 2 sh. 50 cents a head. They wanted to break that racket. I think all the genuine spies had left by the end of the course.

Against the advice of the Registrar of Co-operative Societies, Sir Andrew Cohen decided that reforms were needed in the official Co-operative Movement in Uganda. A Commission of Enquiry which had been set up after the 1949 riots had made criticisms of the Government officers supervising the Department on the grounds that they had run it as a department working for the benefit of the Government rather than for the benefit of the co-operative farmers. The Registrar of Co-operative Societies himself made a very revealing remark to the Commission. When he was asked whether he thought the Registrar should be a non-official, he replied, 'No, I think he should be a Government servant.' The Chairman asked why, and the Registrar replied, 'Because there are not only the interests of the members of the co-operative society to be safeguarded, but also the interests of the public who are dealing with them.'

The Commission felt that he should confine his attention to the welfare of the co-operative societies and that the Government should look after the welfare of the general public. The Commission's report recognised the resentment of the farmers towards the Co-operative Department. Africans suspected that their co-operative societies were about as free as communal farms under communism, for they were only agencies of the Government. It became evident that societies would succeed as genuine democratic bodies, expressing the initiative of the farmers locally and giving them a share of responsibility, only if the structure of Governmental control was changed.

Sir Andrew Cohen realised the need and went some way towards meeting it. A Co-operative Council, which would have on it representatives of the major co-operative unions and others interested in the promotion of co-operation, was set up and the office of Registrar was abolished. The legal functions of registration were taken over by the Administrator General, and a new position of Commissioner for Co-operative Development created to assist the day-to-day working of the societies, without actually controlling them. It was also agreed that unofficial groups of farmers who wished to maintain their identity would be allowed to register as co-operative societies rather than be forced to split up and join other official societies.

This was a decisive victory for the political campaign of the

Federation of Uganda African Farmers. The way was now open for this body to be wound up and its groups of supporters advised to form into registered co-operative societies. A special general meeting called to discuss these proposals was held at the Aggrey Memorial School just by the site of the Kabaka's Lake and a stone's throw from the Lubiri.

Over two hundred farmers' representatives came from all parts of the Protectorate—Buganda, Busoga, Lango, Acholi, Teso. In view of the background of inter-tribal rivalries it was a remarkable achievement for all these men from different tribes to feel linked together in a common purpose. Presiding over the meeting was Ignatius Musazi, facing a most difficult task. He was in favour of accepting the Government's recommendations, for winding up FUAF and forming the co-operative societies. But against him was a sizeable group of his co-directors who wanted to keep the private company in existence and to have no truck with the Co-operative set-up. The meeting went on for two days. No time had been fixed for it to finish. By common consent it was agreed that it should go on until everybody who wanted to speak had had a chance to do so. This custom in African meetings leads to tedious, long drawn-out meetings and the stamina of those attending is quite incredible. The discussion went on without a break.

Most of the speeches were made in Luganda, but others were translated from different vernaculars into English. The issues which had to be decided were not altogether uncomplicated. Many delegates did not realise that some of the directors who were opposed to change had a vested personal interest in maintaining the private company. I had come across some of their corrupt practices behind the scenes quite by chance.

In a remote village the truck broke down and, while waiting for a spare part to be collected, I noticed one of the directors who was with me handing out leaflets to some African bystanders. While he was in the village I retrieved one of the leaflets and had it translated. It turned out to be a prospectus for a private company which was proposing to operate a soap factory. One of the Federation Directors was named as the Managing Director; his colleagues on the self-appointed Board were other FUAF directors or employees. For months money had been collected for the non-existent soap factory and there was absolutely nothing to show for it.

I took it up later with a full meeting of the directors. At first the soap factory promoters denied all knowledge but when the leaflet was produced they admitted their guilt and promised to stop. However, they never gave up their fiddling with these private activities; the facilities of

FUAF were used for them on a wide scale. Badly needed trucks were 'borrowed' to transport goods for their private companies, and sometimes farmers who subscribed money towards what they thought was a co-operative set-up discovered afterwards that they had donated towards a private soap factory which had not been built and was never likely to be built.

Once when in the remote north I discovered that the driver, while the rest of us were engaged at a meeting, had been peddling his own make of patent medicines among the villagers. His customers had assumed that his mixtures would be particularly efficacious as the pedlar appeared to have the approval of Ignatius Musazi, the political leader.

The minority of the directors who were using FUAF for their own purposes were encouraging some of the employees to do the same. It was impossible, however, to pin them down. When the matters were raised at directors' meetings they pleaded poverty and promised good behaviour in the future; but other petty swindling cropped up again and again.

The honest directors were appalled by these activities and they were anxious that FUAF should be wound up and co-operative societies registered as quickly as possible. But because of the confusion which had been sown among the ordinary members and their delegates by the corrupt directors who were playing on the fears and suspicions of the Government, the issue at the special general meeting was very much in doubt.

The turning point in the meeting came when a young farmer, speaking persuasively and with an oratory which surpassed that of even the usually eloquent Baganda, moved the delegates to an appreciation of their opportunity. I was unable to follow it all as my translator himself was so moved that I could only pick up odd sentences here and there. In effect what the young farmer said was that for years FUAF had been planting seeds of discontent because of the Government's measures against co-operative farmers. But now the plants had grown and bore fruit, a beautiful crop which all could enjoy. Now it was the opportunity for those who had worked so hard in spreading the seeds to reap the harvest of reward.

When it was put to the vote a substantial majority was in favour of winding up FUAF and forming genuine co-operative societies. I was heartily relieved and now felt that my work was worth while. I could not have stayed in Uganda if the vote had gone the other way.

Within a few weeks I realised that some directors were not accepting the result of the vote and were making it as difficult as they could for the groups in the districts to re-form as co-operatives. The official Co-operative Department itself was not always as willing to help as it should have been. It was almost as resentful of the changes, which limited its power and authority, as were the corrupt directors within our own organisation. When we asked them for copies of the model bye-laws they only had a few available and to speed up the conversions we had hundreds printed at our own expense. I went on many long safaris with Musazi to speak at meetings of farmers to explain the new conditions and to push their registrations through.

The extent of the rearguard action being fought by some of the other directors was made evident to Musazi and me when we once arrived late for a meeting in the Teso district, which is north of the lake Kioga formed by the slow flowing Nile. Sir Andrew and Lady Cohen had invited Barbara and me to one of their musical evenings at Government House on the evening before the meeting was due to be held, and Musazi thought it important that we should accept the invitation in order to keep up good relations with the Governor. He thought good relations were important, as ill-informed action by the Government could ruin the chances of persuading the farmers to co-operate.

As soon as I returned from the evening at Government House I changed into my safari clothes and at midnight we set off on a 300-mile drive, taking turns at the wheel. We took turns in sleeping too, but sitting up in the cab and knocking our heads against the window as the truck lurched over the bad roads was not an ideal way of spending a night.

During the morning we arrived at the meeting place to find a crowd still waiting patiently. We learned that some of the other directors who were against forming co-operative societies had been in the area spreading slander against Musazi, saying he was a dupe of the Europeans and was not to be trusted. At the meeting the position was explained to the satisfaction of the majority but there was an element of discontent and we knew that after we had left more attempts would be made to confuse the people.

I remember one meeting, which was addressed by a Government Co-operative Officer and myself, where one member was particularly insistent in asking questions. It was the custom to allow every questioner to pursue his cross-examination of a speaker until the inquisitor was completely satisfied. The people were gathered at a crossroads under a tree, and as the sun went round almost all were exposed to it. It was really hot and under cross-examination the Co-operative Officer became more and more exasperated. He asked the chairman of the meeting, a very impressive local leader, to stop the questioner, whose questions he protested had already been answered half a dozen times. But oh, no, the chairman said, the people would want that man to have satisfaction before he went on to the next question. So he allowed the man to put his question yet again.

This the questioner did, quite politely, standing in his open-necked shirt and holding his large floppy hat in front of him. But when he repeated, once more, virtually the same question which had already received half-a-dozen replies, the Co-operative Officer's nerve broke. He shot up from his seat, shouted that he was not going to stand for any more of that, and rushed to his car, revving it up ominously. The crowd, in confusion, stood up, wondering what was going to happen next. It was fortunate for them that they had, as the Officer let the car into gear and tore at the crowd, who scattered in all directions. The last we saw of him was a cloud of dust.

I could appreciate his exasperation, for it certainly needed infinite patience to handle a meeting of Africans who were distrustful of Government. In many places they were even distrustful of me, although I was not a Government official. I was, in fact, their employee, but many of them had been taught to beware of Europeans in any circumstances. It took a long time to get their confidence, but once established it was a firm bond. Part of the explanation for my good relations with most of the Africans, who were prepared to accept my advice even against that of the directors who were dishonest, was the way in which I identified myself with them by staying in their homes, eating with them and working side by side with them on the long safaris.

We began to feel that we were on the right lines as several new co-operative societies were established. Meanwhile we were carrying on with the commitments for the marketing of maize and later, during the season, cotton. We wanted the Africans to have confidence in the marketing activities as a basis for successful co-operatives, though in the course of these activities we uncovered a lot of snags, and a few more crooks. But what was so heartening was the fact that most of the ordinary farmer members were honest and trusting and prepared to hand over their crops and wait months for payment. Fortunately most of the leaders they elected were also honest, but a minority plainly were not.

One outstanding chouser in Busoga made several hundred pounds. As a local farmers' chairman he persuaded his followers to collect their maize in a godown to which he alone had the key. He promised them that he would sell it to Indians for a very favourable price. This, apparently, he did for the maize disappeared from the godown; the farmers, however, never saw the colour of their money. In their simple trusting way they had put the maize in the warehouse without obtaining any receipts. When the maize disappeared the chairman brazened the whole thing out, nor could any Indian merchant be found to admit buying the maize which had so mysteriously disappeared.

Some local officials took share money which they had collected with forged receipts; one who had decamped with a large sum turned up months later working in Kenya as a Jehovah Witness. But perhaps the most audacious of all the crooked petty officials was the one who decided to build himself a house and a shop at the expense of the organisation. With a local Sikh fundi he signed a contract for building what he said was going to be the local headquarters of FUAF. He held no important FUAF position and had no right to act on its behalf, but the Sikh made no attempt to check his status and went ahead with the work. It was nearly completed before the builder realised that he would have trouble getting his money and he brought an action in the local court. When notice was served on the local official in the name of the Federation of Uganda African Farmers it was completely ignored and, in his absence, the court made an order against FUAF for payment of the sum due.

I first heard of all this when the fundi arrived at our Kampala office followed by a court official with authority to seize property to the value of £1,500. I was flabbergasted, and I think my incredulity convinced the court official that we were genuine in saying we knew nothing about the building. Eventually the problem was solved but it was a headache while it lasted.

We were also in the throes of sorting out the tangles of the marketing system. The maize marketing programme had been so successful in Bugerere that the godowns were full to overflowing. Every time I went to the area I found the golden harvest piling up higher in mountains between the mud walls until it looked as though the pressure would cause them to collapse. There were not sufficient gunny bags to pack all the maize and added to that there were immense difficulties with transport.

The narrow road to Bugerere which I had learned to know so well during many safaris was quite unsuitable for heavy traffic and something invariably went wrong with the trucks. Often after a rainstorm they were stuck in the glutinous mud. It was quite a hectic business clearing a bogged-down truck. Two or three banana trees would have to be

5. Members of the Mathira Coffee Co-operative Society, Kenya,
sorting beans

6. (*right*) Young Uganda

(*below*) Young Rhodesia—children in the water accumulated in a caved area, Mufulira Copper Mines, Northern Rhodesia

stripped to form a carpet on which the tyres could grip. It was lucky that the villagers from nearby volunteered to help push and pull the vehicle out of the quagmire. They always did this quite willingly and only very occasionally asked for payment, although sometimes they were working for two hours on the job.

The maize position in Bugerere became really desperate and the maize mountain in one godown was ten feet high. We tried hiring extra lorries to bring the crop to Kampala, but as everybody else was in the same position transport was just not available. We also faced a go-slow campaign on the part of the local members who were reluctant to bag the maize at the speed necessary to clear the high piles of golden grain. If the maize was left for long in this condition it would become weevil-infested. After warnings about the danger of the position the farmers were willing enough to work, but after a day or so they became lethargic, through lack of enthusiastic leadership.

Dr Cazziol saved the day; he volunteered to live in the area for the weeks necessary to supervise the operation and threw his heart, soul and shoulders into the job. Not only did he organise the work but he set an example by filling and loading the 200 lb. sacks himself. The example of a European doing this work so shook the Africans that Cazziol was able to get their wholehearted co-operation to complete the job.

As we had feared, the crop at the bottom of the pile on the ground was so infested that it had to be thrown away. It was a dead loss. But when I delivered some of the good maize to the Indian millers I was horrified to see that their stocks of grain were much worse than the maize which we had discarded. The piles of maize ready to be milled were literally running with black weevils; there were more weevils than maize grains. When I complained to the Indian he replied nonchalantly that it was quite usual to see infested maize. 'Don't worry yourself about it; when it is milled it will be quite palatable for Africans. They are not worried by weevils, they eat ants anyway.'

When the cotton season came there were more organisational head-aches. While we were trying to cope with the crop we were also advising the members on the steps to be taken for the formation of registered co-operative societies. If we had been able to organise the cotton buying purely as a business operation it would have been straightforward and probably quite profitable, but it was bedevilled by 'political' considerations. The local committees often felt that loyalty demanded that it was necessary to send a truck ten or fifteen miles to collect a member's crop even if it consisted of only a few bags.

Almost all the £20,000,000 crop of cotton in Uganda is grown by

F

African farmers on three- to ten-acre plots. The season comes about Christmas time and the little balls of cotton fluff growing on the bushes look rather like snow flakes. The handpicking of the crops takes several weeks and the whole country is in a flurry of excitement as the economy depends so much on this major crop. When his own crop is picked the farmer stuffs it into sacks or wraps it in pieces of cloth and carries it on his head, or on his wife's head, or on his bicycle, to a ginnery where it is sold to the Indian traders. If he belongs to a co-operative group the crops are collected and sold in bulk for a commission.

The ginneries become the centres of activity as hundreds of people congregate for their sacks to be weighed and the cash to be handed over. Although bank notes are used the peasants prefer to be paid in silver shillings and the ten cent pieces with holes in the middle. The holes are useful for making necklaces or bangles and for accounting purposes the pieces can be tied in tens to make a shilling. The demand for coin during the season is phenomenal; to keep up with it the banks have to send lorry loads of money to the cotton districts. There are few robberies and only one European cashier usually accompanies the load. After they have been paid the farmers spend the money on a coveted bicycle, cloth for the wife (or, perhaps, wives), or beer. Many dig a large part of it into the ground—the peasants' savings bank. The money brought to the towns to make a big purchase is sometimes green after the long sojourn in the earth.

The Government has made repeated attempts to persuade farmers to save their money through post offices or the Uganda Credit and Savings Bank, as well as through commercial banks, but most Africans live tens of miles from the nearest town and even the post offices may be a day's walk away.

Most Africans do not trust the pieces of paper given to them as receipts for bank payments; they prefer hard coin. Some have made the mistake of burying paper money in the ground along with silver, only to dig it up half eaten by insects. Older Africans can remember the days when cowrie shells were in regular circulation as money and paper does not seem nearly so valuable. Cheque books are a mystery.

Once collected the cotton is fed into gins where the lint is separated from the seed and baled for shipment overseas. The prices paid to the grower are fixed by the Government every season to avoid wasteful competition and swindling by the buyers. Africans must sell their cotton to the nearest ginnery, although some co-operative societies which have acquired ginneries under the compulsory acquisition scheme are allowed to collect from members over a wider field. The ginneries are paid according to a formula which calculates the out-turn of lint cotton. This may change from year to year but the ginneries are virtually guaranteed a reasonable profit. The Africans resented this, demanded a share in the monopoly, and are now operating thirteen ginneries through co-operative unions.

Cotton is politics in Uganda. One of the reasons for the growth of the unofficial movements was the fact that co-operative societies were forbidden to engage in any political activity. Now that restriction is not so onerous and the societies have a useful share in the processing side of the industry.

Dr Cazziol was very keen to use his knowledge and energy in the development of a genuine co-operative farm—that is, one where the land is pooled by a group of farmers who work it communally and share the crops. At the first stage we knew it would be impossible to persuade the individualistic Baganda to give up completely their individually owned plots in favour of such a scheme so we arranged a pilot project on which a group of farmers would work together only part-time, keeping their own plots separate. Under Cazziol's super-vision they would be able to learn new farming methods which might be adopted by other farmers in the area. We had great hopes for this co-operative scheme. Through the experiment we learnt a great deal about Baganda psychology.

Those Baganda who own land are very proud of the *mailo* title they hold under the native law. But most farmers live as tenants on large estates and pay a tribute to the landowner. Private landlordism was introduced by the British, as under the Buganda Agreement in 1900 half the land was allocated to the Kabaka's Chiefs. In the last half century the larger estates have been split up by death and by the sale of land but there are still many large landowners. The land cannot be sold to non-Africans, which is some protection to the indigenous people. Neverthe-less many of them suffer poverty because of the tribute in crops demanded by the landlord, which in some places is as much as one third of a tenant's crop. Many landowners are extremely rich. It is one of the incongruous sights in Uganda to see sleek new Humber Super Snipes in the remote country areas parked outside mud houses. No hire purchase is necessary here, for the cars are paid for cash down. These rich Africans are the best customers of the motor dealers.

Their affluence is in striking contrast to the abject poverty and, indeed, near starvation of some of their tenants or of the immigrant workers who are employed at very low wages on their estates. Many of the big landowners are opposed to co-operative societies as they fear that they will give the peasant farmers too much power. For the same reason they are opposed to democratic political advance and are the biggest stalwarts of the quasi-aristocratic rule of the Kabaka's Ministers. They hate the newfangled politicians who preach one man one vote and would rather co-operate with the British Government than with their fellow Africans who want independence. Although the peasant farmers oppose landlord politics they have acquired a taste for private land ownership. Buganda is an acquisitive society and the idea of a co-operative farm was therefore revolutionary. It could, if it succeeded, make a big impact on Baganda land custom.

Musazi's father, a venerable gentleman over ninety years old, who even at that age was not senile (he could remember clearly the very early days of British infiltration, when he was an important Saza Chief), came to our aid. He understood the significance of the co-operative ideal and, encouraged by his son, he agreed to allocate part of his considerable land holdings to the experiment.

Roger installed himself in old Musazi's home (it would compare very favourably with any village house in southern Italy), and took ample supplies of spaghetti and tomato sauce with him. His job became a trial of patience and faith. The farmers agreed willingly enough to become partners in the co-operative farm but when the first task of clearing the site ready for the tractor and plough was put to them they had second thoughts. Some of them sent immigrant labourers to do the work, which was far from the object of the co-operative scheme, and others protested that they wanted to see the successful beginnings before they soiled their own hands.

Roger was driven to distraction but he overcame the first stage by paying some labourers himself. When the whole area was ploughed ready for planting more of the farmers came forward to plant and to hoe but gradually they dwindled away to their own private plots and Roger was left once more to see the project through.

He left the maize to grow, returning to Kampala for other work, and telling the farmers that he would return when the first harvest was ready. When he did so he found that they had already harvested the crop and pocketed the money.

Let me hasten to add that although this co-operative scheme was such a failure, as the ground was soon overgrown again, in other parts of Uganda, particularly in Acholi where the land has always been communally owned, co-operative farming has been more successful. Even in Buganda the idea still has great possibilities.

8

Kampala to Katwe

GEORGE and Shirley Shepherd wanted to return to America at the end of their first two years, Shirley to have her second baby and George to stimulate American interest in Africa and, particularly, to raise money for projects in Uganda. Before leaving he asked me to take over responsibility for FUAF, to which I agreed, providing the directors were willing to wind it up as quickly as possible. Already most of the groups of members were following our advice and forming co-operative societies. I wanted to speed up this process and remove the temptation from the corrupt directors who were taking advantage of the facilities offered by FUAF to make money on the side. Their petty swindling was difficult to stamp out. Fortunately it was confined to only a small group of 'Directors-at-Large' and most of the lower officials were quite honest.

With his misplaced sense of service to the Africans George had refused to understand the extent to which the corruptors were undermining his own efforts. I thought that while he was in America it would be possible to speed up the process of winding up, but shortly after his departure those directors who wanted to carry on held a meeting and reversed the decision to wind up the company. They claimed that the Government was impeding the formation of societies in some areas. Some of the Government officials were cautious or even obstructive but that was not a sufficient reason to change the agreed policy. I had no other course but to hand in my resignation.

The other directors who were as anxious as I was to complete the change-over to co-operatives asked me to stay on and complete my two years by helping to extend African participation in trade and establish a basis for consumer co-operation. I agreed to this suggestion, although at this time I also had an offer from a British company operating in Uganda, as well as strong inclination to return home to resume political activities.

It was about this time too that we became very worried about the

85

health of Jane, our elder daughter, then aged four, as tests at the local hospital had shown the early stages of TB. We decided to try to leave the Kitemerike House where there was no water or sanitation—but we could not afford another house as my own salary was minimal. Fortunately Barbara, who was working as a secretary for a British construction company, was offered a smart company bungalow in a mixed European and Indian area and we were able to move from Mengo into comparative luxury. It was a real delight to turn on a water tap and revel in the clean gushing flow but it seemed very extravagant to have baths whenever we wanted them. The children had a wonderful time playing in the bathroom for two days.

We were sad to leave the Kitemerike House where our life was never without some incident to enliven it. When I returned from safari there were Africans waiting to see me, either with some grievance they wanted to discuss or simply on a social call. The house was always full of people and children.

Our own daughters made friends with the nieces and nephews of the landlady, who lived with her for months at a time. Some of them were orphans, but there were no orphanages in Uganda and the children are always taken over by relatives or close friends of the family. One of their playmates was Princess Dorothy, also a niece of Mrs Kitemerike and the daughter of the Kabaka, who was about the same age as our own children and who lived just across the road. She would invariably arrive in the morning dressed in a beautiful pale blue nylon or white organdie dress, but usually returned home for lunch minus a button or with her sashes dangling down her back after her frolics with all the other children in the Kitemerike's enormous garden and banana shamba.

The house itself was not easy to live in. For one thing the cockroaches were more plentiful than usual and Barbara's first job every morning before preparing breakfast was to sweep up the hundreds which had died in the night as a result of the DDT spraying the evening before. The live ones would scamper away between the floorboards. Breakfast could then be cooked on an ancient oil stove which more than once spluttered in protest, throwing out flames which singed her hair and eyebrows. Washing was fraught with difficulties, not only because the water was so short, but because the balcony on which a bathroom had been specially built for us was a haven for bats. Sometimes the shrieks from Barbara or Shirley would shatter the neighbourhood as the bats dived down at them in their baths. (For some reason or another the famous radar system which bats are supposed to have either didn't work in Africa or girls just do not vibrate with bats.)

Enormous flying beetles were another menace, not to mention flying ants which are attracted to the light, flying in at the windows and knocking themselves senseless on the light bulbs.

Every evening from our balcony we could see Africans gathering around the enormous ant hills, which they covered with old clothes or a piece of bark cloth, leaving only a small opening for the ants to emerge through, lined with banana leaf. Soon hundreds of flying ants would pour out—only to be clapped in the hands of the bunch of Africans waiting outside for them, and devoured immediately.

As Barbara was working during the day we had an 'ayah' to care for the children. The first one, Maria, was recommended to us by a lecturer at Makerere College who had employed her to care for his own children. She was a practising Roman Catholic and when the local priest visited some of the villagers who lived nearby she would run out asking for a blessing and could often be found sitting on the balcony fingering her rosary. Maria was quite efficient, but we later discovered that she had more than one profession. Her other profession was the oldest in the world. One evening we noticed two cars in the drive with a European at each wheel. We thought at first that they were calling on us, but in fact they were each waiting their turn to visit Maria in her little house. We replaced her the next morning, but it was not the last we saw of her. Months after, at a students' dance at Makerere, she re-appeared, very well dressed, obviously tipsy, and addressing us like long lost friends.

There were many prostitutes in Kampala. At the bottom of our hill there was a positive den of them and at night time they would stand on the roadside or at the doors of their huts touting for business. During the day their activities included the brewing of a very potent local beer called 'pombi'. Others were in great demand as dancers, Kiganda style. For this they had tremendous talent and tremendous energy. They could keep going all night, only stopping to pick up the coins thrown by their enthusiastic audiences, and as the night wore on the sound of the shillings and 50 cent pieces which they dropped down the front of their dress bodices would rattle to the rhythm of their bodies. They shook and wriggled with all their might, their only accompaniment a set of drums.

Fenner Brockway and Leslie Hale came to see us at the Kitemerike House after their visit to Kenya during the Mau Mau period and a great garden party was organised for them by the Africans. There were at least five hundred guests and among the entertainers were a schoolgirls' choir, jugglers, a trick cyclist, and the dancing girls. The party continued all through the night, long after Fenner and Leslie and the rest of us had retired to our beds, and the girls danced through until four o'clock in the morning. Some uninvited guests, incidentally, included a truck load of police who stationed themselves just outside the house, but they left soon after the entertainments had begun as there was obviously no trouble brewing.

Once when we returned home we found two Europeans waiting for us instead of the usual Africans. One of these was a young English doctor engaged in research work into Africans' diets who was one of the devoted team of junior officers who had sacrificed a career at home to work in Africa. His research into the diets of children revealed the appalling extent of malnutrition, for although malaria is the major cause of death, lack of good food is the second reason why four out of ten children die before they reach fourteen years of age. Dr McFie has vigorously complained that there has been no programme for improving the diets of the Africans and that even when presented with the facts the Government has no real plan to cope with the situation. Fish has been exported in large quantities, although needed in Uganda, and only token amounts of milk powder have been imported, even though New Zealand, to take one example, has big surpluses. Once when Dr McFie asked for permission to write articles in the vernacular press advising Africans how to improve their diets, he was reprimanded by his superiors, who told him that if he wanted to help Africans he would be better employed teaching them boxing and football to give them a healthy outlet for their energies, instead of making friends with African editors.

The other visitor was a large American lady from the American Deep South who was doing her bit to improve race relations through the Young Women's Christian Association. She had only recently arrived in the Protectorate to establish girls' clubs and was looking for helpers. Barbara explained that she was out at work each day and had a family to look after, and asked if more recruits could not be found among the many European women in Kampala who did not work, as well as among those who went to the local church every Sunday. Miss Stile, however, had already tried them and had found them to be unenthusiastic. So Barbara agreed and once a week rushed home to feed, bath and bed the children before walking the couple of miles down Mengo hill and up to the top of Mulago hill where she established a club among the nurses of the hospital. When the club was over it was always dark and the roads, which were unlit, were pitch black. Barbara would never set off without an enormous torch 'in case of snakes'.

At a meeting of club leaders Barbara found that three of the four white women helping to get the YWCA going were not Christians, although all the African women were and of course so was the one Goan lady, who was a Roman Catholic. But it says a lot for the go-ahead American that she was prepared to get her scheme under way using whoever was willing to help, and that today her success has been crowned by the establishment of a most up-to-date hostel for working girls in Kampala.

Like most young Africans the girls at Barbara's club were eager to assimilate Western ideas and habits and thrived on such things as dress-making, learning to dance 'western style', learning to use a typewriter, and invading our house for tea-parties 'western style'. On her side Barbara learned a lot about them. The nurses were involved in a conflict between modern science and tribal witchcraft. One experience really worried them. Apparently an educated husband, estranged from his wife, had gone to a witch-doctor in order to end his wife's pregnancy. When the wife suddenly became very ill friends rushed her to hospital and found that everything that could be done for her was done, includ-ing blood transfusions. But she died. Not only the nurses, but even one of the African doctors, thought that the witch-doctor was stronger than modern medicine.

One of the early morning sounds at the Kitemerike House was the noise of George Shepherd, philosopher-cum-missionary, at work on his typewriter. He was writing a new book on philosophy called *The Evolution of Revolutions*. He was up sometimes as early as five o'clock in the morning before starting on the daily task of helping Africans towards their practical evolution. Writing philosophy was one way in which George kept himself in touch with the western way of life in the middle of Africa. Another way in which Shirley and George sought to escape from Africa was via the harp. Their favourite tune was 'Danny Boy'—Shirley playing, George singing, just as though they were in some Boston drawing-room. Although it was pleasant enough, this was not quite the brand of culture Barbara and I had anticipated when we had taken the trouble of bringing the harp with us all the way from Britain.

From the other side of the house other musical noises could be heard practically all day long coming from a portable gramophone which Shirley had helped her houseboy, Simon, to buy. We were more appreciative of his choice, however, which ranged from New Orleans jazz to African 'highlife' tunes.

We were very fond of the African family below us, the Kitemerikes. The old lady was tall and stately and moved like a queen. She had two daughters living with her, both tall and pretty. One of them, Cissie, was a girl in her early twenties and was the technician around the house, more at home with her head under the bonnet of a car than in a kitchen. She had a most attractive, gentle personality which was oddly at variance with her command of things mechanical. With the usual Baganda charm she was ever ready to help and was a great friend and comfort to Shirley and Barbara. The sitting-room of the Kitemerikes was the most African room in the household and a really exciting find for small children. Here were the trophies of the old Saza Chief himself. Spears and shields covered the walls, alongside fading pictures of the old Chief in full tribal regalia. Over the chairs and floor were the skins of leopards and other wild animals and neat arrangements of walking sticks and switches made from the manes of lions.

*   *   *   *

A big job was waiting to be done in breaking the Asian monopoly in the import and retail trade. Practically all consumer goods imported into Uganda go through Asian business houses situated in Mombasa, Nairobi, or Kampala itself. The Africans strongly resented this grasp on the economy by the 60,000 Asians. They still do, and it makes for bitter passions. Recently when Mr Leonard Basude, the Buganda Minister for Agriculture, was in Bombay he had this to say: 'Asians in Africa are like the baby chicks sheltering under mother hen's wings, thinking the hawk cannot see them. Mother hen is Britain. When Britain goes, we, the hawk, can swoop on those baby chicks. When Uganda gains independence in two years her Asians must use their profits for the benefit of their adopted country or all industries, now Asian controlled, will be nationalised.' Mr Basude went on to claim that nearly all the wealth being made by Indians in Uganda was being sent back to India and that the total in 1958 was £750,000. He claimed that none of the Indian wealth was being used to help Africans.

The Hindus and Khojas (followers of the Aga Khan) are very successful businessmen, not through astute methods but by their sheer hard work supplemented by family connections which support a trader over his bad mistakes. Many are not traders at all; gambling by over-trading is notorious. In a good crop year the orders booked for the following year are always greatly in excess of the real needs of the consuming public. The market is in a perpetual state of boom and slump even at the best of times and as it takes about six months for goods to arrive from Britain, India, or Japan, the main sources of supply, the market is cut off from external influences. It operates in an East African vacuum, although some enterprising traders are trying to break it by using air freight.

The Asian importer works on credit, and it is incredible how much can be generated on a single consignment of goods. The order given to a British firm is covered by the confirming house in London, giving credit of three to six months, during the actual time of the sea and rail journey. The goods are then sold to a wholesaler who never pays in cash, but signs a promissory note payable in three months. The importer discounts the note at a bank and collects his money. The wholesaler sells to a series of sub-wholesalers who pay him by promissory notes which are likewise discounted and the sub-wholesalers sell to retailers who also sign notes. Some retailers also sell to other retailers.

The goods can go through six or seven hands before they reach the consumer and there is credit given on every transaction except the final one, and even sometimes then. The trading mechanism is such a maze it can cover up an immense amount of financial intrigue. Africans find it difficult to enter the game as the banks do not regard them as credit-worthy.

When Asian traders face financial crises, which they do frequently, a convenient trick used is the exchanging of promissory notes with other friendly traders. No goods are involved, but they get the credit they need from the banks on the fictitious transactions. One enterprising Indian trader in Nairobi was able to save himself from bankruptcy by operating two subsidiary companies and three bank accounts between which he exchanged an astonishing number of promissory notes and cheques, keeping all his companies in existence on fraudulent credit. The bank managers were very surprised to find out how they had been duped.

The credit system is built up on the prestige of the importing house, which in turn depends on the standing of the firms in Britain prepared to do business with it. When a representative or a director of such a U.K. firm visits Uganda he is greeted as a Very Important Person by the Indian proprietors. I have known traders hardly able to afford a cup of coffee and up to their necks in debt entertain visiting British representatives to sundowners and dinner parties on a scale fit for the Governor himself. At these sundowners I learnt a lot about the methods of the Asians as they were always very voluble—about business.

The biggest trade is in textiles, which comprises about a fifth of total imports, and choosing printed cottons and rayons is the skilled part of the business. Women in Uganda are very sophisticated customers; they will not wear the brash designs which sell well in other parts of Africa, but want delicate and subtle designs in a variety of shades of sky blues, flamingo pinks, lavender, and for special occasions, deep purples and cherry reds. The wrong choice could lead an importer into a loss of thousands. Large Lancashire firms like Tootals employ designers to keep pace with this part of their export trade, and every year new patterns and shades are brought out to please the fastidious ladies of Buganda.

The dress they wear is of ankle length and was designed originally by the missionaries, with square neck and short sleeves, tied at the waist with a gorgeous silk sash which alone could cost two or three pounds. The length of cloth needed is usually six yards and the better quality cloth costs seven or eight shillings a yard; some women pay up to twenty-five shillings a yard and a few buy exquisite French velvet costing over £3 a yard. Dressing the Baganda ladies is a major and expensive industry.

Most of the women are loyal to Lancashire; brand names like Tootal's Tobralco and Lystav have a special appeal and customers insist on them, spending hours over their purchases to choose the right design. Japan, which already has a hold on the market for cheaper cloth, is breaking into the better class market. They are quick competitors. I have known designs left by representatives in the safekeeping of their agents in Kampala find their way to Japan within days to be copied—with the result that the Japanese cloth, practically identical to the British product, reached Uganda weeks before the original orders to the British firm were fulfilled. So concerned were the British textile manufacturers by such activities and by the encroachments of the Germans or even the Spanish on their traditional markets, that they sent a high-powered textile mission to Uganda. When the mission arrived they had real VIP treatment, but their principal hosts were the very people engaged in importing Japanese goods.

One British firm were very jealous of their good name in the market and they were alarmed one season to find that thousands of yards of seconds were being sold, undermining the reputation of the trade mark. Foolishly they had sold the seconds to a firm in Aden, but should have realised that a little colony of poverty-stricken people could never absorb such quantities. The goods were transhipped to East Africa, and the representatives of the British firm were given the job of visiting the shops of Kenya, Uganda, and Tanganyika, buying up the seconds wherever they could find them.

Besides the importers who actually handle the goods there are hundreds of indenting houses in Kampala and Nairobi. They are usually one-roomed affairs with thousands of samples crammed to the ceilings, tinned food, German tools, Swiss watches, Japanese ball-point pens, bicycles, portable gramophones, Italian blankets, and farm tools. Theirs is the cut-throat business of collecting orders for a one per cent commission. Ultimately the needs of the remote African peasant are satisfied, but he would not have enough fingers to count the number of middlemen he employs.

The Asian community were a fascinating study. Anthropologists at Makerere, who were thirsty for knowledge about the customs of primitive man, also set up a special survey into the caste system and social habits of the Asian minority. Mr Morris, who conducted it, found some interesting facts.

The children, and even grandchildren, of immigrant families are usually married according to the villages in Mother India from which their parents originally came. Although Asians have lived in East Africa for over fifty years there has been almost no inter-marrying with Africans, and hardly any marriages between the different castes. Many of the marriages are contracted as business arrangements when the children are quite young. In African custom the parents of the bride collect a payment from the bridegroom of cattle or goats (known as the bride price or more accurately as the marriage-insurance), but according to Hindu custom the payment is made by the bride's parents. To marry off a family of daughters is an expensive business but it is certainly profitable to have sons. Some of this money is paid when the prospective bridegroom is still only a child of seven or eight. Morris learned more about the Asian community than any other anthropologist but much was told to him in strictest confidence and that part of his findings can never be published.

In the patchwork quilt of races in Uganda is the Goan community of two thousand who are Roman Catholics and loyal, honest, hardworking people. In trade they specialise as grocers, but most are employed as Government clerks and administrators.

The outstanding Goan was Norman Godinho, who went to Uganda with a Portuguese passport and tremendous energy but no money and set about building half the commercial capital. He had formidable business acumen but one foible; he had an acute aversion to accounts and kept most of his business transactions in his head. When he died suddenly of heart failure and his son Carlos was called back from a Cambridge law course to take over the reins of a business with which he was in no way familiar, the enterprise looked like disintegrating. But with his legal training and his capacity for hard work Carlos was true to the family tradition and kept the company in being.

Besides paying the death duties he has pioneered new, exciting projects. His wide screen 'Norman' cinema excels anything in East Africa and is well up to the best West End standards. On the roof of the cinema is a fabulous restaurant and night-club where, like the cinema, there is no colour bar. It is very popular with all races and an example to the dull and dreary places which open their doors to whites only.

It is well known that the network of Asian enterprise has been a virtual conspiracy against the African consumer. Exploitation was easiest in the remote villages as the peasants had no idea of the prices prevailing in the towns and all the shops were owned by Asians in league with each other to keep prices at fantastic levels. Our job was to break down this practice and give the African consumer a fair deal. Later we hoped to establish consumer co-operative societies in the villages. We opened three shops in the principal townships and this had an immediate effect in reducing prices. For the country districts trucks were sent out laden with goods which were sold by the yard or by the dozen on the roadside but miles away from the trading centres. Nevertheless the Indian traders soon felt the competition. Fujiette shirts from Hong Kong which cost 1 sh. 50 cents to import had been sold for 25sh. a piece, but these prices soon dropped.

When the news about our organisation spread people walked from miles around to buy from our mobile shops. When I went on safari I worked alongside the devoted salesmen, who were idealists as well as employees, selling thousands of yards of cloth and shorts and shirts by the hundred, standing under the burning sun for eight or nine hours a day.

I gathered around me a fine band of young men. They were of all religions and none, but they worked together with an almost spiritual fervour, dedicated as they were to giving practical help to African advancement.

One of them was Dionysus Mukibi (nicknamed Bacchus), who had never had a formal education beyond primary school; but he was intelligent, sensitive and wholly sincere. I had many long walks with him around Mengo hill in the cool of the late evening when he would unfold to me his philosophy of life, which was as deep and as moving as anything I have ever heard. He had become an agnostic not because of a pagan upbringing but through, as he called it, 'thinking it all out'.

In a sense he was an 'angry young man'—angry with the Government for not really understanding Africans or really bothering to try; angry with Government officers because they invariably adopted a paternalist approach and always kept the Africans at an intellectual arms length; and angry with his own tribal customs which he thought were holding back the people. He vowed to me once that he would never get married unless the girl he chose was prepared to take him without a bride price. He would have no truck with a system of inferior wives and wanted a partner with whom he could share a rich relationship. He was very interested in politics of course, but was very keen that politicians should turn their attention to the practical problem of helping Africans to share in the web of local government and in the running of affairs which affected their everyday lives, as well as struggling to get the British out.

He often used to tell me that there was no point in having freedom from the British if it meant being under the domination of a feudal clique of landlords around the Kabaka. Nor did he want the business life of the country to be always in alien hands. These were the reasons why he had become a socialist, and passionately believed that democracy and social ownership—particularly through co-operatives—would be the practical way for Africans to express their aspirations for a better way of life. Bacchus was a very sober young man—life was a serious affair to him—but he could appreciate a good joke and when he heard one he threw back his head and laughed huskily and heartily.

Between people in the older generation there are bitter rivalries about religion, which is partly explained by the passionate competition between the mission organisations themselves. One early report of a Protestant group woefully records that the Roman Catholics had been making big inroads in the conversion of heathen Africans but qualifies the sorrow by the comment that even the RCs were better than 'those shocking Mohammedans who have in some places already picked up most of the conversions'.

There was none of this old fashioned rivalry between the members of our loyal team. Roman Salli, for instance, was a devout Catholic and had been educated at a Catholic secondary school and was employed by a leading British firm at quite a high salary when he volunteered to join our organisation. He felt the change would help him to express his sense of idealism. He took on a most arduous job and went on long safaris, working all hours of the day and night if necessary, driving, selling and supervising the shops in the outlying districts. Like all the other members of the staff (except one) he was completely reliable.

At the end of each safari of a mobile shop the stocks, cash and receipts were meticulously checked. The transactions ran into thousands of pounds, but only one case of open dishonesty ever occurred. The team itself was so keen that the integrity of Africans should be demonstrated that they advised me themselves if anyone on the staff was unreliable.

The accountant, who was the kingpin of the organisation, was a Muslim, Mulani Katende. Steadfastly and painstakingly he worked on the books. He was a quiet, undemonstrative young man, but he had a very strong character. He was a devoted husband; unlike some other Muslims he only had one wife, a beautiful young woman with a large, radiant smile. Mulani built a house for her on the outskirts of Kampala and at the week-end was quite a handyman, adding bits and pieces to it. Gradually he saved up enough money to buy corrugated iron sheets for the roof and then cemented the walls and whitewashed them. Within a year he had a very respectable little house and a garden which looked very much like a well-kept English allotment, where he grew a large part of the food they needed.

Mulani was no politician, but he belonged to the generation of young Africans who felt, as a matter of principle, that they had to demonstrate by their industriousness and reliability that they were capable of accepting responsibility. They wanted desperately to be recognised as individual human beings. The greatest injury which some Europeans caused them was to treat Africans as though they were an amorphous mob without individual personalities. This attitude often came from the well meaning paternalist who could not grasp the fact that no two Africans are alike, just as no two white men are alike, and that every individual wants to be recognised as such on his own merits. I think one of the reasons why I had such friendly understanding from them was because I knew them all as individuals and enjoyed the company of each because each could be rich in companionship.

The comic of our team was a tall, lanky Lango man, who could put everyone into fits of laughter. He had had practically no education at all, perhaps a year or two in a primary school, but he had taught himself English and was able to write. His most extraordinary wit often landed him in trouble. Once in his own home town he got into an argument with a local Headman who did not appreciate his brand of humour and, as a result, he landed up in the local jail for the night. He wrote a letter to me apologising for his enforced delay in a rather illiterate but very appealing way, and starting; 'This is the first time I have spoken to you through this white stuff. . . .'

As I went on long safaris with them, encircling the whole of the Protectorate, I learned to understand these young men as well as I understand my best friends. In time I was absolutely oblivious to the fact that they had black skins and I had a white one, and I believe that

. Joshua Nkomo, President of the South-
rn Rhodesia African National Congress

Julius Nyerere, Leader of the Tanganyika
African National Union

Dr. Hastings Banda, President of the
Nyasaland African National Congress

Tom Mboya, Member of Kenya
Legislative Council

8. Sir Roy Welensky, Federal Prime Minister, with Garfield Todd, former Prime Minister of Southern Rhodesia

Sir Edgar Whitehead, present Prime Minister of Southern Rhodesia

Michael Blundell, New Kenya Party

they also forgot the colour difference because the relationship we had, one with another, was on a level where colour does not play any part. I did not think of them as Africans, only as individuals. I knew them for what they were, happy when things were going well, eager always to make a success of what they were doing, deeply moved by emotional experiences, and inspired by philosophical ideals.

It is a mistake to think that Africans operate on a lower, shallower plane than Europeans. Their sensitivity of feeling can be as developed as that of the white products of western civilisation. Of course, I have known Africans, many Africans, who are dull and stupid, but there are many Europeans like that too, and unfortunately an awful lot of them find their way to Africa, which is perhaps why relationships between the races are sometimes so bad.

Most Europeans cut themselves off in isolated communities and the nearest they get to an African is when they give an order to an employee or tell the houseboy to wash up. It is ludicrous how many Europeans believe they know Africa simply because they have lived there most of their lives. They may know the physical environment, but of Africans they know practically nothing. Many have never eaten a meal with them nor attempted to hold an intelligent conversation with them.

Fortunately the attitude of Europeans was not reflected by their children. When our own children had a birthday party and European and African children were invited they were all great friends together. Some of the other European children were playing with Africans for the first time, but this did not seem to affect their ability to mix without colour consciousness. One little eight-year-old white boy made fast friends with an African of the same age but his father was a prejudiced bigot and probably would have been very angry if he had known that his son was playing with Africans. I remember the father was always complaining about African encroachments on European privileges; once he became incredibly angry because some Africans came and sat next to him in the expensive seats at the cinema.

Compulsory segregation is the biggest curse in Africa. It begins in the schools and follows through to the clubs. It is an artificial barrier which denies both sides the benefit of contact. While we were in Uganda the colour bar in the hotels was gradually breaking up and we tried to encourage its end by taking our friends into the hotels. Some Africans took the initiative themselves.

Once when we were at a dinner dance at the Imperial Hotel Apollo Kironde, a barrister, and his wife came in, both of them beautifully dressed. An embarrassed head waiter began to show them to a table in

G

the furthermost corner of the room where they would be half hidden. They joined us, however, at a table right in the centre of the room, much to the curiosity of the other diners. Although there was no unpleasantness it needed courageous people like the Kirondes to break into the supercilious atmosphere of colour privilege, which the whites had gradually evolved. Thank goodness the colour bar is now almost finished in Uganda. If only that could be said for the rest of Africa further south!

When I was on safari I invariably stayed in the homes of Africans, but in the towns we sometimes called in at the hotels for meals. In some of the smallest towns, where there were only tiny European communities, I came across the worst colour prejudice of all. At one place in particular there was a rambling hotel, which could well have passed for a shooting lodge, filled with a nasty atmosphere and Victorian bric-a-brac. I walked in for a meal with Stanley Kabuga, a smart young assistant. The proprietress came up to us as we sat at a table in the dining-room, in a state of near apoplexy. She screamed at me: 'That African should clear out of here. Don't you know that this is a European hotel?'

We studiously ignored her. Stanley was obviously under great strain but was completely controlled and eventually the woman went away and we were served very courteously by the African waiters. A few months later I went back to this hotel with some African friends and there were no incidents whatsoever. The colour bar had ended.

Journeys to Lake George and the south-western corner of Uganda were always a delightful experience. The winding road to Fort Portal took us through swamp, forest, tea plantations and all the variations of the African scene as we drove towards the foothills of the Mountains of the Moon. From Fort Portal itself, the capital of the native kingdom of Toro, I could see the majestic snow-capped mountains, the legendary Ruwenzori. These were once thought to be the source of the Nile and the ancient Egyptians knew all about them. In the mountains is a world of mystery with weird and wonderful vegetation growing to giant heights in the strange climatic conditions of an equatorial paradise of contrasts. The icy glaciers up there are real enough, but so is the heat in the foothills below.

One day I took the road around the mountain towards a corner of Toro which is completely isolated from the rest of Uganda. The road hugging the sharp mountain drop was so dangerous that cars were forbidden to travel the route out of Fort Portal between two and four in the afternoon, when the local bus was travelling in the opposite direction. Bitter experience had imposed this rule; several buses had disappeared over the edge when they had met oncoming traffic. Along that road, which descends into the thick steaming jungle, I saw near-naked pygmies who came down to the roadside to watch and to stare, looking so sad with their little wizened faces. They offered arrow heads in exchange for cigarettes or other delights to tickle the fancy of these children of the jungle. The arrow heads, made from iron ore found in the jungle, have been used by the Pygmies as a means of barter with the surrounding tribes for generations. Higher up the mountain live the gorillas, but they never came to the roadside.

Along the route we came to a crude market near Bundibugyo where my young Muganda assistant, who had never been this far from home before, was revolted by the hundreds of primitive tribespeople who crowded around dressed in skins and smelling abominably. His Buganda sensitivity was affronted by the tangible evidence of primitivism which offended all his senses.

On the way back at dusk we stopped along the road climbing through the foothills of the Ruwenzori to see the bubbling hot springs which Africans visit to cure all ailments. I was glad to leave the sulphurous fumes and climb again into the cool air of the mountain. It became suddenly dark and we picked out the winding track with our headlights; to our right the steep wooded slopes of the mountain and on the left a sharp drop hundreds of feet to the plain. As the truck rounded a bend a lioness jumped on the bonnet, crouching there only a few seconds before leaping down towards the night prey below.

On another safari, when I was due to visit Bundibugyo, we were delayed in Fort Portal so long that the plans had to be changed so as to avoid meeting the oncoming bus at the dangerous bends. Instead we headed towards the south in the direction of Lake George. It was fortunate indeed that we did so, for an hour's journey out of Fort Portal the brakes of the truck suddenly failed. We were able to pull into the side of the road, but if we had been on the original route hugging the Ruwenzori the truck would certainly have crashed over the side and fallen hundreds of feet towards the Semliki Plain below.

The journey to Lake George was like travelling through an open zoo; 1,500 square miles of the area has been designated as the Queen Elizabeth National Park, and elephants, buffalo, rhinoceros, lion, hippopotami and leopard wander freely. It was incongruous to see Africans riding nonchalantly along on their bicycles while a herd of buffalo grazed only a few yards away. They are most dangerous beasts. Once, when with Barbara and the children on a visit to this park, we had stopped the car to watch a wild boar feeding its young when a great herd of two hundred buffalo stampeded across the road just a few feet away; I can hear the roar of their hooves to this day.

Near to Katwe, the little fishing village on Lake Edward, I passed Hippo Bay where dozens of hippopotami were cavorting in the water, making their strange coughing sounds and yawning widely. I had borrowed a cine-camera and tried to get a shot of them at close quarters. I assumed, in my ignorance, that they were very slow and cumbersome on land and I advanced within a few feet of the water with the camera whirring. (Later, to my chagrin, I found that the film had run out!) When the thing began to lumber out of the water I thought I was quite safe and quietly walked back to the car. My nonchalance was shattered, however, when I saw another hippopotomus about a hundred yards away come out of the water at flying speed, looking at least as nimble on land as a carthorse. I made a mental note never to go so near a hippo again—in or out of water.

The folklore of the Lake has many stories about the hippo, which once, according to legend, had an argument with the gods of fire and of the sun. Then the hippo was a land creature but as he wanted to escape from the sun during daylight he went to the water to find an ally. The Lake agreed that the hippo could make his home in the water on condition that he never harmed any of the water creatures. The bargain is kept to this day; the hippo does not eat fish, nor does it attack fishing vessels except, very occasionally, in fear. It only leaves the vicinity of the water during the darkness, when it roams for miles away from the lake in search of food.

Katwe was one of my pleasant surprises in Africa. The neat little village nestling by the lake has mud houses, whitewashed, which have the appearance of the little stone cottages in west Wales. The fishermen work together on a co-operative basis. Their catches are pooled and the profits distributed equally. The operations of the marketing company are entirely directed by Africans who not only catch the fish but pack and sell it. Much of the catch goes to the Belgian Congo; the Muganda director is astute in his business deals with the Belgian and Greek traders across the border.

I stayed many times in this little village, sleeping in one of the whitewashed houses, and once I saw the catch come in at one o'clock in the morning. The fishermen had been out far longer than usual and the catch was heavy; they were all smiling, although tired. On the lakeside I watched the wives cleaning and throwing the fish in their hundreds into the crates to await salting the next morning. They were working by the light of Tilly lamps with the cool breezes blowing off the lake and the ominous jet black night all around. It was unusual for them to have a white visitor at that hour of the morning but they were not put off by my presence; they sang, laughed, and joked, as happy a group of people as I have ever seen at work.

During the day the scene was picturesque; the nets hanging up to dry, the occasional boat drawn up for repairs, and walking between the huts the huge, grotesque scavenger birds looking for pieces of fish. These birds were part of the everyday scene and taken for granted by everyone, but I had never seen them anywhere else. They looked like a cross between a pelican and an ostrich and stood about two or three feet high. I saw one once in the grocer's shop, standing on one leg on a crate of Pepsi-Cola and looking very solemn, almost mournful.

Half a mile away was a great dried-up salt lake where contractors still collect the salt which has been dug there for hundreds of years. Katwe salt was a source of inter-tribal trade long before the British arrived.

It was on a return from Katwe to Kampala that I had one of my few driving mishaps when I drove the truck, half laden, on to the railway line. I should say in mitigation that it was in the middle of a black night and the road had many sharp bends. The nearest town was miles away and, of course, there was no other traffic except the early morning train from Kampala due about 6 a.m. It was then about 2 a.m. The truck was too heavy for the two of us to move; after two hours of trying we scoured the neighbourhood and found some huts. The people came willingly, looking like ghosts in their long white kanzus, and with their help the truck was eventually shifted just before the train came.

On another night journey, which will live in my memory, I was carrying over a £1,000 worth of coins in a sack and my lights failed and then I had a puncture. It was in a tsetse area near the great swamp of Lake Kyoga. That time I was on my own and when I tried to change the wheel I discovered that there was no jack. I climbed back into the cabin and dozed off to sleep for I did not expect to see another vehicle in the next twelve hours. But after only an hour of snoozing the reflector mirror dazzled me with the headlights of another car. I stopped it and six young Indians, who had been on a jaunt to the Murchison Falls, changed my wheel with alacrity. But when I started again the wheel fell off, its clattering noise breaking the heavy silence of the night. Perhaps we were so anxious about the lions prowling around that diligence was sacrificed. But the Indians did not despair; they put the truck into running order and I reached Kampala safely soon after dawn.

I can remember a kaleidoscope of such experiences when I look back on my years in Uganda; the goodwill from ex-Chief Okwerede, with whom I stayed in remote Teso, who always gave me his only decent lamp so that I could read *The Times* or the *New Statesman* sitting up in bed at the end of a hectic day; the fifty peasants who spontaneously ran to my aid when the truck slipped off the road into a swamp and who heaved for an hour to lift it out; the hospitality from the many who expected nothing in return. These experiences taught me that the bonds of humanity can still be strong even in a country where deep political conflict is heightened by racialist distrust.

9

The Kabaka Debacle

SERETSE KHAMA gave me an introduction to the Kabaka before I left London, but I thought it wise to wait some weeks before using it as so many Africans were resentful of the Kabaka's feudalism and I did not want to be identified with it. But the meeting came earlier than expected.

Barbara and I were invited to a sundowner at the Imperial Hotel to welcome a visiting Pakistani dignitary. Almost all the guests were Asian or European but I noticed, sitting at a table by himself, a smart young African who looked rather lonely. I assumed that he was being neglected by the other guests and went over to sit at his table. After I had introduced myself he mumbled something, which I did not understand. We exchanged pleasantries for several minutes before I realised with a shock that he was Kabaka Mutesa II. He insisted that I stayed at his table throughout the evening.

I tried to discuss politics and economics in Africa with him. This had been possible with Seretse, who was intensely interested, but it soon became evident that the Kabaka was not. He had none of the fervour and enthusiasm of Seretse, although he was in a position to do so much more for his people than Seretse could do for the Bamangwato of Bechuanaland.

I soon discovered that most of the progressive Africans resented this indifference of the Kabaka to the real problems of Buganda. They criticised him for his playboy approach to the throne and complained that he was more interested in hunting parties than in economic problems and spent too much money on Rolls Royces.

The strongest critics of the Kabaka were in the Uganda National Congress, a political party which brought many tribes together and was gaining increasing strength under the leadership of Ignatius Musazi. Its first General Secretary was Abu Mayanja, a gifted student at Makerere College, who had come from a simple peasant background. Abu spent many days at our flat in Kitemerike House; he studied in a spare room

103

because his own home was full of goats and chickens by day and at night he had to work by candlelight. He was a delight to be with, playing his guitar as brilliantly as he quoted Shakespeare. Abu, a Mohammedan, had one great failing—particularly in Barbara's eyes— he thought that women were inferior in status and that they should have no part to play in political and economic affairs. 'Woman's place is in the home' was his theme and whenever he wanted to goad Barbara into an argument he knew just the way to start one.

Abu was always getting himself into trouble because of his forthright manner and his unwillingness to knuckle under when he had a grievance. At Makerere College he was suspected (probably correctly!) of leading a strike of students against the poor food in the refectories and because of this he was expelled. Sir Andrew Cohen, although bitterly attacked by him, had a soft spot for Mayanja and arranged a grant to enable him to go to Cambridge University. After a successful course there Abu was called to the Bar and has now returned to Uganda after a world tour which took in Cairo, Moscow and Peking. The part he is to play in the affairs of Uganda may not be unlike that of Nkrumah in the Gold Coast. When he was still a student he drew up the constitution of the Uganda National Congress and had it launched before he left for Cambridge. He had left the country when events took place which shook the whole of Buganda and shattered the confidence of Africans in British colonial rule.

On the 30 June 1953, Mr Oliver Lyttelton, (now Lord Chandos), who was then Secretary of State for the Colonies, made a speech to the East African Dinner Club in which he referred to the Central African Federation and said, 'Nor should we exclude from our minds the evolution, as time goes on, of still larger measures of unification, and possibly still larger measures of Federation of the whole East African territories.'

This was taken up by the *East African Standard* in Nairobi, the settlers' paper, and the remark was represented as an indication that the Government was planning political federation in East Africa.

The Kabaka had not yet returned from his Coronation visit to Britain and the three Ministers of the Buganda Government took it upon themselves to write a letter to the Governor drawing attention to the threat of Federation, saying that it would 'shake the foundations of trust among our people and will also badly damage the good relations which hitherto obtained between the Baganda and the British'. Behind this was the fear that East African Federation would mean the domination of Uganda by the Kenya white settlers in much the same way as the

Nyasa Africans feared being brought under the domination of the Southern Rhodesian whites by the experiment in Central African Federation.

The Governor replied that the Colonial Secretary's speech did not indicate any change of policy and that the future development of Uganda and other East African territories must be guided by local public opinion.

When the Kabaka returned to his palace on Mengo he sent a message to the Governor, countersigned by his Ministers on behalf of the Lukiko, which pointedly referred to Nyasaland as the reason for the Africans' fears in Uganda. It threw the assurance of the Governor that 'the future would be guided by local public opinion' right back in his face by saying:

'As regards the statement which has appeared in your letter, setting out a condition in the event of a political union of the three territories namely that such a union can only come about by the desire and the express of public opinion of the majority of local peoples, my people and Government have this to comment, that recent happenings in Central Africa have shown that however many there may be Africans opposing a proposal, the wishes of the minority who are generally non-Africans must necessarily prevail, no matter what petitions, deputations, and representatives are sent to the authorities by the Africans. Some African deputations from Central Africa were recently not even shown the courtesy of being received in London and the Federation has merely been imposed upon them, however much it goes against their will. It will not be unreasonable to compare the destiny of Uganda to that which has overtaken Nyasaland, both countries being Treaty states and Protectorates, but Nyasaland has been forced into the Central African Federation. This evidently suggests that local opinion seems to mean the opinion of the least section of the population as long as that section happens to be the most vocal.'

Accompanying the Kabaka's letter was a memorandum by the Great Lukiko which described how in 1894 the then Kabaka, Mwanga, had entered into a free Agreement with Queen Victoria, which resulted in the declaration of the British Protectorate. Uganda was then under the care of the Foreign Office but was transferred to the Colonial Office in 1902. This, the Lukiko complained, meant lowering of the status of Buganda. They said, 'We are not a colony, we have never been a colony', and as an example of the lower status referred to the treatment given to the Kabaka at the Coronation of Queen Elizabeth. They claimed that he was treated no differently from other colonial guests, whereas in 1902 when a Sir Apolo Kagwa, who was Prime Minister and Regent, was the guest at the Coronation of King Edward VII, he was recognised as a distinguished foreign guest, as distinct from the colonial guests. The Lukiko also complained about the setting up of the East African High Commission, which pooled the economic resources of Uganda without consulting the Great Lukiko of Buganda.

The memorandum referred to the celebrated speech of Mr Lyttelton's and to 'the fact that it followed soon after the imposition of Federation over Central Africa against African opinion and the disregard of the Nyasaland status as a Protectorate', and emphasised that the Great Lukiko was 'compelled to take steps to safeguard their future'. They demanded that the affairs of Buganda should revert to the Foreign Office and that a time limit be set for their independence within the Commonwealth, making it crystal clear that they strongly opposed any form of political union with the neighbouring territories.

That was on the 6 August 1953. The Governor did not reply until the 27 October, by which time tension was growing in the country. Like many others I had to make a re-assessment of the Kabaka, for he was showing extraordinary courage in reflecting what was undoubtedly the feeling of the majority of the Baganda people. I had assumed that he was a playboy, but he was not prepared to sell-out what he considered to be the interests of his own people.

When the Governor's reply eventually arrived it said that Her Majesty's Government had no intention of raising the issue of East African Federation either at the present time or while local public opinion on the issue 'remains as it is at the present time'. Sir Andrew also remarked caustically that the Colonial Secretary did not propose to comment on the remarks about Central Africa although 'this must not be taken as meaning he accepts those remarks'. The request to transfer Buganda affairs to the Foreign Office was similarly rejected on the grounds that under the 1900 Agreement Buganda was clearly stated to rank as a province forming part of the Uganda Protectorate.

Within a month the Governor asked the Kabaka to sign a statement that he would accept the decisions of Her Majesty's Government and that he would inform the Great Lukiko publicly at its next meeting that those decisions must be accepted. On the very next day the Kabaka replied to the Governor, refusing to sign the document without first consulting the Great Lukiko itself. He said:

'Were I to affix my signature to the document in question I should be nullifying my whole position with my people as their Kabaka and acting contrary to the democratic principles which are supposed to motivate Her Majesty's Government.'

The Kabaka also wanted a cable to be sent to this effect to the Colonial Secretary in London, asking for an early reply as the Lukiko was meeting shortly; and as the Governor had arranged a further meeting with him, he took the text of the cable with him and asked the Governor to despatch it. Little did he know when he drove into Entebbe that fateful morning of 30 November that he was going into a trap.

From ten o'clock the Governor did his best for three hours to persuade the Kabaka to accept the British Government's ultimatum but the Kabaka insisted that he should consult the Great Lukiko. This was the advice he had from his Ministers who were waiting in another room in Government House, and whom he consulted twice.

Because the Kabaka was adamant the Governor ordered him to be escorted to the airport, put on a RAF aeroplane and deported from the Protectorate. He was put into this position because, at that stage, he tried to be a constitutional monarch, paying some heed to democracy, and not being merely a British stooge. He was not even allowed to pack his clothes or say goodbye to his wife. Sir Andrew was showing his mailed fist.

Public opinion in Buganda was stunned. I was in Katwe, near Kampala, when the news first broke. People were walking around dazed, unable to believe the news that their king had been flown away against his will. There was a wave of support for the Kabaka; even those who did not understand the issues involved or who were opposed to the feudal nature of the office were solidly behind him.

The active politicians in the Uganda National Congress who had been opposed to the Kabaka because of his dilettantism and apathy were now as firmly in his support as any other section of the community. It was feared that further arrests would now follow, particularly as it became evident that the political leaders were in support of the Kabaka, and not opposed to him as the Government had thought. Ignatius Musazi was particularly worried as he was being watched by the Special Branch and he urged me to see him at the Lukiko office to discuss the position. I went up to Mengo hill and was shown into the Lukiko by the sentries. In a sparsely furnished room I found Ignatius and Amos Sempa (a Minister in the Buganda Government) engaged in an earnest discussion. They switched to English as soon as I came in and Sempa told me of his fears that if the politicians organised demonstrations, which would be attended by hundreds of thousands, the Govern-

ment would take repressive measures against the people. This they
wanted to avoid at all costs; although the Baganda people were shaken
to the core they wanted to make their protest against the British
Government's action in a dignified and responsible way. He thought
that Musazi, as the leading political figure in the country, should go to
Britain and make known the opinions of the Baganda there. Ignatius
then intervened. He knew that he was being watched and that if he went
to Entebbe airport to catch a plane he would be arrested. The Government were probably only watching for him to make a move before they
swooped on him. I advised him to leave the country by another route,
and as quickly as possible.

Secretly we arranged for a hired car and late that night Musazi was
driven towards the northern frontier and across into the Sudan,
following the route I had taken the year before. He reached Juba and
was given facilities in the Sudan, travelling up the Nile by steamer.
Reaching Egypt, he obtained further help from President Nasser. An
eye disease, which he caught on the Nile, delayed his journey and he
did not reach London until some weeks later. When he did arrive he
held a press conference at the House of Commons.

Uganda had been looked upon as a model colony, gradually pro-
gressing towards independence. Parliament was amazed that this
tranquil country should suddenly be the centre of a clash between the
colonial government and Africans. Newspaper correspondents arrived
in Kampala by the score and we met many of them—Colin Legum and
Hugh Latimer of the *Observer*, Alexander Campbell of *Time/Life*,
Philip Goodhart* of the *Telegraph*, and many others. In their wake
came Members of Parliament.

Most of the newspapermen summed up the situation well but one or
two came to the most dogmatic conclusions; the MPs limited themselves to talking painstakingly to the string of political leaders and other
dignitaries introduced to them by the Government. One exception was
a Parliamentarian who did not know much about Africa but who went
out of his way to interview the whole executive of the Uganda National
Congress. Barbara and I were very surprised when he came back afterwards and told us about the Congress policy for the constitution of
Uganda. We knew that Congress had no such policy as it was involved
in the clash between the conceptions of a unitary and a federal structure;
in the context of the Kabaka issue it was impossible to get the Congress
politicians to think this problem out clearly. But the MP had one
meeting with them and found a policy. With his agile brain working

* Later elected Conservative Member of Parliament for Beckenham.

overtime he could cut through the growth of confusion and emotion which overwhelmed the Africans he was interviewing. Later we heard how his interviews were conducted.

'Would it be true to say so-and-so and so-and-so?' he would ask. The Africans nodded in an agreeable way as they were thinking out the implications of the question and in the case of those whose English was shaky, translating it back into their own language. But before they had had time to do all this and give a considered reply the MP had snapped at them again.

'Yes, I thought you did. Ahem. Then you also think so-and-so and so-and-so?' After thirty minutes of this the Africans were thoroughly perplexed by his quick-fire interrogation and had hardly had time to say anything for themselves at all. We tried to make it clear to the MP that Congress had not worked out its policy but he was sure that he had found out something which had been denied to others.

Meanwhile the Baganda were expressing their opposition to the Government's action by every non-violent means; they behaved with incredible restraint. As a sign of their disgust with the Governor they took to wearing bark cloth and growing beards. Every other man in Kampala went to work with a beard and all my assistants grew them. Everyone wore something made of bark cloth; some sported scarves or ties of it but several enterprising men went further and had complete suits made of bark cloth which looked as smart as wool, though its keeping qualities were distinctly inferior. The Nabagereka (the Kabaka's wife), wore bark cloth dresses and native dress and discarded her West End fashions from Messrs. Marshall and Snelgrove.

The Acting President of the Uganda National Congress, Mr S. M. Sekabanja, started a boycott of all non-African goods and non-African shops. The boycott was almost immediately effective. The sales of bread, cloth, bicycles and other goods fell within a few weeks to a mere fraction of what they had been before. The Asian traders who had built up big stocks in the expectation of a good cotton season found it difficult to meet their debts. In an attempt to win back trade they slashed their prices below cost; traders in Buganda hired vehicles and took their goods miles outside the province to areas where the boycott was not in force to engage in bitter and slashing competition among themselves to win the limited custom available. Even merchants as far afield as Nairobi and Mombasa were affected. They had imported goods in expectation of big demands in Uganda and when the orders did not materialise they sent their own vehicles 600 miles or more in an attempt to dispose of their goods in small lots by travelling from shop to shop.

Although we were not immediately affected by an African boycott our own consumers' organisation soon began to suffer as we were unable to sell goods at fair prices and they had to be disposed of below cost. The boycott went on throughout the early months of 1954 but the economic effects of it lasted well over a year. Many traders received a death blow from it.

The Government did not ban the Uganda National Congress but restrictions were placed on the size of meetings and the freedom of the press was gravely affected by prosecutions for sedition. One of those accused was Ddamba, the Acting Editor of the *Uganda Post* in the absence of Joseph Kiwanuka in England. Kiwanuka was chairman of the Uganda National Congress and the Government wanted to hit at him through the *Uganda Post*. Ddamba had reprinted an article on the Uganda crisis from the *Socialist Leader* by George Padmore, the Negro writer who was then in London but who became Adviser on African Affairs to Dr Nkrumah in Ghana. There was really nothing exceptional about the article, but the Attorney General decided on a prosecution. Defending Counsel was David Lubogo, who had been a fellow student of mine at the London School of Economics. He asked me to appear as a witness for the defence, and I gladly did. The case was taken before an Asian magistrate, Mr Saldanha, and Ddamba, as everyone expected, was found guilty.

When Joseph Kiwanuka returned from Britain he was allowed to travel around freely for some time, but the freedom was shortlived; he was rusticated to a remote area of Uganda in the north-west on the boundary of the Belgian Congo. I visited him once on a safari and found that he was having a wonderful time as a rusticate. He had a house to himself and had put his guard to work in the garden. He rode a Government bicycle into Arua to play tennis with the local District Commissioner who apparently found him good company. Kiwanuka is one of the most flamboyant characters in Uganda. His bow tie and gruff, aggressive manner are well known there—he is an African Lord Boothby. He is now a leader of the Uganda National Congress, although it has suffered so many successive splits that one cannot be sure which is the genuine Congress. Kiwanuka has had much help from President Nasser for his group and this has incurred the severe displeasure of the Governor. When he returned from a visit to Moscow and Peking he had his passport impounded.

The Lukiko secretary showed me copies of the secret correspondence between the Kabaka and the other rulers concerning the rights of the Agreement states. Apparently Cohen was most concerned when he

heard about these negotiations between the kings, although he did not
see the letters. They were the first sign of the Kabaka's intransigence.
The Governor could not deal with more than one unruly ruler at a time
and faced with unity of the kings the position of Britain as the imperial
power would soon have become intolerable. The minutes which I saw
of the Kabaka's meetings made it clear that the negotiations had reached
quite an advanced level.

The Omukama of Toro, ruler in the far west of the Protectorate near
the Mountains of the Moon, asked me to have a talk with him. I knew
him quite well. When we were living in the Kitemerike House he
arrived one morning while I was out and was invited by Barbara to have
something to eat. He ended up by eating all the lunch before I had even
arrived. That created a bond of friendship! He is a giant of a man;
certainly the tallest and biggest man I saw in Uganda, even bigger than
Cohen, and when he spoke in a whisper it was possible to hear him in
the next room. This is probably why he behaved so oddly when I
called on him. As I drove up to the house of the Baganda Minister with
whom he was staying the Omukama rushed out of the front door
towards my car, waving to me to stay in the seat. He opened the car
door, plonked into the seat beside me, and told me to drive away
quickly. Then he directed me to a lonely little house where we could
not be overheard.

He told me that he was furious with the Government for taking away
the Kabaka. 'This action has struck at our loyalty to the British.' Now
the Government had taken this action against the leading king of the
Protectorate the others did not feel at all safe if they spoke out for the
rights of the people. In Toro, he complained, the British had given vast
areas of land for a National Park for the protection of game while
human beings were land hungry. 'But how can we make our grievances
known to the British Government when they take dictatorial action like
deporting the Kabaka? And,' he added, bending over towards me with
a confidential look and holding a large fat finger against his lips as if to
motion me to complete secrecy, 'do you know that I am being followed?
I have to take great care now what I do. That is why I brought you
here, because I am sure you cannot trust anyone these days. You cannot
even trust some of these Baganda Ministers, telling the Governor what
the Africans are saying!'

I was rather surprised that he should treat me as his confidant at all,
and can only assume that he was desperate for advice or that he thought
I would be able to communicate with the Labour Opposition in
Parliament.

The crisis became more acute when Mr Henry Hopkinson (now Lord Colyton), who was then Minister of State for the Colonies, said in a debate in the House of Commons that the 'possibility of the Kabaka being able to return to Uganda must be discounted'. It is fortunate for all concerned that this remark did not have the same disastrous effects on Uganda as a similar one which Mr Hopkinson made about Cyprus had on that unhappy island. But tension developed in Buganda when more statements were made by Protectorate officials to the effect that the deportation of the Kabaka was irrevocable.

There were rumours that the Government intended to impose a new Kabaka on Buganda and they were undoubtedly true, but the Governor had to take account of the almost unanimous opposition of the Baganda. He announced that it was not his intention to impose a new Kabaka against the will of the people. A special constitutional commission was appointed in order to break the impasse under the guidance of Sir Keith Hancock, a professor of Commonwealth Affairs. The Lukiko appointed a committee to meet him.

Meanwhile the judgment in a case brought before the Uganda High Court by the Lukiko shook the Government. It said that the decision to withdraw recognition from the Kabaka was justified but that the withdrawal of recognition under Article 6 of the Agreement was an error. The Baganda sensed a victory and soon after, when the Governor drove to the Lukiko meeting to make an announcement about Government decisions, he could not make his speech because of shouts and the stones thrown at his car.

Nevertheless, the speech was published and it was revealed that the constitutional recommendations of the Hancock Commission were accepted by the Government and that the Kabakaship would be transformed into something like a constitutional monarchy. The Kabaka could return nine months after the Lukiko had put the recommendations into effect.

Kabaka Mutesa II eventually returned in October 1955, within two years of the speech of Mr Henry Hopkinson. It would be a mistake, however, to assume that relationships in Uganda have been happy since that year. The Baganda are now intensely suspicious of the Government following the high-handed way in which their Kabaka was treated. Sir Andrew Cohen was very badly advised indeed when he was led to believe, partly by Uganda's Attorney General (who is still in office today) and partly by the Special Branch, that popular political opinion among the Baganda would be on the Governor's side against the Kabaka.

They had assumed this because of the rivalries between the up and coming politicians like Musazi and Kiwanuka and the leading members of the Lukiko. There had been an incident in Katwe only a short time before the deportation when a picture of the Kabaka had been defaced and a poster of a monkey put in its place. The poster, nailed to a tree, had then been pelted with rotten mangoes. But such demonstrations of public hostility to the Kabaka were never repeated after the Governor's action. Although the Kabaka may have been disliked personally by some elements he was a symbol of Baganda independence and prestige and the removal of the Kabaka was felt to be an affront to the whole nation.

When Sir Andrew was faced with the inevitable difficulties of negotiations with the Kabaka and the undemocratic Lukiko his wisest course would have been to continue the negotiations whilst pushing through the reforms of the Legislative Council and allowing for direct elections on a fairly wide franchise. This would have cut the ground from right under the feet of the feudalists and would have given a platform for the progressives in an enlarged and vastly more important central Legislature. The reforms, however, were held back—perhaps the reaction on nearby Kenya, where the white settlers were desperately afraid of the Africans being given increased political responsibility, was feared.

When direct elections eventually came to Uganda they were a great success. Over 80 per cent of the registered voters went to the polls, but because of the aftermath of suspicion and mistrust, Buganda did not participate in the direct elections and to this day there are difficulties in securing the representation of the Buganda district in the Legislature.

As soon as the Kabaka had settled back into the throne the political parties were again organised, but this time on an increasingly divergent scale. Mr E. M. K. Mulira, a very moderate editor of a vernacular newspaper and a former research worker, became the President of the Progressive Party, which had the support of many young intellectuals. The Roman Catholics organised the Democratic Party, with active support from the White Fathers, while Ignatius Musazi's Uganda National Congress has had three major splits. The Uganda National Movement, a new phenomenon, largely confined to Buganda, has brought under its wing all the political parties except the Uganda National Congress and the Democratic Party, in an attempt to consolidate public political interest in Buganda.

Another boycott campaign of non-African shops was set under way and the Uganda Government, under a new Governor, Sir Frederick

H

Crawford, came down very strongly against it. The Uganda National Movement was banned; so were its successors, the Freedom Movement and the Freedom Convention, and the six principal leaders rusticated to remote areas; and a Bill to ban trade boycotts was introduced.

These actions solve nothing, of course. They only sow far wider the seeds of hatred and discontent. The only answer to Uganda's political problems is a clear time-table towards independence as an African state, with a central Assembly elected on the basis of universal adult suffrage, and the provinces, such as Buganda, having locally elected councils, like the Lukiko, which would be responsible for local services.

For the success of such a political framework it is necessary to have national political movements which can unite the tribes but allow for local political activity and expression. If the African peasantry are to play their part in this new democracy their participation should not be limited; they should have a say through co-operatives in the villages and trade unions in the towns, and, of course, within the political parties themselves, as well as using the vote. There is a danger of power being collected in the hands of a few autocrats who destroy the democratic heritage for their own prestige. In Buganda itself autocrats have been much in evidence and the Lukiko itself has been opposed to democratic elections because it fears that democracy would sweep the present incumbents out of office.

In the transition from British colonial paternalism to a thriving, lively social democracy there are many difficult stages to be overcome. One should never assume that they are easy to overcome, but the colonial power should be quite frank with the Africans as to the way they are being tackled. They cannot treat a Protectorate as a kindergarten, as though Africans had no right to know what is going to happen to them and should be smacked if they reach out for the fruit too quickly. They must be allowed to know how the transition is being effected and given ample opportunity to make their suggestions about the matter which affects them far more deeply than it affects us. To keep them in the dark creates enmity and suspicion.

On 23 December 1959 the Wild Committee of the Uganda Legislative Council recommended a new National Assembly of seventy-nine Members to be elected early in 1961 on a common roll with universal adult suffrage. It would therefore have an overwhelming African majority. It is to be hoped that the Government will implement the report and pave the way for Uganda's self-government on a democratic basis.

10

Court Room in the Wilderness

WHILE I was in Uganda, from 1952 to the middle of 1954, neighbouring Kenya was in the grip of a complex struggle between democracy and justice, and privilege, racialism and primitivism. None of these five attributes was confined to any one of the many factions. The situation was made almost impossibly complicated to the outside world by the fact that neither side, if in this the Kenya Government and the Mau Mau can be considered *sides*, had a monopoly of virtue or sin. The Kenya Government and the loyalists included many who were striving for a decent order of society for Africans and Europeans; but also within Mau Mau there were men who, because they felt completely frustrated as other legitimate ways of expressing their grievances had been closed to them, resorted to violence as a means of securing a remedy.

They could be compared to the gunmen of the Stern gang who committed atrocities as a means to the end of establishing national independence in Israel. The numbers of such men supporting or condoning Mau Mau became fewer as the movement became more addicted to revolting sexual ceremonies and the atrocities themselves became increasingly pointless. The Kenya Government and the white minority in Kenya must, however, accept a large part of the blame for the growth of Mau Mau as a mass revolt of the Kikuyu. Early concessions to legitimate African grievances about land and political representation would have removed much of its motive force.

In addition to those who felt the political appeal there were many Africans who were attracted by the mysticism. Those who besmirch Africans as a race because in Kenya and other countries they have used mystical and bestial practices should be reminded that 'civilised' countries also have their secret societies and also that mass horror has been the hallmark of Hitler, Franco, Stalin, and always ostensibly in the interests of 'high ideals'. Mau Mau atrocities, hideous as they have been, pale into insignificance against Belsen, Buchenwald and Auschwitz, yet Germany has now, to all intents and purposes, been admitted to the comity of nations and the past has been disregarded. Similarly the past of Mau Mau should not be used as an excuse for denying legitimate African aspirations.

There were those in the Kenya Government and among the white settlers who used the campaign against Mau Mau as a means of suppressing African demands for reform. Many of these settlers, particularly, had no respect for the dignity of the African individual and saw themselves as the master race in Kenya. The growth of the Kenya African Union appeared to them to be a threat to their privilege.

There were, however, some settlers as well as Government officers who were sincerely interested in helping the Africans to advance and were prepared to give them an increasing stake in the government. But there was almost no meeting point between the African nationalists who expressed the desires of the black millions, and the few progressives among the whites. Frustration grew to fever pitch when in 1952 the KAU deputation led by Mbiyu Koinange and Achieng Oneko, its General Secretary, asking for the opening up of the White Highlands for African farming, achieved nothing. Restrictions were put on African meetings and on the collection of subscriptions, which deepened the sense of hopelessness. Africans who had heard of India's independence and the developments in the Gold Coast feared that in Kenya, because of the white settlers, they were to be denied political advancement and kept under white domination in perpetuity.

It was in that atmosphere of frustration and growing hatred of the European that the Mau Mau made converts. There is an element in all tribes which hankers to return to sheer primitivism but only in the worst conditions will it gain support and develop a cult of hideous brutality. We knew that in Buganda. A section of the tribe supporting the Bataka Party was in favour of primitive rites and developed an anti-European psychosis, but it was never able to secure a grip on the tribe as a whole because after the Kabaka debacle the Government showed itself willing to negotiate. In Kenya all means of negotiations were abandoned and nearly all the political leaders detained with, or mostly without, trial. This may well have forced some African nationalists to ally themselves with the Mau Mau, although they hated the primitive aspects of it. In any case, the events bred in them a deep distrust of the white man.

The Europeans in East Africa vied with each other in finding reasons for the phenomenon of Mau Mau. It gave them an opportunity to analyse the African personality, which few of them had really attempted before. Although they might have lived in Africa for two or three decades, they almost invariably accepted Africans merely as servants and made no attempt to understand them as individuals or to evaluate their attitude to life. I have often heard Europeans who have lived in Africa for years claiming that they know Africans so well and then they say, 'Only the other day my houseboy said to me. . . .' The only Africans with whom they have any real contact are servants, who themselves are hardly ever in a position to say exactly how they think and feel.

The 'state of the African mind' was a favourite topic of conversation in the bars and the clubs where Europeans forgathered. In such circles it was generally accepted that the African brain is smaller than the European and that it 'has less wrinkles'. These misconceptions and some variations have been found repeated in pseudo-serious books. Mr C. T. Stoneham, who is a Kenya settler of more than thirty years' standing, gives the following priceless information in his book *Out of Barbarism*:

'If six people are living in a house and an African servant is accustomed to make tea for them, he will continue to provide exactly the same quantity of tea after four of them have left. If a dish is served and the bwana requests a second helping, he will receive twice as much as at first, it being evident that he did not get enough the first time. If the master finds an article in a position unsuitable for him and moves it daily, it will invariably be returned to its first position, even if he goes on doing this for months. An African always places a trunk or suitcase with the locks against the wall so that it cannot be opened, and generally he puts it upside down. He may be able to read and write English, but he will still do this; as he will usually put books into a bookcase the wrong way up.'

This is, of course, an exaggerated and misrepresentative account. I cannot help comparing this cynical attitude with the careful, well written applications I used to receive for jobs and the way in which Africans carry out responsible jobs, ranging from bar stewards to barristers. Environment makes the man, and this is true of the European as well as the African. Many decent Europeans going to Africa as settlers find themselves in a situation in which the white man is regarded as master and the black as servant. His fellow Europeans preach a doctrine of race superiority; within time he falls a victim to this environmental influence, even if his outlook had been progressive before. This shaping of the personalities of white settlers is one of the plagues of Africa. It was very much at work during the Mau Mau period when many Europeans in Kenya—but happily, not all—developed an acute hatred of all Africans, partly through fear. This developed into physical cruelty in some cases and the attitude of the European mind in Kenya at that time certainly influenced Government officers to the excessive use of repressive powers. Powers of detention were certainly abused, many thousands of innocent people were rounded up.

One of them was Achieng Oneko who was charged with being a Mau Mau organiser. By taking action against some of the leading politicians the Kenya Government hoped to separate them from their followers and destroy the strength of the African political movement, but instead their action has consolidated African opposition to the Government. The trial of Achieng and others will be remembered as one of the historic events in Africa. Few Africans believed it was a fair trial and most Europeans thought that some aspects of it were distinctly unsatisfactory. The recriminations about the trial will go on for a long time to come, at least until those who were found guilty and have completed their sentences are allowed to return from life banishment.

Principal among the accused was Jomo Kenyatta, 'the flaming spear', now over sixty years of age and broken, but in his earlier days a dynamic African leader. To avoid expected demonstrations outside the court the trial was arranged to take place at an isolated village called Kapenguria instead of in Nairobi. The world's Press made a pilgrimage to the scene of the trial, which was news for months.

When I heard that Achieng had been arrested and was accused of being responsible for a movement which used the most bestial of tortures, I was flabbergasted. I had known him as a well-meaning, moderate man who was always quite gentle in his approach, although a determined political campaigner. I volunteered to give a character witness on his behalf and the evening before I was due to be called by defending counsel, D. N. Pritt, I drove the two hundred miles from Kampala towards Kitale. Night fell long before I left Uganda and I crossed the border into the White Highlands to find it apparently completely deserted. It was an eerie experience to pass through villages without a light showing and covered in a shroud of silence. But about midnight I saw a man with two women trudging along the roadside. One of the women was pregnant and obviously ill; I gave them a lift to the nearest dispensary, which saved them a walk of twenty miles.

I reached Kitale early in the morning and woke up the sleepy night porter in the town's only hotel. Next morning I met D. N. Pritt at breakfast; he was still preparing the defence case for yet another day of the long-drawn-out trial. There was another group of witnesses to produce at the court and he asked me to drive the whole party to

Kapenguria in a hired Consul. We set off along the rutted road, strain-
ing the springs of the overladen car. Some miles out of Kitale we were
stopped at a police post and the passes were carefully examined. I got
through without a pass; as I was the driver there were few questions
asked.

The courtroom turned out to be in a European style school building.
Troops with rifles and sub-machine-guns were all round it, presumably
to guard the court from a possible Mau Mau attack. I waited outside on
the road for my turn to be called as a witness and I overheard an
armoured car sending a radio signal down to Nairobi. It was a
request for someone down there to take care of a police officer's
dogs.

It was surprising how small the courtroom was, yet in this little
schoolroom was being played out a drama of months which affected
the lives of millions. The 'public gallery' was occupied by a few white
farmers' wives who had driven up for the day from the European
farms around Kitale. There were no Africans there as it was practically
impossible for them to reach Kapenguria, which was in the closed area.
The seven accused sat in a dock together with an armed askari at each
end and a European police officer stood at the door. The Press were also
there, and the lawyers for both sides.

After I had given my evidence of Achieng's character the prosecution
asked for an adjournment of the court to enable them to prepare a cross-
examination of me, but when I returned to the witness box Mr Somer-
hough, the Prosecuting Counsel, said 'No questions'. I took a
seat in the public gallery and watched the rest of the day's proceedings.

At the lunch break D. N. Pritt and I ate sandwiches and drank coffee
with all the accused, without any police supervision. I met Jomo
Kenyatta for the first and last time. He was in surprisingly good spirits,
almost jovial, and looked relaxed in a weatherbeaten bush jacket and
corduroy trousers. I sat with Achieng in a corner of the room and had
a confidential talk. He again protested his innocence and said that he
had publicly condemned Mau Mau, but that he could not be sure about
one of his colleagues.

At the end of that first hearing Judge Thacker found all the accused
guilty and sentenced them to long terms of imprisonment, but later,
on appeal to the Kenya Supreme Court, Achieng was acquitted. In spite
of his acquittal, however, he was immediately re-arrested under the
Emergency Regulations and kept with hard core Mau Mau detainees
in various camps, including the notorious Manda Island. I have since

heard from him many times in letters smuggled out by friendly warders. He not only complained about his own imprisonment, which was unjustified, but gave details of ill-treatment of detainees and prisoners by the authorities. He was not even allowed a visit from his wife until I raised his case in Parliament in 1957. He was then able to see her for the first time in five years. In 1958 he was eventually released from detention, after six years, but is still 'restricted'.

When the news was published in the *Uganda Herald* that I had been a witness for one of the accused at the Kapenguria trial, some of the Europeans began to mutter that I was a supporter of Mau Mau. By then we were quite familiar with their shallow interpretation of politics and a curious moral ethic which gave them the capacity to see issues only in black and white. The attitude, based as it was on fear, probably had much in common with the fear psychosis of McCarthyism in the United States, and it prevented them from understanding why anyone should put himself out to try to prevent an African from being wrongly imprisoned. A poetic equation appeared in the *Uganda Herald* from a Scottish businessman, who formed an organisation similar to the League of Empire Loyalists, which accused Barbara and me and the Shepherds of being active supporters of Mau Mau. We dismissed it as pathetic nonsense, but another businessman of better repute rushed to our defence. Within the European business community there were some who approved of the line we had taken.

Later we discovered that some others did *not* approve. We had decided to take the children on a much needed holiday to see the sea at Mombasa and were intending to drive the thousand miles to the coast to relax by the Indian Ocean. But when we went to the Immigration Officer to go through the formality of having our passports endorsed for travel to Kenya, he looked at his list and told me that I had been declared a Prohibited Immigrant in Kenya. I said, incredulously, 'Why in heaven's name should they want to prohibit me from having a holiday in Kenya?'

The Immigration Officer shrugged his shoulders and said, 'We are never given any reasons why these orders are given.'

But he promised to make inquiries to see if we could get to Mombasa.

The reply was favourable, but we had to report to the police during our stay. We learnt later that the Kenya Government's action had been taken because of my friendship with Achieng Oneko and my plea on his behalf at the Kapenguria trial; the authorities did not look with favour on those who were identified with Africans.

PART TWO

II

Return to Africa

The landscape and the people of Africa are attractions enough, but to me Africa displays another aspect. The challenge is very real. It is like an arrow pointed at the soul of Europe.

The European powers have squabbled about Africa; they have colonised; they have sent their missionaries and traders; settlers, engineers, professors and others in search of service, adventure or profit have travelled in their thousands to Africa. But can any one of us yet say that he *knows* Africa? The diversity confuses and the mind fumbles with the problems of political and economic evolution. But Europe, over several centuries, had been embroiled in Africa; the responsibility for helping to conquer the problems cannot be given up lightly.

Africa is dynamic; the land and the people can be changed by the building of a factory, or a railway, or a dam, or even a road. A track can open up the contact for a primitive people and within a few years they can be transformed by the civilising influence from outside. Some tribes do still stand aloof, whatever influences are brought to bear on them. The Karamojong in the north-east of Uganda are living today in much the same way as they did centuries ago, before the British arrived. Like the Masai in Kenya and Tanganyika, they live off their cattle. Not for them the complicated business of growing crops to sell for money. They use their cattle as a form of wealth and for their food drink the blood and the milk of their animals.

But these backward tribes are the exception; most of the people in Africa are developing at a pace which keeps them in step with the economic and social changes going on around them. Indeed, in many places they stimulate change by their own initiative. The Wachagga, for instance, on the slopes of Mount Kilimanjaro who, through their successful co-operative marketing of coffee, have made thousands of pounds which have been allocated to educational facilities for their members. Their great new education centre, built with their own

money, is a monument to their determination to instil a sense of purpose in the new African man.

Because Africa is changing so quickly and so dramatically it is vitally
necessary to keep in touch. After I was elected a Member of Parliament
for the Wednesbury constituency, at a by-election in February, 1957,
and started asking questions in the House of Commons, I had a shoal of
correspondence from British territories. Every week requests came in
from people with personal grievances to ventilate. Many of them could
not be ventilated or remedied locally. The Mother of Parliaments must
pursue these cases, even though the post office at the Palace of Westminster is cluttered up with the mail from all the towns and villages of
British Africa. It is ironical that the Colonial Office diligently considers
each individual case, although when major political issues are at stake
the rights of the individual are pushed aside without adequate consideration being given to them.

I was glad when opportunities came for me to revisit Africa as a
Member of Parliament. Sitting in the Palace of Westminster reading
letters or even meeting scores of visitors from Africa cannot be a
substitute for seeing the situations at first hand. In the Spring of 1958
I returned to Uganda to advise coffee Co-operatives, and within a year
I was arranging to visit Africa yet again. This time I was going to study
the political and racial problems of Central Africa, which had given so
much concern to people in Britain. I also wanted to see the situation in
Kenya and Tanganyika—especially the Kenya detention camps, about
which I had received horrifying accounts.

I left on Friday the 13th February, 1959, by BOAC Britannia. The
aeroplane, destination Johannesburg, was full with returning tourists
and students, some businessmen, and probably one or two newspaper
correspondents. The aeroplane was bound for the black continent, but
every one of the passengers, except for a Kenya Asian, was white. But of
course there was no colour bar on the aircraft. Many South Africans sit
down with negroes for the first time on a BOAC aircraft and such travel
certainly broadens their minds.

Rome was the last stopping place before leaving Europe and
because of an engine failure we spent a day there on a conducted
tour as guests of BOAC. The next stage of the journey would
take us into Africa, to Khartoum, the capital of the Sudan. After a meal
served by the stewards, we settled down to an uneasy sleep. Below, the
Mediterranean and the tail of Italy disappeared behind us. Ahead,
the darkness of Africa. Above, a great bowl of a sky glowing with
stars of unusual intensity. Outside, a quiet, unreal world. Inside, the

passengers sleeping uncomfortably to the drone of the aircraft.

We landed at the tiny oasis of twinkling lights of Khartoum and the passengers were surprised by the heat at two hours after midnight. In the airport restaurant we were served with coffee and cold drinks by soft-footed waiters who never seemed to be tired. Other Arabs outside, dressed in a strange assortment of ex-army clothing, were struggling with the luggage of the disembarking passengers. There was much shoving and shouting. Standing in a curio shop in the corner of the lounge was a tall Sudanese gentleman. His business is open twenty-four hours a day to receive the passengers who want to carry away souvenirs of their half-an-hour on Sudan soil.

We reached Nairobi airport shortly after dawn. Waiting at the barrier for me was J. M. Desai, who had been up half the night expecting a message giving the time of arrival of the delayed aeroplane. We shook hands warmly—it had been five years since we had last met; J. M. had tried to keep the spirit of inter-racial friendship alive in the midst of Mau Mau hatred. From the airport we drove to call on Tom Mboya in the African location. The roads through Nairobi were deserted except for a few askaris sitting in the doorways of the shops, dressed in their great long coats and carrying long sticks.

People were beginning to stir as we arrived at Tom's little bungalow in the Nairobi Council estate. We knocked on his door lightly and a sleepy Tom in his pyjamas and dressing-gown opened the door. We went in and he explained that he had been up late the night before as some of his supporters had been arrested. We arranged to meet later that day and went off to J. M. Desai's house for breakfast.

Mr Amin, the President of the Kenya Indian National Congress, was there, a short but impressive man who is a leader of a religious sect as well as a politician. His has been the difficult task of co-ordinating the aspirations of the heterogeneous collection of Indian businessmen, professional people and craftsmen and finding an agreed policy for them in the complex state of politics in Kenya. The Indians have felt squeezed between the African masses and the Europeans who, until very recently, had all the political power. Most Indians, however, are only anxious to have an easy, happy life. Politics is of no direct concern to them. But most feel an emotional sympathy with the Africans in their fight for political rights. They themselves were enthusiasts in the struggle for India's freedom. In their offices, shops and sitting-rooms are photographs of the leaders, Nehru, Ghandi, and Bose, who was labelled a traitor by the British during the war for his broadcasts from the enemy.

We went to the Kaloleni Hall in the afternoon; the Nairobi Peoples

Convention Party were putting on an afternoon show to welcome me to Kenya. Tom, now in an embroidered fez and carrying a beautiful switch, was a confident and commanding figure; the crowds surged around him, calling 'Freedom' and, in Swahili, 'Uhuru', holding up their right arms with clenched fists in salute. Thirty-year-old Mboya is a leader of his people. Although Luo by birth, and coming from the Nyanza province, he is supported by the other tribes, including the Kikuyu who are the strongest in and around Nairobi.

He was born into a peasant family but left Nyanza to find work in Nairobi, where he became a health worker for the City Council. While he went from house to house checking mosquitoes his thoughts were on the low pay and poor conditions of the municipal employees and he decided to help them form a trade union. This took him into full time trade unionism, organising the dock workers of Mombasa, where he established a reputation as a negotiator with employers and employees alike. The Workers Travel Association, whose officers include Mr Arthur Creech Jones, gave financial help for the young Mboya to go to Ruskin College, Oxford.

Since then he has not looked back; he became, successively, General Secretary of the Kenya Federation of Labour, Member of the Kenya Legislative Council and Chairman of the Accra Conference; he was fêted by Vice-President Nixon of the United States when he visited Washington, and is now an honorary Doctor of Laws of an American University.

But when we met his supporters inside the hall I found that Mboya still had the common touch. There were several hundred people sitting tightly together, leaving a space for the dancers. As we entered they shrieked out greetings, 'Freedom', 'Uhuru'; the women ululating. They cheered everyone who came in, even the newspaper correspondents. The visitors included the Commissioner for the Government of India, Mr Badahur Singh, and his elegantly dressed wife, whose beautiful sari was an exotic contrast to the clothes of the African women who were mostly dressed in cheap cottons.

Political meetings were banned by the Kenya Government. It was the time of the Queen Mother's visit to Kenya and the Government said that the police would be too busy to supervise political meetings. To circumvent the restriction Tom organised a tribal dance and a choir recital. The singing was powerful and tremendously moving and the songs reminiscent of those of the Welsh valleys or of the workers of Vienna. One of them was about the African leaders, with separate verses in praise of Jomo Kenyatta, Tom Mboya, and Mbiyu Koinange, the words of which evoked shouts of approval from the audience. The hall was vibrant with noise and enthusiasm, further intensified when the dancers came on. But it was not the place for a tribal dance; they can only be shown off effectively in a bush clearing—a hall is claustrophobic and inhibits the exuberant energies of the excited dancers.

The dancers were dressed in a fantastic assortment of clothes. Some had tribal headgear, made up of birds' feathers, and having skins draped over their khaki shorts but wearing incongruously heavy boots. Others were dressed in ordinary town clothes, shirts and shorts. Several had tins tied on their knees, making a noisy clatter, and one had a poster advertising Coca-Cola tied to his back. They stamped out their dance and the passion of the crowd grew; several old women in the audience, gripped by the rhythm, threw themselves forward to join in it. Then they all filed away, stamping.

'Now,' said the M.C., 'we will have dancing in the civilised style.'

This was the time for the young men and women to come forward. The African jazz band played for the shapely girls, with pouting lips, dressed in pretty cotton frocks or skirts and blouses, and the young men in their shirts and slacks and polished brown shoes. They danced in the disdainful manner of some British teenagers, mostly old-fashioned jiving, but some in a genteel quickstep—the partners holding each other at arms' length. The old people looked rather bored with all this and were obviously hoping that the tribal dancing would soon be brought back.

Tom, however, was determined to speak to the people, ban or no ban. He started off by warning them that he could not make a political speech but his words were as near to the political as they possibly could be. The crowd roared their approval at this. He introduced me and I said a few polite words in reply. The choir, without accompaniment, followed us by singing a dramatic song, during which they held each of their limbs as they symbolically dedicated themselves to the cause of Kenya, ending on their knees with arms outstretched, shouting 'Uhuru'.

During the singing I was approached by a young Kikuyu, shabbily dressed, who had none of the exuberance of the other young men. He told me that he had recently been released from detention after being in prison for five years without trial. He said that whilst in detention camps he had been beaten, as were many other Africans, and to confirm his allegation he rolled up his trouser leg to show scars on the calf. He had taken the Mau Mau oath and admitted his guilt to the screening teams. His name, he told me, was Josiah Kariuki.

A few months later I was reminded of this conversation. Kariuki wrote to me from Kandongu Detention camp; he had been picked up by the police and detained again without trial only seven days after our meeting at that tribal dance. His letter, which had been smuggled out of the detention camp by a friendly warder, alleged that he had been detained again because of our conversation in Nairobi. When I asked the Colonial Secretary in the House of Commons about the reasons for Kariuki's detention he replied that the Governor considered he should be detained in the interests of public order. No other reason was considered necessary.

When Tom Mboya and the visitors left the hall the crowd surged forward again, pressing our hands in greeting.

That night I talked to Mboya and his lieutenants until past midnight. He told me of the incredible difficulties under which their party was organised. No national party was allowed and his own was restricted to Nairobi. The collection of subscriptions and other work was handicapped by the arbitrary arrest of party officials on trumped-up charges. One night the police had surrounded a house in which some members of the choir were singing as the officers objected to the references to Jomo Kenyatta in the songs. The police burst into the house and took all the men to a police station where they were locked up for the night. When Mboya heard about the incident and complained he was told by the officer-in-charge that they had been arrested for singing illegal songs. Mboya protested that it is not illegal to sing songs. Next morning he heard that the men had been charged with contravening the pass regulations; they had left their papers in the house when the police arrested them.

On the following day I met all the members of the PCP executive committee. They were eager young people, and none of them could have been over thirty years of age. For two hours they plied me with questions.

'What is the Labour Party's policy for Kenya?'

'What are you going to do about Central African Federation?'

'Don't you think that detainees should be released from prison or put on trial?'

'Are you going to open up the White Highlands for Africans?'

None of them approached the intellectual calibre of Tom Mboya himself. They were all young because most of the older generation with political inclinations were in detention camps or had been released only on condition that they did not return to politics.

I also met Dr Gikonyo Kiano, the graduate of an American univer-

9. (*above*) Southern Rhodesia: Batonka moving from the Zambezi

(*below*) Storing grain

10. An African worker in the Roan Antelope Copper Mines, Northern Rhodesia

sity, with an alert, piercing intellect. He has the neat appearance and
stature of the Japanese, but an American taste in ties. Once Colonel
Grogan, one of the pioneers of the white settlers, met Kiano in the
Legislative Council lounge.

'Oh, you are a Kikuyu, are you?' said Grogan. 'A degraded race.'

'Don't be silly,' said Kiano. 'Come on, let's go and have a drink.'

When Kiano returned from the United States to take up a teaching
post near Nairobi, he also entered politics as the Member for Central
Province. Some white politicians, anxious to destroy the leadership of
Tom Mboya, spread the rumour that a conflict existed between the two
men and that Kiano was determined to oust Mboya from the active
political leadership. As he was a member of the most politically advanced
tribe, the Kikuyu, this story sounded plausible. It was also said that the
two men were on unfriendly terms. This is unlikely, as Kiano and
Mboya work together very closely and throughout recent negotiations
they have issued joint policy statements. Some of the other African
elected members, particularly Mr Muliro, are trying to create an inter-
racial front with Mr Shifley Cooke, the European politician with a progressive outlook. Kiano and Mboya are still working together with an
undiluted demand for 'one man, one vote', despite a temporary split in
the African elected group on the Legislative Council.

The political climate in Kenya has changed out of all recognition in
ten years. A decade ago the white settlers were asking for independence
from the Colonial Office on the Southern Rhodesian pattern; now the
position is completely reversed and the settlers are asking for Colonial
Office rule to continue until agreed political changes can be made with
the co-operation of all the races. There is no apathy among the
Africans, but the European politicians are only too well aware that
among the whites who live in Nairobi there is a lackadaisical approach
to politics. The 4,000 farmers in the Highlands are determined to
protect what they have, but for Europeans in Nairobi, many of whom
are not genuinely 'settled' in Kenya, politics are a bore.

A letter to the *East African Standard* brought this out. In the by-
election of a European Member for the Legislative Council, only 873
went to the poll out of an electorate of 2,100—a 41.6 per cent poll—and
the votes were apportioned as follows: Howard-Williams 20.6, Boswell
14.3, and Cameron 6.7. The correspondent added plaintively: '. . . it
appears perfectly ridiculous that any man is chosen to represent a
constituency with only a 20.6 per cent backing.'

Air Commodore Howard-Williams is a colourful addition to the
Legislature, although, with only 400 votes, he is not particularly repre-

I

sentative. He is very fond of writing to the Press; his most celebrated letter was one in which he replied to a speech made by Sir Roy Welensky at the Kenya Agricultural Show, saying, 'The White Highlanders applaud your stirring speech, which has given us the lead we need to build the New Kenya in your likeness. . . .' Then he flew to Salisbury to seek military help from the Federal Prime Minister; he said to Sir Roy, 'It is no good waiting on events. You should be prepared. The future may depend on sending troops to Kenya on training exercises. The Federation should not just be ready to go North if the occasion arose but should send troops there for training.'

Group Captain Briggs, another European elected Member, also made the journey south to see Sir Roy to discuss the possibility of convening a 'White Settler All Africa Conference'. He said on his return to Nairobi, 'Sir Roy Welensky, Prime Minister of the Federation of Rhodesia and Nyasaland, is determined that the position of the European in East and Central Africa and the social, political and economic standards he has set shall not be sacrificed in the course of the political changes which are now going on.'

The exploits of the Air Commodore and the Group Captain were considered so dangerous to the position of the white minority that a special convention of the District Associations was called. This is a body which represents most white opinion in the colony and I attended their meeting, held in Nairobi Town Hall. The speeches were tedious and one had the impression that the white community were, to all intents and purposes, leaderless. The only really daring speech was one calling for the retention of the White Highlands, which was enthusiastically received. But the two hundred delegates looked rather like lost sheep who had found their way into the wrong pen. The sheer effectiveness of the African politicians (which they acknowledged) had prevented the achievement of a white-dominated Kenya. They each realised that such a policy was out of all realms of practical possibility because of the growth of African awareness, but they had no policy to put in its place.

The only speech which showed a glimmer of fresh thinking was made by Michael Blundell, who soon after the meeting set up the New Kenya Group and resigned as Minister of Agriculture. But the only Africans in the Legislative Council who will support his New Group are the 'specially elected' Members. They are elected to the Legislative Council by the other Members, rather like an Aldermanic bench. But as the African Members who are elected from the constituencies refused to vote for any 'specially elected' Members because the European Members, including the 'officials', had a majority of votes anyway, the 'specially elected' Africans are considered to be stooges of the Europeans, dependent completely on European votes.

But Kenya's future constitutional position is, as I write, in the lap of the gods and of the Constitutional Conference which will take place in 1960. Mr Lennox-Boyd, then the Colonial Secretary, only agreed to the Round Table Talks which Tom Mboya had requested after much pressure from Africans and Asians, representing 99 per cent of Kenya's population. The Conference should help to clean the muddy waters of the pool of Kenya politics, but it remains to be seen whether Mr Macleod will seize the opportunity to establish a timetable for independence.

I called to meet the aristocrat in Government House, Sir Evelyn Baring, who had been attacked as a weak, vacillating Governor by both Africans and Europeans. I found him to be a most charming man, but I had the impression that he preferred to keep problems at arm's length. He placed great reliance on his Ministers, many of whom were Government civil servants and were not endowed with outstanding abilities. A few were shown to be quite incompetent—particularly by the Hola Camp affair.

Kenya is in a period of transition and Sir Evelyn's successor, Sir Patrick Renison, fresh from handling Dr Cheddi Jagan, should be well equipped to take on the task of building up Ministerial responsibility whilst retaining his own authority at Government House until the Legislative Council is properly constituted and able to take over the reins.

Sir Evelyn's greatest failure, in my judgment, was his handling of Mau Mau. Instead of accepting the economic and political reasons for the early strength of this movement he treated the whole nationalist movement as a subversive organisation. Many men who were not in favour of violence were rounded up with the Mau Mau and tainted by it. The treatment of these detainees has been a blot on the British colonial record which it will be hard to rub out. Hola in particular will be remembered, not only for eleven dead men but for the meeting of Ministers, over which Sir Evelyn presided, which issued the Press statement to the effect that the deaths had occurred after the detainees had drunk contaminated water. It was more than a case of ineptitude.

When I was in Kenya again, some weeks later, I met some of the officers concerned in the issue of this communiqué and I was struck by the nonchalant way in which they regarded the affair. It was about a week after Hola. I did not see Hola but they did arrange for me to visit the Aguthi Detention Camp, where 222 Mau Mau detainees were kept.

It is a few miles south-west of Mount Kenya and to reach it we travelled through miles of Kikuyu Reserve.

This land is some of the most densely populated in Kenya. In the Fort Hall district the area of 585 square miles has a population of 384,000 people, almost all of whom are trying to eke out an existence from the land. The allocation works out at under one acre per head. Elsewhere it is the same story. In Kiambu there are 388,000 people in an area of 615 square miles, or one acre per head.

Much of the land, of course, as we saw from the roadway, is steep and cannot be cultivated, which brings the actual fertile area of land available down considerably. No wonder the Kikuyu feel bitter about the land question when they know that the whole area of White Highlands of some 16,500 square miles of land is allocated to only 4,000 white farmers, 4 square miles per family. There are 250,000 Africans living in the Highlands but they have no rights there except as labourers for the Europeans; the wages they receive are about thirty shillings a month.

Those who look at the map of Kenya and imagine that there are vast areas available for African farming should be reminded that most of the area north and east of Mount Kenya is virtually uninhabitable except by nomads. The Royal Commission on Land in East Africa reported that land should have about twenty inches of rain to be productive. According to the rain maps there are 24,380 square miles of land which have such a rainfall. As 4,700 of these are Forest Reserve, there are only 19,680 square miles available for farming in Kenya. The amount of that in the White Highlands for Europeans is 5,900 square miles; which means that about 30 per cent of the good land in Kenya is reserved for the Europeans. Even if all the commercial people and the Civil Servants are included in the total of Europeans they number only 1 per cent of the population; 60,000 out of 6,000,000. It is not surprising that Africans should feel bitter!

Later, in October 1959, the Kenya Government announced that in future its policy would be 'the progressive disappearance of racial land barriers'. The White Highlands would be opened to Africans and Asians of proved competence as farmers and a Central Board, composed of members equally from the three races, would advise the Governor on land transfers.

This long overdue concession to Africans is limited in its effectiveness as European farmers may not be willing to sell or lease land to non-Europeans and few Africans, without Government help, command the necessary resources to buy it. What is still needed is an imaginative plan for the development of the Highlands. The Gezira scheme in the

Southern Sudan, which provides capital and assists and supervises the farming operations of the tenant cotton-farmers, is an example which might well be adapted to Kenya conditions.

When I arrived at the Aguthi Camp I met some of the most bitter Africans of all. These were the so-called 'hard-core' Mau Mau detainees, who refused to do any work except that connected with their own domestic requirements. Six of them were kept in a separate barbed-wire compound. When our party of visitors walked into the compound they stood and looked at us with hostility. They were dressed in prison regulation clothing of white shirts and white shorts and looked fairly fit. We walked up to them but they refused to speak, only staring with glazed eyes. Through an interpreter I told one of the detainees that I had come from the House of Commons and that if he wanted to speak to me he should feel free to do so. Then he began to speak in Kikuyu, but the Prison Officer cut him short and told me, 'I'm afraid they are not allowed to speak to visitors.'

The Officer, I suppose, was worried because there were several newspapermen with us. As the prisons and detention camps had been closed for so long to the Press I had asked that they should be able to make the visit as well as myself, but it looked as though that request had undermined the effectiveness of my visit.

Although there is so much bitterness and hate between the races, there is still hope that these can be overcome. It would be wrong to assume that no progress has been made in the last few years. Despite Mau Mau and its aftermath Africans have a much bigger say in political matters and some other opportunities have also been opened up to them. In 1952 my African friends were turned out of the New Stanley Hotel, but on my last visit I went with Tom Mboya to the exclusive grill room of the New Stanley and the dozens of Europeans eating lunch hardly batted an eyelid when we walked to our table, accompanied also by another Kenya African, an American negro journalist for *Look* magazine, and his white photographer. Three years before the three dark-skinned members of our party would have been thrown out; that day we were all accepted. More than any other incident which I experienced, this proved to me that Kenya is now, at last, on the road to sanity.

The Haven of Peace

TRAVELLING out of the tight political bitterness of Kenya into the vastness of Tanganyika is like coming out of a thick fog into the bright sunlight. Tanganyika is altogether a happier and racially healthier place. Of the six British territories in East and Central Africa Tanganyika is nearest to solving its political and racial problems.

It has reached that position by a combination of good luck and good politicians. For good luck it has fewer white farmers than the 4,000 in Kenya and they have been less, much less, short-sighted than their fellows across the frontier. Although some of the sisal barons who live along the coast at Tanga have entertained ideas of white political rule, most of the farmers have eschewed politics, perhaps because most of them are hardworking Germans and are not as interested in politics as the ex-Indian Army types in Kenya; good luck, also, because Tanganyika has been a Trustee Territory under the United Nations.

Rumour has it—quoted by John Gunther *—that just before World War II the Chamberlain government was prepared to do a deal with Germany and give Tanganyika back to them. The Germans would have nothing to do with it; not only were they too busy colonising Europe, but also they knew that 9,000,000 Africans would be too difficult to handle 5,000 miles away from Germany. Once the Germans had put down a rebellion by the Magi Magi tribe by exterminating people over a vast area, so the return of Tanganyika to Germany would not have been a very popular move among the Africans themselves. The territory remained under British trusteeship and almost forgotten but since the war the United Nations has taken an ever increasing interest and has sent many investigating missions. This, in turn, has helped to create a favourable atmosphere for political advance.

Good luck also gave Tanganyika an energetic and lovable Governor in the person of Sir Edward Twining. He was not a stickler for protocol and was fond of wandering around the front of Dar es Salaam, gazing benignly at everyone. Africans were concerned when he was succeeded by Sir Richard Turnball; they feared that it would be a change for the

* *Inside Africa.*

worse. Sir Richard had been in Kenya, as Chief Secretary during the
Mau Mau period, and this made him highly suspect. But Sir Richard
has stepped very nicely into his predecessor's shoes. He has listened
courteously to African opinions; has made African friends and has
influenced people by a speech advocating non-racialism. That speech
pleased the Africans very much; they look upon words like 'multi-
racial' or 'partnership' as excuses for giving most privileges and the
political power to the minority whites.

Outstanding among the good politicians in Tanganyika is Julius K.
Nyerere, graduate of Edinburgh University and a Roman Catholic. He
is looked upon by his fellows with reverence. He is the most dynamic
African politician in East Africa, but he is a practical one. In little over
a year he built the Tanganyika African National Union into an effective
political force. It now has branches even in the remotest villages where
it was unheard of a few years ago.

The beautiful capital of Tanganyika, Dar es Salaam, is a much
friendlier place than its sister capital, Nairobi. Perhaps the reason for
this is the fact that Dar es Salaam is a port and has had, over the years,
the benefits of cosmopolitan influences. It is hot and humid, just like a
Turkish bath. As soon as I walked off the aeroplane it hit me. Nobody
wears a coat or tie until the evening and when I met the Government
officers, including the Governor himself, they were in shirt sleeves. But
the sea breezes from the Indian Ocean are cooling. It was across these
seas that the Arab *dhows* came and established a port which they called
The Haven of Peace, a name which it justly deserves. A tall, handsome
Government officer who met me at the airport had transferred recently
from a Pacific Island and wasn't sure whether he liked the change.
'There is far more work in Tanganyika than in the sleepy Pacific', he
complained, although fortunately for him there is not much change in
the climate.

After I was installed in an airy flat in the building reserved for
Members of the Legislative Council, I went off to visit the executive
committee of TANU. They were celebrating an astonishing election
victory. Under the arrangements made by Sir Edward Twining before
he retired as Governor, ten constituencies had been drawn up and in
each of these three Members had been elected; one African, one
European, and one Asian in each. Qualifications for the common roll
of electors were low—Standard VIII in education or an annual
income of £150—and many more Africans were enrolled than for
the other races; each had to cast three votes, one for each race.

Julius Nyerere's organisation supported European and Asian candi-

dates as well as their own African nominees. As African voters were in
the majority in all the constituencies, except Dar es Salaam, the TANU-
nominated candidates were all elected. In the capital Asian electors
supported the TANU-Asian Association united front candidates. As a
result, the United Tanganyika Party, which was set up by white settlers,
was swept completely out of existence. Julius Nyerere now leads a
group of thirty elected Members, two-thirds of whom are of a different
race but who recognise him as the leader.

When I met the TANU executive committee they were discussing
the policy to be adopted after these phenomenal election results. Julius
Nyerere had a difficult job in controlling one or two of the extremists,
who wanted no truck with the other races, but almost all of the executive
committee supported him in his intelligent handling of the racial situation. Eventually Nyerere will achieve his ambition of admitting
individual non-Africans as members of TANU.

That evening I attended a party which was held to celebrate the
TANU victory. It was held at the Patel Club—a club mainly for
Indians, but the party was attended by members of all races, and they
mixed together without embarrassment or artificiality. These people
were feeling like Tanganyikans, not members of their own individual
races. TANU was obviously wielding a force of non-racial co-operation
which is a lesson to all countries in Africa where different communities
live side by side. I met the leaders of the Asian Association who together
with Julius Nyerere must be given the credit for the tremendous
advance in race relations in Tanganyika. In 1954 that Association
published a policy document called 'The Right Road for Tanganyika'
which made a courageous declaration:

'We reiterate that all men are born equal and are entitled to an equal
opportunity wherever they may be. In Tanganyika each of us has a
great opportunity to do his utmost to put this human and democratic
ideal in practice and not pay it a mere lip service. Tanganyika has the
opportunity and can give a lead to the rest of Africa in creating a non-
racial secular state wherein all the peoples whom destiny has brought
together can live as proud citizens without being hampered by racial
privileges, handicaps and prejudices.'

A committee of the Legislative Council has, since the election, been
studying proposals for constitutional changes in Tanganyika. The
Asian Association, true to its own policy declaration, is asking that
there should be no minority privileges for the Asians. They do not
want special reserved seats in the Legislative Council or special educational facilities for Asian children; they are prepared to sink their

identity with that of the African masses. Strangely enough it is Julius Nyerere and the African leaders in Tanganyika who are asking that the Asian minority and also the Europeans should each have special safe-guarded status. Julius says this is necessary to avoid giving the impression to the outside world that in Tanganyika the Africans are going to ride roughshod over the wishes of the minorities.

The leaders of the new Tanganyika are remarkable men. Amir Jamal, for instance, an Asian elected Member and son of a prosperous business man; he has a fine intellect and a striking appearance, rather like Cheddi Jagan of Guiana. George Kahama, who was trained as a Co-operative Manager at the Co-operative College at Loughborough, returned to organise the Bukoba Co-operative Union and succeeded in building up their reserves to half-a-million pounds; he is now a Minister, one of those chosen by Julius to enter the Government during the transition period. Mahmud Rattansey, a lively, engaging personality, who is Secretary of the Asian Association, has guided the Association into close working with the Africans. Then there is Paul Bomani, a very large, dominating African, General Manager of another successful Co-op on the east side of Lake Victoria in an area where cotton production has been increased five-fold in five years and where the entire crop of 175,000 bales is being marketed co-operatively. And Julius himself, respected and admired by all the others because of his outstanding intellect and his dignified manner, and yet possessing a very warm feeling for humanity.

At the party we drank Pepsi-Cola, and some other stronger beverages, and ate hot Indian curries with chapatis. Everyone was in extremely good spirits, Africans, Asians and Europeans slapping each other on the back and exchanging jokes.

I found that the rank and file Indians supported the idea of equality with Africans as keenly as their leaders did. The Asians I had known in Uganda had not expressed much interest in the plight of Africans and most of them expected the British to give Asians special privileges as they considered themselves to be a cut above the Africans. Not so in Tanganyika: the contrast between Asian attitudes in the two countries was very great.

The difference has been due to the remarkable influence of a few outstanding men and women of all three races. Most of them were at that party, including Mr R. M. Kawawa, the twenty-nine-year-old General Secretary of the Federation of Labour and the youngest Member of the Legislative Council, Mr Douglas Heath, formerly in the Nigerian colonial service and now a TANU-supported Member of Legislative

Council and, by no means least, Miss Bebetiti, the women's leader. In any gathering she would stand out as the largest and happiest person. Once she had an inferiority complex because she could not speak English; she lost all that when she attended a women's conference in New Delhi, where she was delighted to find that most of the women delegates could not understand English either. She went back to Tanganyika and has been twice as effective in her speech-making—in Swahili.

After the party a few of us drove to the coastline north of Dar es Salaam. We parked the car along a beautiful bay of sand and looked at the palm trees gently waving in the breeze and the moonlit Indian Ocean. Rattansey said, 'We have created a miracle here in Tanganyika. We have brought the three races together and can forge a new nation without animosity. This can be a new Brazil in Africa.'

Then Julius, leaning on his black stick, said, 'Yes, all we want now is our independence so we can get on with the job. Those chaps in Government House are holding things up. How can they take decisions for the future of Tanganyika when they know that in a few years' time they will be out and we will be in power? Many of them are near retirement, anyway, and are only waiting for their pensions.'

We went on to talk about Tanganyika's economic problems. This vast nation of 9,000,000 people is bigger than the whole of Central Africa, but its resources are limited. The Williamson Diamond Mines produce a major source of income, and cotton, coffee and sisal also make a big contribution, but vast areas of Tanganyika are completely undeveloped, either because of lack of roads and communications or because of tsetse fly, or simply because the peasants have not yet acquired the will to improve their lot.

'We can do something about these difficulties,' said Julius. 'We can let the people know that they have within their own hands the chance to improve their lives. They cannot do it under colonialism. They need their own Government to show them and guide them to the way ahead. We need a lot of outside capital, but that is more likely to come when investors know what the future political position will be and only we can assure them about that. The British Government, by hanging on without giving a clear time-table for independence, are putting obstacles in the way of getting outside investment.'

I asked Julius about the white settlers, what did he think about their future in the country? He assured me that there would be no action taken against them. 'We are not interested in the piffling bit of land which they occupy,' he said. 'I went to them at the election time when we were asking for support for our candidates and I am sure many of their people voted for our nominees. We have got too much to worry about in Tanganyika as a whole without worrying about the few white settlers. They can carry on as they are.'

Julius's main concern was with the future of the peasant Africans, whose incomes are, on average, about £12 a year and who, he believes, need the dynamic force of political independence to wake them from their lethargy. Certainly one thing TANU has done is to give these people a sense of nationhood. In this vast country there are 127 different tribes and it is a mark of TANU's success that it has achieved a sense of equality between the advanced tribes like the Wachagga, who have a well developed culture, and the more primitive tribes like the Daroma. This is every bit as important as achieving a sense of equality between Africans, Europeans and Asians. Given capital aid from outside, and new development schemes, Tanganyika could indeed be a Brazil in Africa, a place where to do the possible will be easy, but where the impossible will take a little longer.

On another evening I went with Julius and his associates to one of Dar es Salaam's open air night clubs. Most of the little tables were occupied by Africans with their wives or girl friends but there was a sprinkling of Indians and one or two Europeans. As Julius walked in almost all the people stood up as a sign of respect. Julius replied with a salute, rather like a Roman emperor. The three-piece band played Arabic music and the singer chanted an Egyptian song with an exotic lilt. I mused, as I listened, on what would be the relations between Egypt and an East African Federation of, say, forty millions, (with Julius Nyerere as President) in twenty years' time? Both nations would have an interest in the Nile but Sudan would be a buffer state.

Then the singer introduced another song, in praise of Nyerere. I realised that in more ways than one this engaging philosopher-politician is becoming the symbol of Tanganyika's independence. Even match-boxes show his face on the cover. But he is an unlikely man to succumb to the cult of personality.

I called on the Chief Secretary, a paternal character—even in his shirt sleeves. Mr Grattan-Bellew, CMG, QC, was a member of the old generation of civil servants and had the kindly air of an ageing Head-master. When I talked to him about the future he wanted to bring me down to earth and practical realities.

'What can we do on a budget of £18,000,000?' he said. 'We cannot even afford to pay for extensions in the education services. Every improvement costs money and we simply haven't got it in the till.

Development of new industries is a real headache because a sound economic base is needed and we haven't that yet. Take cement, for instance, we use only 75,000 tons a year and import that, but a factory needs at least an output of 100,000 tons to be economic.'

He realised that political advances had to come, but even the elections themselves were expensive. The last ones, he said, cost £60,000. Two of his officers had to travel three days by Land Rover, boat and canoe to collect only five votes. He commented, 'You cannot hold elections too frequently at that price.'

The Government offices were ramshackle and as I walked down the wooden steps from his first floor office I thought to myself that it would be a very long time before they could be rebuilt if the financial situation was that bad.

But Tanganyika is a young country and if education could be given to the children, even if only of a primitive kind, their energies could be translated into productive, useful effort on the land; Tanganyika could eventually produce the wealth needed to pay for the improvements she needs. Of the 9,000,000 Africans in Tanganyika, 4,000,000 are children under sixteen. But child mortality figures are very high; in some areas six children out of ten will die before they reach fourteen years of age. There are only 123 doctors in Government Service and 75 working for the missions; that is one doctor for each 45,000 people.

Education is mainly in the hands of the missions, to which the Government pays grants-in-aid. The Roman Catholics had the biggest slice of £686,000 in 1957, the Church of England schools had £280,000 and a hotch potch of other denominations received varying amounts, including £30,000 which went to the Church of Sweden.

It is mainly through economic co-operation that the advances will be made and Africans have shown that where they have the chance of helping themselves through co-operatives they make an outstanding success of it. Co-operatives market a large part of the principal cash crops of cotton and coffee. First in this field were the Wachagga, who established the Kilimanjaro Native Co-operative Union on the slopes of the mountain of that name and have made it the shrine of successful Co-operation in Africa. It is African-controlled, although it has had excellent help from Mr Bennett, seconded to them as adviser from the colonial service. With the profits they have built a wonderful education centre—an example to the other Tanganyikan tribes.

Co-operative endeavour has even been extended to leper colonies. There are 5,000 people in leprosaria and in one of them, at Makete in the Southern Province, the inmates have a co-operative for making craft goods. They learn a skill and also something about co-operative methods, both of which are useful to them when they return home to their villages. Africans are finding that it is by self-help and mutual aid that they can best build up their own new Tanganyika. They cannot wait for charity.

Rattansey was very insistent that I should meet the Asian Association executive committee as he was eager that I should be convinced about their sincerity in putting forward a non-racial policy. I met them around a table in a small hall just off the Dar es Salaam bazaar. The Chairman went round the table and introduced every one of his twenty-man committee by name and occupation. He managed to say something complimentary or humorous about every single one. There was Mr Shah, a lawyer ('We have a lot of lawyers in Dar es Salaam, you know, we need them!'); Councillor Devani, the Mayor of Dar es Salaam, ('We're very proud of him'); Mr Patel, builder, ('He's a real worker'), and so on—businessmen, traders, professional men—a good cross-section of the community.

They emphasised that they feel Tanganyika is their home and that they are prepared to put everything they have into it. They sincerely wanted the Africans to advance. 'We realise our future is tied up with them and it is immoral that any Tanganyikans should live in poverty.'

They wanted to know from me about Labour Party policy on Africa and their most searching questions were about Central Africa. They saw the Rhodesian federation as the most serious threat to their conception of non-racial democracy.

'The way Federation has been imposed has been a shock to us all,' said one eager man, who expressed the anxieties of his fellow executive members. 'We cannot be happy when right on our borders that dictatorship is being imposed on Africans and Asians.'

On 15 December 1959, it was announced in Dar es Salaam that new elections would be held in September 1960 and that major constitutional changes, based on the recommendations of the Post Elections Committee, would be implemented. The new Legislative Council will consist of a few nominated Members, plus seventy-one elected seats (eleven of which will be for Asians and ten for Europeans), elected by a largely African electorate. The number of voters will be dramatically increased from 60,000 to 1,500,000 by reducing the qualifications to £75 annual income and knowledge of English or Swahili. Virtual democratic home rule so soon in Tanganyika will certainly frighten many whites in the Rhodesias; but the Africans there will say, 'Why not us too?'

Southern Rhodesian Maelstrom

IN the Customs Hall at Salisbury airport, where passengers wait for their luggage to be trundled from the aircraft, there is a poster on the wall—'Settlers welcome to the Federation.' Another gives details of a welfare centre where the new settlers can go for assistance.

The dozen or so passengers were standing around exchanging friendly words with each other, waiting for their cases.

'Staying long in Salisbury?'

'No, I'm driving off to Umtali tomorrow, got to be back on my farm. Been away for six weeks, you can't tell what can happen in that time,' said one brawny traveller with a bushwhacker hat.

Another passenger, an open air type, turned to me and said, 'Great to be back isn't it old boy? Damned annoying, though, waiting around for the suitcases like this.'

'Unfortunately, I only have a week in Southern Rhodesia,' I replied, 'then I'm off to Northern Rhodesia and Nyasaland.'

'Pity you're not staying,' he said. 'Great country, this, wonderful future—if we don't have any trouble with the blacks.'

Out in the reception hall three Africans, leaders of the Southern Rhodesian African National Congress, stepped forward to greet me, smiling broadly. After we exchanged greetings I asked how they had recognised me so quickly.

'Our friend pointed you out to us,' they said with more smiles. 'He's with the Special Branch, down here to keep an eye on things.'

We walked out together to a large car. I noticed that my erstwhile fellow-travellers were eyeing me with some surprise and obvious disapproval, even anger.

Then we drove along the wide roads towards the city centre; it was early evening and there were many cars about but it seemed that all of them contained Europeans. I looked out onto the streets to see shops and buildings with none of the brashness of a pioneer town—this could well have been a city in Europe. But, unlike Europe, the pavements were deserted. All the people were in cars and there were no Africans to be seen. I wondered where they all were. After all, the total white population of Southern Rhodesia is less than that of the Borough of Islington, where I live in London.

At the end of a tree-lined road we parked the car by a grass verge and walked into the new, plushy, Jameson Hotel. The European reception-ist looked up, a little surprised, but said nothing, and we went upstairs to the lounge and ordered some beer. The African waiter went away with the order, but a European under-manager came back.

'Sorry sir,' he said to me, 'we are not allowed to serve beer to Africans.'

'For goodness' sake, why not?' I asked.

'Well, they have their own places, and until the Multi-racial Hotel Bill goes through we have to be very careful, we don't want to have any trouble.'

So we all had orange squash.

'This place is the exception,' said Robert Chikerema, the Congress Vice-President. 'At least we can come in here. The other hotels won't admit us at all.'

I looked around the lounge. There were ten or a dozen Europeans and no other Africans.

Paul Mushonga, the Treasurer, looked smart in his well cut suit and bow tie. His composed face and lively eyes and soft-spoken manner disclosed an intelligent, sensitive personality. He and Robert Chikerema settled back in the easy chairs trying to look relaxed. I was reminded of Uganda in 1952 when Africans were daring to sit in the hotel lounges for the first time. So long had they been kept out that there was a feeling of unease. But in Kampala, in Nairobi, and in Dar es Salaam the Africans had come into their own and except for some places in Kenya, there was no colour bar in the hotels.

George Nyandoro, with a beard and a slightly husky voice, showed no signs of uneasiness. His ebullient personality would make him feel at home anywhere. He was fast talking, and fast thinking. As I was to learn later, he was the life and soul of the Party, besides being its General Secretary. Paul Mushonga was the serious one of the trio, composed, thoughtful, and with an intense feeling.

We discussed where I should stay during my week in Southern Rhodesia. As I wanted to make as many official contacts as possible it was agreed that for the first three days, and for the last two, I should stay with a white member of the Southern Rhodesian African National Congress in Salisbury itself. But as the meetings and functions at which

I could meet Africans had been arranged in the African township of Highfield on the outskirts of Salisbury and also in Bulawayo, I should stay with Paul Mushonga during the week-end in between.

I was told about the legislation which bolsters up the colour bar in Southern Rhodesia. In Salisbury itself or in the suburbs for whites it is impossible for Africans to live, except as house servants, when they stay in little brick boxes at the bottom of the European garden. No African can operate a business or practice any profession in Salisbury, with just one exception. Herbert Chitepo, a barrister, is the only privileged African and a special Act was passed in the Southern Rhodesian Legislature to enable him to rent an office. It is impossible for a white family to invite a dark skinned friend to stay with them overnight. Intermarriage presents insuperable difficulties. When Patrick Matimba returned from his student years in Europe with a young Dutch wife he found himself in an impossible situation. He could not live in the European area, nor could he take his wife to live in the African area. Almost everywhere in Southern Rhodesia it is illegal for an African and a white wife to live together in holy matrimony. But they found a haven at St Faith's Mission Farm where Guy Clutton Brock gave them accommodation to live together. Patrick later moved into Salisbury to set up a printing press. He did this in defiance of the authorities and described his wife as the owner and himself as her servant.

However, I saw no reason myself to adopt the colour prejudice imposed by the law of the Southern Rhodesians. To accept 'apartheid' is to condone it. The discriminatory legislation had been passed by a Legislature on which Africans were not represented. Southern Rhodesia, I discovered, is an autocracy, and the Land Apportionment Act is the principal weapon used to consolidate the control of 2,500,000 Africans by the white minority of 200,000.

In all my discussions with Africans I was constantly reminded of the land problem, as the allocation of land between Africans and Europeans is bitterly resented. The 1930 Act allocated the land between Africans and Europeans, despite the fact that the Orders in Council of 1894 and 1898, which established Company Rule in Rhodesia, required that 'A native may acquire, hold, encumber and dispose of the land on the same conditions as a person who is not a native.' Until 1930 and the Land Apportionment Act Africans were allowed to buy and occupy land anywhere in the colony.

Some white politicians claim that the Act has been as much in the interests of Africans as Europeans, in that African land holdings have been protected. But the Native Reserves owe their existence and status not to the Land Apportionment Act but to a Land Commission in 1914

11. (*above*) An aerial view of Kariba Dam, nearing completion
in June 1959

(*below*) African workers at Kariba Dam

12. The author with his wife after arrival at London Airport
from the Rhodesias, March 1959

which set aside 21,000,000 acres for tribal areas. And in the 1923 Constitution these reserves were 'set apart for the sole and exclusive use and occupation of the indigenous native inhabitants of the colony'. It was in 1924 that it was decided to consolidate white control of the land and the Carter Commission was set up to report on the desirability and practicability of dividing the land outside the Reserves into European and African areas. The great carve-up had begun.

Following the Commission's Report the vicious Act was passed in 1930. About 43% of the land in Southern Rhodesia, including the Reserves, was set aside for the exclusive use of Africans, but 53% was allocated to Europeans. The other 4% was barren forest or other unassigned land. The final assignment of land, following a new Apportionment Act in 1941, shows the allocation as follows:

> 51,987,000 acres to European use (of which 4,000,000 acres are game reserves).
> 41,950,000 acres to Native areas.
> 3,129,000 acres to forest areas.
> 57,000 acres to undetermined areas.

This shows less than 20 acres per head of the African population and more than 250 acres per head of the European population. And most of the Europeans live in the towns.

A paper* from Mr K. E. Brown, who was in the Native Affairs Department of Southern Rhodesia as a Land Development Officer for five years, gives more details to demonstrate the discriminatory nature of the land allocation. According to Mr Brown, most of the African area is poor soil, usually the poorer types of granite sand known technically as Class III land, while the European area contains all the areas of fertile soil in the colony, e.g. the red clays overlying dolomite, greensand and banded ironstone, the 'Glendale' soils and the Lmagundi Sediments. He says, 'In many parts of the country it is quite embarrassing (if you are a European) to drive through a European Area into a Native Area. The change in soil type coincides almost exactly with the boundary line and is startlingly obvious. . . .'

Most of the African areas are situated well away from the main roads and railways, making transport to markets a difficulty, but European farms are mainly adjacent to the railway or main roads.

Some 8,000,000 acres within the area allocated to Africans is designated as Native Purchase Area, where Africans are able to buy land for freehold tenure. The principle that Africans should be entitled to own

* Now published by Africa Bureau.

K

freehold land has therefore been recognised, and could well be applied
to the tracts of European land which are under-utilised. The overcrowding in the Native Reserves is very serious and is officially recognised in the Southern Rhodesian Government's pamphlet on the Land
Husbandry Act, which reads:

'From 1926 the history of native agriculture in Southern Rhodesia
had been that of a continuous battle between the steady increasing
pressure of growing population on the restricted land Reserves. . . .'

Africans should be allowed to buy land in the European areas where,
according to the Select Committee on Unimproved Land reporting in
1957, only 1,100,000 acres are actually under crops.

The Land Apportionment Act applies in the towns too and the
commercial centre and suburbs of Salisbury are wholly European. No
African is allowed to own or occupy any property in the town of
Salisbury. Two years ago George Nyandoro had the temerity to open
an office for Congress in the middle of Salisbury. He soon had to leave
and move to the back room of Paul Mushonga's shop in the African
township of Highfield.

The European home where I stayed was in a suburb of Salisbury. The
house was a bungalow type and there were hundreds of similar houses
all around with their own little back-and-front gardens. The residents
in the neighbourhood had travelled to Rhodesia during the last ten
years. Most were from Britain, some from South Africa and a few from
other European countries. My hosts were different from their neighbours. They wanted to meet and understand Africans, while most of
the other new immigrants mixed only with whites and had no contact
with Africans except at work. The others had a typical suburban
existence, driving into town in a stream of traffic in the mornings and
back again in the evening, complaining about the cost of living and
struggling to keep up the mortgage repayments. Except for an
occasional trip into the country they saw little or nothing of Africa,
and probably have never seen how a typical African family lives.

My host was a clerk in Salisbury, in a comparatively humble job. He
had no ambitions in politics but, with his wife, had become a member of
the African Congress because he believed that its policies would be
most likely to achieve Christian harmony among the races in Southern
Rhodesia. He abominated the racialist policies of the United Federal
Party (UFP) of Welensky and Whitehead, and had absolutely no
respect for the Dominion Party, which was 'at least frank in its belief
in "apartheid"'. He told me that the slogans of 'partnership' and 'equal
rights for all civilised men' were nothing more than tricks to bemuse

British public opinion and to keep the Africans quiet until such time as the white minority had achieved the political independence which it desired for Central Africa. Privately—and indeed, on occasions, publicly—the white politicians of the two main parties had boasted that Africans would never have real political power within the foreseeable future.

There are liberals, like my hosts, among the white minority but they are only a handful compared to the many who accept the policies of racial privileges. The white supremacy makes sense because it means for them a better standard of living than they had at home and a higher status in life than they expected.

'We have seen many new immigrants from Britain change within a matter of months,' my host explained. 'It is not long before their friends at the office or on the building site tell them where they are going wrong. They are warned if they speak to Africans in too friendly a way. They are actively discouraged from having African friends.'

Before long even the immigrant who once had firm convictions about human justice knuckles under to the accepted way of life. Even he finds that he can get satisfaction from being in a superior social caste, and so enjoying privileges which only he and his fellow whites have reserved for them. He, and she, find that it is comforting to have a houseboy or a cook to undertake, dutifully, the household chores, accepting the master as some sort of demi-god. So unaccustomed are they to the idea of servants that it can only make sense to them if the Africans are regarded as inferior beings. Servants are, indeed, a big factor. The total European population of Salisbury is 60,000 and the number of African domestics 30,000.

The standard of living also appeals to the immigrant. It is much higher than what he has been accustomed to in Britain and his wages are much higher than those paid to Africans. The figures for the manufacturing industries of the Federation of Rhodesia and Nyasaland demonstrate this. Seventeen thousand Europeans employed in these undertakings received a total income in wages and salaries of £15,000,000 a year. The 100,000 Africans employed in the same factories received a total of £8,000,000 a year. The average white wage is £22 a week and the average African wage is £1 12s. od. No African is given a job superior to a European.

The immigrant finds that he can afford more luxuries than he had back in Britain. Income tax is lower, and his house and a car are easier to afford. His wages are on average over ten times as much as those of the

African with whom he works; in time he begins to believe that his higher standards can only be maintained if the African is kept in his place. Then, despite his earlier inclinations, he accepts the industrial colour bar and the discrimination against Africans which cuts right through Southern Rhodesian life. The immigrant, in fact, has been condemned to accept a system which his better judgment would truly reject in another social environment.

My hosts told me of some of their difficulties in living in this situation. When they had African children to play with their own children at Christmas parties, the neighbours objected. Although they had African friends in to tea, they could never ask the neighbours in too. At work my host could not discuss his attitude with his colleagues but he had to listen in silence as between themselves they engaged in the customary abuse of Africans, who are commonly called 'munts'. My host said that they put themselves into the same mental category as the white Americans who call the negroes 'niggers', and the fascists who talk about 'yids'.

There were twelve European members of Congress, several of whom were with Guy Clutton Brock at St Faith's farm at Rusape, where a daring experiment in inter-racial co-operative farming had been so successful. Only a few others, like my hosts, were brave enough to identify themselves openly with the Africans. But there were others with a liberal outlook; some, indeed, were South Africans who had travelled north of the Limpopo to escape from Afrikanerdom.

These liberals (and I was able to meet many of them while I was in Salisbury) are a gallant band of people. Despite ostracism and much open hatred from other Europeans, they are prepared to advocate the cause of the under-privileged. It is an act of courage in Salisbury to be seen mixing with Africans and there are few opportunities for it. One of the few places where it is possible for the races to mix is in the Capital Club, where University people, a few journalists, and professional people get together. This club was launched by members of the Capricorn Africa Society and it is an oasis in white Salisbury. But the atmosphere is rather artificial. Europeans and Africans do mix in meetings of the UFP but, so I was told, the artificiality is even more pronounced. Africans are tolerated by most of the Europeans, welcomed by a few as a symbol of the 'partnership' about which they preach, but are almost never accepted as genuine equals.

I called on the High Commissioner for the United Kingdom, Mr Metcalf, who seemed perplexed by the Rhodesian situation. He was concerned that I should meet 'African moderates' as well as the Congress leaders, and to this I willingly agreed. They were included in my programme of visits.

My first visit was to Sir Roy Welensky, the burly ex-railwayman who has become the Prime Minister of the Federation. His offices were in the modest corner of a building which had been taken over from the Southern Rhodesian Government, and his own room was on the ground floor, with two large windows looking out on a pavement.

There never has been any suggestion of violence on the part of the Africans in Southern Rhodesia; they are most peaceful and, under the circumstances, most patient. Violence has never been among the tactics adopted by the Southern Rhodesian African National Congress and the leaders are most stern with the members who ever suggest it. Sir Roy Welensky himself realises this and always makes himself accessible and never has a guard.

I found him also a charming man. He poured tea for me, which he drinks in great quantities—he never drinks alcohol—and we talked. But whenever I brought up a matter of policy he quickly changed the subject. Then he described his cabinet problem. 'As you will find out when you are in a cabinet one day, it is not easy to deal with cabinet colleagues. Each of them feels that his own Department's business should be pushed through. I have had to insist that cabinet papers should be circulated several days before we meet; some Ministers were in the habit of handing them out at the last minute before we could give them proper consideration.'

I did not know then that within a week I would have a direct personal interest in the Federal Government's 'proper consideration'.

Sir Roy is a big man physically, has big ambitions, and has always known what he wanted. In 1948 he came to London as Leader of the Unofficial Members of the Legislative Council in Northern Rhodesia and asked the Labour Government to give them closer union with Southern Rhodesia. By a reporter he was asked what he would do if Federation were made impossible. Mr Maclear Bate quotes the reply in his *Report from the Rhodesias*: 'If we do not get federation do you know what I'm going to do? I am going to do everything in my power to bring more Europeans into Northern Rhodesia. I don't care where they will come from, Great Britain, Holland, Germany, South Africa, Australia, America—it doesn't matter a damn—just let them have a white skin and be willing to work. The very day we have 100,000 in the country WE WILL DEMAND DOMINION STATUS!'

Welensky's father was a Polish Jew who emigrated to South Africa and married an Afrikaner girl. They crossed the Limpopo into

Mashonaland in 1890 with Cecil Rhodes' Pioneers. Seventeen years later their son Roland was born in Salisbury, which had become the capital of Southern Rhodesia. He went to work at fourteen, first as a barman and then on the railway. He took up boxing and wound up as Southern Rhodesia's heavyweight champion. In Bulawayo he became active in the white railwaymen's union but the railway bosses banished him to Broken Hill in Northern Rhodesia, then a bleak place, to get rid of him.

Some of the rowdies there once plastered his cab with anti-semitic slogans. Welensky got the better of them, revived the white union and found his way into the colony's Legislature. In politics he fought against the copper barons and the Colonial Office and this made him the hero of the white voters. But of his relations with Africans, who are 96 per cent of the Federation's population, Frank Barton, who as former editor of the *Central African Post* knows Welensky well, has this to say *:

'The simple truth is that, born and bred in the country though he is, he understands them no better than he does the Eskimos. Only lately has the truth slowly broken upon him that he cannot carry them with him on the same tide of oratory, bluff and charm that won and keeps for him the bulk of European support.'

I next called on an ex-member of the Suez group of Tory rebels who has settled in the Rhodesias. Captain Charles Waterhouse was the Member for South-East Leicester when I took my seat in the House after the by-election at Wednesbury. A week later I made my maiden speech and immediately following it Waterhouse made his last.

His office was at the top of a giant skyscraper built for Tanganyika Concessions, of which he is Managing Director. I took the lift (not to be used by Africans) and found Captain Waterhouse sitting in shirt sleeves and braces behind a large desk. He was frank and surprisingly progressive about African advancement.

'If we give them more economic opportunity here we will be expanding the market and establishing a strong basis for the economy', was his theme.

He said that some of the restrictions against Africans taking on skilled jobs were ridiculous. He went on: 'Why, in the Belgian Congo it is possible to go into a bank and to see a whole line of bank clerks who are Africans, but one is always served by European bank clerks here. Even in the railway workshops in Angola Africans are doing skilled jobs, which are not open to them in the Rhodesias.'

I asked him about his attitude to segregated housing.

* *Africa South*, issue of July/Sept. 1959.

'Ah, that's a little more difficult,' he said, 'but eventually Africans will have to move into Salisbury to live amongst us.'

He was in favour of opening up a better-class African housing area within the European township. When I asked him about the economic possibilities for the Federation as a whole he answered by quoting the trends in the price of copper; the inflationary housing boom in Southern Rhodesia did not impress him.

I came away encouraged that a champion of capitalism should have been so outspoken about breaking down the colour discriminations. He did not go as far as my liberal friends, but I found that he was not the only capitalist to hold such opinions. Many others realise that the only hope for the expansion of Rhodesia lies in African advancement and many of them are quite prepared that the colour bar discriminations, which are in part a product of the conspiracy to keep the Africans in a permanent subordinate position, should also go.

Unlike the artisans, the capitalists will always be able to buy privilege and seclusion, so they do not fear so much the breaking down of colour discrimination. In Britain they have been buying privilege for generations. For them it is not really a colour problem, it is a class question. But the white artisans and the farmers have most of the votes and they dictate the political policies to be pursued in Rhodesia.

I meant to call briefly at the offices of the *African Daily News* to see the Editor-in-Chief, Mr Lawrence Vambe, but I stayed for two hours and we both missed lunch. He had been represented to me as a 'moderate', but I came away with the feeling that if this were 'moderation' then the whites in Rhodesia are sitting on a volcano. Mr Vambe is a tall, sober-looking man with dreamy eyes. He was most bitter about colour discrimination and was sure that the Land Apportionment Act would have to be amended if the Africans were to be mollified. About discrimination on the railways he was particularly outspoken. He referred to the agreement reached between African railway workers and the European Railwaymen's Union for African advancement into certain categories of work. He said it was only a limited advance, but it was something. But the Government were not pushing it, although they had had the agreement before them for over a year. Africans are prevented from driving trains or acting as firemen, although these jobs are done perfectly capably by Africans in neighbouring territories such as the Belgian Congo. When more engine drivers were needed on the Rhodesian railways white men were especially recruited in Italy to avoid the necessity of promoting Africans to do the job.

On Federation Vambe said he supported it as the only way in which

Africans in Southern Rhodesia could be saved from being absorbed into the Union of South Africa. He feared that without it Africans south of the Zambezi would have no hope. This opinion was not shared by other Africans with whom I spoke. They said that the conditions in Southern Rhodesia were practically as bad as in the Union, and that the only hope Africans in Southern Rhodesia had of achieving any advance was for their black brothers in the two Protectorates to have more responsibility.

However, Vambe, I felt, is no stooge and sincerely believes what he says. But for any man in his position there is the danger of being out of touch with African opinion. The 'African' newspapers are European owned and many Africans look upon them as European propaganda sheets, although Vambe himself was an honest and outspoken editor. Since I met him in Salisbury he has become a Public Relations Officer at Rhodesia House in London, and he has not lost his outspokenness. At a meeting we both addressed in Birmingham he challenged Welensky's policy by saying that there should be no question of the Federation getting dominion status in 1960 and—even more daring—that European immigration should be stopped forthwith.

I went to the Native Commissioner's Office to check the figures on the Land Apportionment Act, so shaken was I by its sheer discriminatory character. Then I called in to see the Southern Rhodesian Parliament in action. I sat in the gallery and looked down on the miniature House of Commons. It had all the paraphernalia of Westminster, including a stern looking Speaker with a wig and a Serjeant-At-Arms with a mace. But there were only thirty MPs and they were sitting at desks. There were no black faces to be seen anywhere, none in the Chamber, none in the public gallery, and none in the Press gallery. I could have been in a European country with a wholly white population, and yet that Parliament legislates for a country in which over nine-tenths of the people are black.

I heard the members discussing a Bill to extend the heavy penalties for stock thieving to include the theft of chinchillas. A year before punishments were also increased for the theft of motor cars and corn-on-the-cob. In that Parliament there was one Member who spoke powerfully against the measure. Mr Holderness, a Salisbury lawyer, gave a vivid description of what corporal punishment for adults involves. Whippings were administered with a rattan cane four feet long and half an inch thick. The prisoner is stripped and tied across a 'triangle'; strokes are administered at the rate of ten to fifteen a minute; and after the whipping surgical dressings may have to be applied. In

Southern Rhodesia the range of offences for which corporal punishment may be administered is much greater than in most other countries, and it is used far more frequently. But farmer members strongly supported whipping as a punishment for the theft of maize on the cob, saying that it was a definite deterrent.

Mr Quinton, former Parliamentary Secretary for Native Affairs, said farmers were losing more than four to five per cent of their maize crops by theft, which meant a loss to each farmer of more than £1,000. Whipping was the only way to stop maize thefts because Africans who were sent to prison returned as 'national heroes'. Sir Patrick Fletcher said that the arguments against whipping had been sentimental, and the Bill was passed with only two votes against.

Mr Holderness, a supporter of Mr Garfield Todd, was defeated at the next election and one of the few voices of liberalism in the Southern Rhodesian Parliament was silenced.

The debate I listened to ended and the Bill to extend yet more punishment was passed with a comfortable majority. When the House rose for tea I met the Prime Minister, Sir Edgar Whitehead. He looks vague and absent-minded, but this may be because he is half blind and half deaf. He has a reputation for being an intellectual but his capacity in office since he was called back from his job as Federal consul in Washington has not been impressive. He was once considered to be a liberal but the repressive Acts against Africans which he has pushed through the Southern Rhodesian Legislature might well be described as fascist. Churchmen and lawyers in Rhodesia itself have been severely critical.

I had tea with Dr Hirsch and Mr Blair Ewing, the youngest Member of Parliament, and saw the only Africans in Parliament. They were the waiters. I asked the two Parliamentarians why there were no Africans as Members.

'Well, you know, they are on the Electoral Roll, we have no colour discrimination in that sense. If they have the qualifications they can vote.'

'But,' I said, 'you put the qualifications up when there was a danger of Africans coming on the roll in large numbers. It appears to us on the outside that you are determined to keep them in a small minority.'

They said, 'We in the UFP are far more liberal than the Dominion Party. They would take away all African political rights. We do let them vote when they have the qualifications.'

I asked them about the Land Apportionment Act and again they gave evasive replies. The Act was represented as the height of liberalism and

in the Africans' best interests. I had the impression that the double-talk
and platitudes of the UFP are more dangerous to the Africans than the
threats of the reactionary Dominion Party.

I left the Southern Rhodesian Legislature feeling that I had been in a
make-believe world. The elected representatives of the minority were
deaf to the black rumblings in their own country and unable to understand the hopes and aspirations of Africans.

Dr Ahren Palley, another MP who was then the spokesman for the
Dominion Party but has since formed his own Party, took me to the
Jameson Hotel. He told me that he would show me an example of an
inter-racial hotel. Although we sat in the lounge talking for nearly an
hour we did not see any Africans there except for the waiters. Dr Palley
gave me the most recent policy statement of the Dominion Party which
was a frank rejection of the Welensky conception of Federation. He
reminded me that at the last territorial elections in Southern Rhodesia
the Dominion Party had more votes than the UFP and that the
majority of white voters were opposed to Whitehead and Welensky.

Later I checked on the figures. Dr Palley was quite right. In
Southern Rhodesia, where over two-thirds of the settlers of Central
Africa live, the United Federal Party polled a total in all constituencies
of only 16,840 first preference votes. Their total of votes is, in fact, less
than that polled individually by the average MP in Britain.

The Dominion Party had a total of 18,142 first preference votes but
lost the election because most of the 4,663 votes cast for the United
Rhodesia Party, who were bottom of the poll in most constituencies,
were redistributed to the UFP, under the electoral system which called
for an over-all majority for each successful candidate. This redistribu-
tion gave the UFP seventeen seats against the Dominion Party's
thirteen.

The United Rhodesia Party has now been renamed the Central
Africa Party under the leadership of Mr Garfield Todd, a New
Zealander, who started work as a missionary in Southern Rhodesia at
the age of twenty-six. He entered politics in 1946 as United Party
Member for Insiza in the Southern Rhodesian Parliament; seven years
later he took over as Prime Minister when Sir Godfrey Huggins (now
Lord Malvern) was elevated to the Federal political sphere.

Always a blunt and forthright man—even in high office—Todd
made several attacks on the economic policies of the Federal Government in 1955 and 1956. These attacks hastened moves to merge the
United Party, which controlled Southern Rhodesia, and the Federal
Party, which had the majority in the Federal Assembly, to prevent open

disagreements between the two Governments. In the negotiations Todd held out for the common roll, on a qualitative franchise, rather than the complicated two-tier system favoured by Welensky. By the end of 1957 they had reached agreement and the merger was arranged for March 1958, when the United Federal Party was born.

Meanwhile, however, the rebels in Todd's cabinet who objected to his liberalism (although it was still not pronounced) planned his political downfall. All four members of the cabinet handed in their resignations in January 1958 and the majority of the Parliamentary Party turned against the Prime Minister. A Special Congress was called and Todd was defeated in favour of the compromise candidate, Sir Edgar Whitehead.

Now Todd is a bitter opponent of Whitehead and many Africans regard him as a champion of their cause. But Mr Chad Chipunza, an African Member of the Federal Assembly for the UFP and a supporter of Welensky, has no such admiration for Todd. Attacking the ex-Prime Minister for calling for the immediate removal of the colour bar Chipunza said, on March 10, 1959, that Todd was 'speaking like a visionary and not a politician' and 'was being unrealistic by demanding that the colour bar be broken massively and immediately'.

Chipunza went on, 'He had four years of leadership in Southern Rhodesia and a very large majority in the House. Why then did he not remove the colour bar massively and immediately?' Chipunza also maintained that Todd, as Prime Minister of Southern Rhodesia, introduced legislation which restricted the inter-territorial movement of non-Europeans within the Federation.

'That legislation was opposed by people of all races, including many of his own supporters,' he said. 'That, in itself, was colour bar. Again, within those four years at his disposal we had the Land Apportionment Act and he ought to have amended the unpleasant aspects of it. If Todd wanted to remove the colour bar then he should have amended the liquor laws.

'Again, under Todd, the franchise qualifications in Southern Rhodesia were raised, making it more difficult for Africans to obtain the vote. Todd's Industrial Conciliation Bill was rejected twice by the Southern Rhodesia House and he did nothing further about it. During those four years he did nothing for African Government employees as far as promotion and conditions of service were concerned.'

Chipunza's speech is a reminder of the difficulties facing liberal politicians who want to implement progressive ideas while they are still dependent on white settler support. Now Todd has been rejected by the settlers he can only make a come-back with the Central Africa Party if more Africans are given the vote.

Dr Palley—or indeed most of the white voters—would not want that. Welensky's supporters want Federation to continue, but firmly under white leadership, but the Dominion Party fears the emerging Africans and does not trust the UFP to keep them in their place. It recommends the division of Central Africa into the separate black Protectorates of Nyasaland and Barotseland and a new European state comprised of Southern Rhodesia, the 'line of rail' to the North and the rich Copperbelt.

But this plan, which keeps the wealthy areas for the whites, sounds too much like the Bantu segregation in South Africa to appeal to Africans. I asked Dr Palley, 'What happens to your plan if uranium is discovered in Barotseland? Will you then want to build a railway there and include it in the white state?'

He seemed temporarily flummoxed, but then came back with a gush of words, from which I gathered that the Africans could have the uranium if they could develop it, but if not, well, then anything could happen!

14

Black Rumblings in Southern Rhodesia

UNTIL three years ago, Africans in Southern Rhodesia had no national political organisation. To the south, in the Union, the African Congress had become a powerful force and Chief Luthuli a recognised African leader. To the north, in Northern Rhodesia and Nyasaland, there were Congresses which had been gradually developing their strength for a decade or more. Ideas were spreading and it was only a question of time before the Southern Rhodesians formed a Congress of their own. But the Government of Southern Rhodesia allowed the movement to exist for only eighteen months. It was formed on 12 September 1957 and banned in February 1959, when the leaders were thrown into gaol. Both the Congresses in Northern Rhodesia and South Africa continued, although under increasing difficulties. The Nyasaland Congress was banned on 3 March 1959, when Dr Banda was arrested and the Colonial Secretary announced that a massacre plot had been discovered.

To be an African political leader in any country south of Tanganyika is a hazardous occupation; there is a 10 to 1 chance of being arrested, and a 1,000,000 to 1 chance of being elected. Notwithstanding the risks the most able Africans helped to form the Southern Rhodesian African National Congress: there were businessmen, trade union organisers, graduates, as well as the more humble workers. There were many bitter grievances they had to pursue—the denial of the vote to all Africans but a thousand, the land allocation, the discrimination in employment and the dictatorial methods of the Native Affairs Department in the Reserves.

Within a few months the Congress found that it was getting mass support, particularly because of its campaign against the Native Land Husbandry Act, which was forcing peasants off their land.

Mr Joshua Nkomo, the President of Congress, voiced the feelings of most Africans when he said that the Act '. . . undermines the security of our small land rights, dispossesses us of our little wealth in the form of cattle, disperses us from our ancestral homes in the reserves and reduces us to the status of vagabonds and a source of cheap labour for the farmers, miners, and industrialists. Such a law will turn the African people against society to the detriment of the peace and progress of this country.'

When the Congress took the Government to Court in cases of the infringement of individual rights the prestige of Congress went up by leaps and bounds. Nothing like it had ever been done before.

The answer of the Government was to pursue cases against the Congress leaders themselves. Principal target was the voluble George Nyandoro. African informers attended all his meetings and made reports which were not noted for their accuracy. A number of convictions were obtained: he was fined £35 for telling women to disobey Native Commissioners when asked to establish fire-guards and for telling a funeral audience that the dead man was killed by Europeans. He was not, however, found guilty of any offence when he was charged with likening Africans to an elephant and Europeans to an ant, nor was he ever given a prison sentence until the Emergency.

It was because such cases taken against Congress leaders were so unsuccessful that the Government decided to destroy the movement by declaring the state of emergency in February 1959. There had been no violence in Southern Rhodesia, nor any suggestion of it when White-head took his extreme measures. Because there have been no massacre plot allegations and no Devlin Commission in Southern Rhodesia, world opinion has tended to forget that hundreds of Africans were rounded up without trial there and that many of them remain in prison. Sir Edgar Whitehead attempted to justify these extreme measures by referring to the situation in Nyasaland. But he has also revealed that preparations for the 'state of emergency' were under way before Christmas 1958 and long before any crisis in Nyasaland.

Despite the long, careful preparations for the *coup* many of the wrong people were swept into custody. Mr Moses Makone of Mabvuku, for instance, was kept in prison for thirty-eight days before he was able to convince the police that he had never been a member of Congress but had been active as local chairman of Mr Garfield Todd's party.

Among those arrested was Paul Mushonga, who was a prosperous African trader and had sacrificed a great deal for his political ideals. His sacrifice gives the lie to the sneer that African politicians enter politics only for what they can get out of it. Mushonga's shops in Highfield, selling groceries and meat, were well conducted and he and his wife very hard-working people. He spent hundreds of pounds for Congress and his car was always at the disposal of the movement. His wife and child were also arrested in the round-up of Congress leaders.

The Congress aims had been simple and democratic, but it was not racialist—and Europeans were supporters and members. Nkomo describes their aims as follows: 'We based our policy on the Universal Declaration of Human Rights, especially the right of adult suffrage and the rights of individuals to property; and we gained the clear support of the African masses. Our aims remain—

1. To recapture human dignity for the Africans, which has been destroyed over a number of years;
2. To restore the land and property rights of Africans; and
3. To gain universal franchise so that the African may play a full part in the political life of the country.'

Congress also opposed Federation because it feared that this would threaten the Africans in Northern Rhodesia and Nyasaland with the political domination of white settlers from which they themselves had suffered. I asked the Congress leaders about the danger of South Africa.

'We believe,' they said, 'that this "bogey" of the Union absorbing Southern Rhodesia was dangled in 1952 to scare the whites into voting for the Federation referendum.'

They admitted that their own greatest hope was the advance of Africans towards political democracy in the two Northern Protectorates. 'It would help us enormously if Africans north of the Zambezi had a greater say in their own affairs.'

They had invited me to speak on Labour Party policy towards Rhodesia in the African segregated area of Highfield and also in Bulawayo. I accepted because I thought Africans were entitled to know about Labour policy and because I wanted to meet as many Africans as possible and hear their reaction.

The Highfield suburb is a miserable-looking estate built for the workers in the factories. Most of its housing is substandard, though better than many African urban dwellings I have seen. The houses are almost all controlled by the white authorities and if a worker loses his job his house goes as well.

As minimum factory wages are only £6 10s. od. a month, it is next to impossible for a worker to maintain his wife and family in Highfield. Many families stay in the reserves. Even the highest paid workers— lorry drivers at £15 a month—find it difficult to make ends meet. The prices in the shops are the same as for the Europeans who are paid on average ten times as much; indeed, a Government enquiry shows that 50 per cent of Highfield inhabitants are living below the poverty line.

The meeting was held on Saturday afternoon, to enable as many workers to attend as possible. When we arrived at the hall the waiting crowd greatly exceeded the expected number and they were moved outside to make room for everybody. About 2,500 Africans were there and ten or so Europeans, who included John Pittman, a Member of the Southern Rhodesian Parliament for the UFP, an Irish barrister who acted for Congress, and journalists. The Africans sat closely packed on the ground outside the hall; some held newspapers to shade their heads against the hot sun, others were hanging on the edge of the building to get a better view, and at the back hundreds were standing. There seemed to be a sea of black faces, all eager and expectant. No uniformed police were present, but some plainclothes men were there.

Although excited, the crowd was just as orderly as the large open air political meetings I have addressed in Britain. The proceedings started with a dramatic singing of 'Mwari Komborera Afrika' (God Bless Africa), a hymn-like anthem used by the nationalist parties in southern Africa. The crowd sang it with feeling. Then I was introduced by Robert Chikerema, the Acting President, and George Nyandoro acted as my interpreter.

To avoid the danger of mistranslation I spoke only a sentence at a time. This also gave an opportunity to the Africans who could follow English to appreciate my meaning more clearly. During my speech I felt that about two-thirds of the audience were able to follow my speech in English, judging by their reaction before Nyandoro had given the Sishona version. I took great care not to make statements which could handicap the Africans in expressing their complaints and aspirations constitutionally. Nor did I wish to obstruct legitimate authority. But I felt it was important that these Africans who lived in a country partly responsible to the United Kingdom Parliament should know the policies and outlook adopted by Her Majesty's Opposition. They were also vitally concerned with the future of the Federation which was, after all, created by the vote of the United Kingdom Parliament and subject to review by that body. Strictly speaking the constitutional future of Central Africa is more the direct responsibility of the Parliament at Westminster than that of the local white politicians. As I saw it the visiting British MP had a duty to exchange views with the people who were so directly interested in the way in which those responsibilities were exercised.

During my speech I also told them about the need for economic development, hard work, and the need to improve living standards. I told them that the Labour Party was very keen on this and had plans to assist the underdeveloped areas of the world by allocating aid. I emphasised that they should not expect too much, for their own standards would be improved mainly by their own efforts. I gave them as a slogan 'Work hard, Educate yourselves, and Organise.'

As there had been reports of incidents in Nyasaland I put the emphasis of the speech on the importance of non-violence. I wanted them to understand that the British Labour movement could not countenance the use of violence and whatever the circumstances they should behave in such a way that their friends overseas could also have respect for them. In some ways it was a platitudinous speech, but the basic points had to be emphasized to avoid any misunderstanding.

When the time came for questions they came in thick and fast. Most of the questions were put to me in English. Some of the more vociferous members of the audience made it all too clear that they understood my appeal for non-violence by refuting the advice. One said, 'Why do you advise us against violence? Britain only understands violence. Look at Ghana and look at Cyprus. Violence worked there.' I said that for every example he could produce of a country which went through a period of violence before reaching independence I could produce another which had achieved independence without it. The Congress leaders also spoke against violence and I felt sure that almost all the people were in favour of following this advice. When I told them that the European settlers in the country were there to stay and that they should make friends with them and not show enmity there was genuine agreement. The meeting could have lasted all evening, but as storm clouds were gathering it was brought to an end as dramatically as it began with another rendering of 'Mwari Komborera Afrika'.

I stayed the night with Paul Mushonga and he arranged a small party for some friends to meet me. His own house was actually two of the usual-sized dwellings with doors knocked in the walls. It was quite comfortable, with large easy chairs and a large carpet in the sitting room, but no electric light had been fitted, although he had often asked the authorities for it. The light was provided by the pressure lamp. Several Europeans came to the party, including some lecturers from the University, and the Irish barrister. I met trade union organisers and the chairman of the Nyasaland African Congress branch in Salisbury, who was a transport worker. He told me that many thousands of Nyasas went to work in Southern Rhodesia and that his branch was a very strong one. 'We are opposed to Federation,' he said, 'because we see discrimination practised here in Southern Rhodesia and we do not want it in Nyasaland.'

L

Others were very anxious to assure me that they did not hate Europeans and that they realised that the whites had a stake in the country and should stay. A Southern Rhodesian said, 'But they cannot expect to stay here at the expense of the majority of the people. We want our rights and we intend to demand them. We will do this by constitutional means, but it is being made difficult for us to do this. The Government has all sorts of ways of hampering us. We want you people in Great Britain to understand how we feel. We ask for nothing more than to have a say in the running of our own affairs.'

I went to bed as soon as I could, for the next morning I had to be up at 4 o'clock to drive the 200-odd miles to Bulawayo for a morning meeting. Paul Mushonga's car is a large American model, but that morning it took over an hour to start. We collected Nyandoro, Chikerema and the Chairman of the Harari branch who were travelling with us and they were most concerned that we should not be late at Bulawayo. We drove as fast as possible through the deserted countryside, through the little European towns of Gatooma and Que Que, and southwards towards Bulawayo, where Lobengula, the King of the Matabele, once reigned supreme. His empire had began to crack in October 1888 when he signed a concession to the emissaries of the imperialist Cecil Rhodes.

It became known as the Rudd concession and formed the basis for the Chartered Company which became Rhodes' vehicle for his expansionist adventures in Central Africa. Rhodes originally bought only the mineral rights for a payment of £100 every month to Lobengula and a gift of 1,000 rifles and 100,000 rounds of ammunition and an armed steamboat for use on the Zambezi. (So much for the peaceful, civilising influence of the pioneers on the Africans.)

But Rhodes was not satisfied with the mineral rights only and found a pretext for a war of conquest against Lobengula. The actual plans for the attack were prepared by that mischievous adventurer Dr Jameson, who wired Rhodes for permission to enter Matabeleland. Rhodes replied, 'Read Luke XIV, 31.' Jameson looked at his Bible and read, 'Or what king, going to make war against another king, sitteth not down first, and consulteth whether he be able with ten thousand to meet him that cometh against him with twenty thousand?'

He sent back a message to Rhodes that he was going in. Lobengula wanted to negotiate but he suspected treachery. Jameson had almost every white man in the country with him; every volunteer was promised a share of the cattle to be looted from the Matabele, twenty gold claims, and each would be given a farm of six thousand acres, which would be valued by the Company at £9,000. The decisive battle of the war took place on the Shangani river; Lobengula was defeated and died soon after; his tribe was broken.

We drove over the Shangani river and on to Bulawayo. At the Stanley Hall, just outside a miserable African housing area, we found a crowd of Africans waiting expectantly. There were also white police in smart khaki uniforms riding on horseback in the roadway and several standing at the back of the hall inside.

The meeting began with 'God Bless Africa'—the Matabele version, 'Nkosi Sikelela Afrika'. Again it was sung with great feeling by the hundreds of men in tattered shorts and shirts or threadbare suits. Almost all of them were Matabele, the sons or grandsons of Lobengula's men. The Mashona had been their enemies, but now they were singing a song of unity not only with the Mashona but with all Africa.

The speeches of the leaders who had come with me from Salisbury had to be made in English and translated into Sindebele by the local officials. The advice they gave was similiar to that given at Highfield.

'Do not use violence. Do not by your actions undermine the success of Congress, but remain firm to our cause and, in the end, we will win.'

George Nyandoro made the most passionate of the speeches. He told the meeting that as their success grew and as Government became more fearful, so the danger increased that the Congress executive would be arrested. 'You must know that even if we are all arrested, the struggle will go on,' he said. 'We cannot rest until all Africans have their rights.'

Although Nyandoro made some bitter remarks about the Government in his speech, there was no emphasis on anti-white feeling, nor in the speecnes of the others. They reiterated that they wanted to be in friendship with the whites who had settled in their country and the crowd approved. 'But,' they said, 'those settlers cannot expect to have privileges which reduce us Africans to a form of slavery.'

I spoke again about the Labour Party's attitude to Central Africa and the anxiety in Britain that there should be peace and understanding between the Europeans and the Africans and that there should be no violence. The questions poured in. One passionate young man said:

'How do we know we can trust you? When you go among your own people won't you say things to them which will please them, and forget what you have said to us about reaching an understanding with the Africans?'

Sitting in the front row of the meeting was a row of 'Coloured' people (of mixed African and white parentage) who were most enthusiastic in their support. I spoke to them afterwards and they turned out

to be school-teachers in the local Coloured school. The Coloured
community is supporting the African cause, they said.

'The Europeans try to keep us apart by giving us separate facilities.
We have a separate area in which to live, we have separate schools, there
are even special rates paid to Coloured nurses in the hospitals. Our rates
are below those of the European nurses, but above those of the
Africans. We do not want to be considered apart, we are throwing in
our lot with the ordinary African people.'

The officials stayed behind for an executive committee meeting and
the school-teachers took me off in a car to have lunch. They stopped at
a restaurant but declined my invitation to lunch. 'No Coloured person
has ever been in that place,' they said. 'We have to live here and it would
be too big a risk to attempt to break down the colour bar by ourselves.'

In the comfortable restaurant I sat by myself and ordered a meal, but
I felt lonely in that atmosphere. The Europeans sitting there had come
into Bulawayo from their farms or suburban homes to enjoy a Sunday
lunch, but they were oblivious of the storm raging outside. The
restaurant was for whites only. The customers were outnumbered by
the waiters who were hovering around, waiting to respond to the
slightest bidding. The service could not have been better, but the
customers seemed to be capable only of regarding the African waiters
with sour, disgruntled looks. One arrogant young man of around
twenty-five years of age lost his temper over some minor complaint
and shouted at the innocent-looking waiter, but none of the other
customers seemed a bit concerned with this ill-mannered exhibition.
That incident seemed typical of the general attitude of white to black.
I was unhappy that my fellow-Europeans were so devoid of feeling for
the people among whom they lived.

We drove straight back to Salisbury and Paul and I took turns in
driving. For miles we saw nothing but the open grazing country. This
was all European farming area and we saw very few Africans. Over the
years all Africans, other than those employed by Europeans, had been
forcibly moved into the Native designated areas even when their
families had always lived in that particular district. Occasionally we
swept through a sleepy township, each one doing its best not to look
like a pioneer outpost with a few shops strung along the high street, a
few brave window displays and one or two neon signs.

When I read the newspapers the next morning I was annoyed to see
grossly distorted reports of my two meetings. Whereas I had been
trying to show the Africans that Europeans had feelings of friendship
and sympathy for them I was represented as 'inflaming the Bantu'. No

newspapers, with the exception of the *African Daily News* (which had as its headline, 'Labour MP Warns Africans Against Using Violence to Achieve Their Aims'), gave a fair account of what I had said. Indeed, sentences were distorted to mislead the readers. After I had spoken about the need for economic development I had said, 'The Labour Party is united with you in the joint struggle against poverty.' In the newspaper reports the last two words were omitted, and no reference was made to my economic theme. Mr Winston Field, the leader of the Dominion Party, had been approached by the newspapers for comment, and he said:

'I consider it the most disgraceful thing I have ever known that any Member of the British Parliament should come to this country and preach open sedition—which is what it amounts to.

'It is time we took a firmer line with people like Mr Stonehouse.

'If they cannot behave themselves in this country we should put them in the same category as other irresponsible agitators and ban them.'

The *Rhodesia Herald*, in an editorial, supported the proposed banning.

I went to see the editor of the *Rhodesia Herald* to complain about the distortions in the reporting of the meetings. When I called he could not see me. Instead I spoke to the Deputy Editor, who turned out to be a most bitter advocate of white racial superiority. 'You should leave us to take care of our own affairs,' he said.

'But it is our affair what you do to two million Africans,' I said. 'The British Parliament still has important responsibilities according to the Southern Rhodesian Constitution.'

'Well, we know what we are doing and we don't want any of you people coming here and interfering. If I had my way I would stop all members of the Labour Party coming into the Federation on visits.'

We could make no progress, so I left.

I called on John Pittman at his request. He is an honest, sincere liberal member of the UFP, a Member of the Southern Rhodesian Parliament and a barrister by profession. I felt that he was completely out of place in the party of Welensky and Whitehead, but I suppose he feels he can do more to influence policies from the inside rather than by joining the Central Africa Party of Garfield Todd, who will never be able to win power on the present franchise. He told me that he thought my speech at Highfield had been first-class and that he agreed with most of it.

Herbert Chitepo, the African barrister, had an office just down the corridor and he told me something of his difficulties. No European clients would instruct him and his African clients could hardly ever afford to pay. Most of his cases were in the native courts so he could not get experience in the major ones. He told me frankly that he was a supporter of Congress and thought that 'those boys' were doing a good job. 'I don't want to come out too openly in support of them yet,' he said. 'I think it is important that first I should build up my practice, but they know that I am with them.' Since the state of emergency was declared, Herbert Chitepo has announced his support of Congress, which in the circumstances was quite a brave thing for him to do. He did it because the Prime Minister had made statements to the effect that the only supporters of Congress were n'er-do-goods.

The more time I spent in Salisbury the more I was aware of the colour bar. There were separate entrances for Africans and Europeans in all the post offices. At a very new one in the suburbs, completed only the year before, I saw the new signs on the brick wall, 'For Africans only', and on another entrance, 'For Europeans Only'. Since I left the Federation it has been announced that these separate entrances are being abolished. My European friends in Rhodesia have written to me warning me not to accept these last-minute concessions to liberalism as a sign of a new progressive outlook on the part of the Government in Central Africa.

It has, after all, taken the Government six years to reach this point, and no attempt has been made to repeal or amend what the Roman Catholic bishops of the Federation at their Conference in October, 1959, called 'statutory law based on race distinction' which includes, of course, the Land Apportionment Act in Southern Rhodesia. Even Mr Jasper Savanhu, who was appointed a Parliamentary Secretary to the Federal Government, has been refused permission to occupy a house in the European-designated area of Salisbury. He could only live in the area if he called himself a servant and got himself taken on the staff of a European resident.

Africans cannot use the bus services run in the town of Salisbury and between the town and the European suburbs. All these buses are reserved for Europeans. A houseboy working in a European household and wanting to get into town would have to walk the whole distance. No public transport is available for him. But there are 'native buses' for the workers travelling between the township of Harari and Highfield and Salisbury itself. Africans can use taxis, but only the second class ones. While I was in Salisbury making visits I borrowed a second class taxi from a Congress supporter. It was a very good car, a Consul, but it was clearly marked on the door '2nd Class'. When people saw me driving around in this they looked at me in amazement. The second class is not meant to describe the car, which was excellent in both appearance and performance, but the driver and passengers.

I went into the main branch of Barclays Bank to cash some travellers' cheques, and found a large reception hall with ten or more clerks waiting to do business. They were all Europeans and there were a few European customers. But on the other side of the barrier in a very much smaller hall were crowds of Africans queueing up to be served by only two clerks. There was nothing 'equal but separate' about that. Even the few prosperous Africans with large bank accounts cannot use the European entrance. This discrimination boomerangs on the European business houses, as almost all the Africans queueing are acting for European firms and sometimes they queue for hours. Africans are now admitted into many of the shops, but seldom receive the treatment given to European customers.

The Multi-racial Hotels Bill had been announced as a great concession to Africans; hotels had been forbidden by law from accommodating any dark-skinned visitor unless provided with special authority signed by Sir Edgar Whitehead, as Minister for Native Affairs, an office he holds with that of Prime Minister. The Act now allows hotels of over a certain value to become 'multi-racial'. But it is worthless; no hotel has applied for registration, not even the Jameson.

Although hotels are forbidden to admit Africans for overnight stay, there is no legal restriction on them admitting Africans to the restaurants for meals. This is left completely to the discretion of the proprietors. The Jameson will admit Africans, but the other places will not. I wanted to give a meal to my friends before I left Salisbury in appreciation of their hospitality, and I booked a table at La Fontaine restaurant at the Meikles Hotel. This is in the new part of the Meikles Hotel, which was first established in the pioneering days; it is one of the citadels of white supremacy.

When I arrived with my three African guests I was told that no table had been booked. We checked the book and sure enough the reservation had been omitted. Whilst I talked to the Under Manager, Nyandoro was speaking to some of the waiters who were highly delighted that some Africans should dare to enter the restaurant. George told me later that the waiters were Congress supporters and so were the cooks. Little did the European customers, staring at us in anger, realise that the food they were eating had been prepared by nationalists, served up by nationalists, and delivered to their tables by nationalists. Probably at no time had a white hand touched the food which they ate.

The Under Manager suggested that we try the old Meikles Hotel which was through a long connecting corridor. We went towards it, assuming that our arrival would be expected, but when we reached the entrance to the old restaurant the European head waiter standing there was genuinely surprised to see us.

'I'm sorry sir, but boys are not allowed in here.'

I said, 'These are not *boys*, these are my friends, and we would like to have a table for dinner.'

'I'm sorry, we cannot let you in here. The other customers might object. I must go and see the Manager. Will you wait please?'

We sat in the lounge and felt a hundred hostile eyes upon us. To be on the safe side, we ordered only soft drinks, but before they were delivered we were summoned to the Manager. He was most apologetic. 'I really would like to help you,' he said, 'but I cannot do it. We hôteliers have to consider what our customers think and if we let you in there would be an uproar.'

The year before my colleague, Barbara Castle, had entertained Wellington Chirwa (who was at that time a Federal Member of Parliament from Nyasaland) to a meal in the Meikles restaurant.

'Ah!' said the Manager, 'we don't want that to happen again.'

When I said that even in Kenya the colour bar was on the way out he replied, 'Yes, I agree, the colour bar will have to break down eventually, but it will be a long time yet. When we do it all hotels will have to act together.'

We left the Meikles and went to the Jameson and there, without any reservations, we sat in the public dining-room and had an excellent meal. We were also joined by my two European hosts. The party of three Africans and three Europeans did not cause any more than passing interest to the other European diners. They accepted the fact that Africans were admitted to that dining room and it did not worry them at all.

I left Salisbury airport ('Southern Rhodesia welcomes you') and flew to Lusaka in Northern Rhodesia. Paul, Robert and George were there to see me off. As I stood with the other passengers by the entrance to the tarmac waiting for the signal to go to the aircraft, which was delayed by some minor repair, I could see nearby a group of about twenty prisoners methodically stamping down a trench with heavy flatteners under the supervision of warders armed with rifles. When I looked up to the balcony I could see George, Robert and Paul waving to me. I waved back, little realising that they—within a week—would be prisoners too.

15

North of the Zambezi

WELENSKY was very anxious that I should visit the Kariba Dam, the symbol of economic advance, and offered to fly me there. Kariba is put forward as one of the political justifications for the rush to impose Federation on unwilling Africans. While I was in Salisbury the workers at the dam site went on strike and the symbol began to look a little tarnished.

The Africans had gone on strike with the slogan, 'We will not die for fourpence an hour', after fourteen Africans and three Italians had died in an accident. It made me wonder about the value of 'economic advance' to Africans in a country where all the factories are owned by European-controlled companies, where Africans are not given the opportunity to rise to skilled positions and where African wage-rates are kept down to about a tenth of the European. I thought also of Paul Mushonga's house in Highfield, still without its electric light bulb. Is there not a danger of worshipping 'economic development' for its own sake, without questioning what advantages it brings to ordinary people?

The national economy of the Union of South Africa looks very respectable on paper and the annual increase in production is impressive, but what really matters is the welfare of the people and the way in which the wealth is distributed. The gold and diamond wealth of South Africa depends very largely on compound labour, which means that workers are taken hundreds of miles away from their homes and kept for years in an unhealthy one-sex community. Who could possibly claim that these men are happier than if they had remained with their families and been helped to live contented peasant lives? If the price paid for 'economic development' is cheap African labour, bad working conditions and separation from family life for years at a time, it is surely too big a price as far as the Africans are concerned. They realise, after all, that the economic empire they are helping to create is a European one. In Central Africa, as in South Africa, the vast economic enterprises are white-owned and white-controlled. The workers on the Kariba Dam site wanted more than fourpence an hour because their wage is their only real stake in the Federation's economic structure.

There are many experts who believe that all Africa's problems could be solved merely by the investment of more capital. That is a great fallacy. More capital invested in an economy which is already controlled by a tiny minority can have the effect of making the rich richer and the poor comparatively poorer. What follows is an increase in the tensions within the community, making a happy life more difficult for everyone to achieve. Investment and economic progress must be linked to a wider degree of participation, stretching down towards the ordinary worker. In terms of agricultural development this means more co-operative societies, giving the Africans a stake in the marketing and processing stages. In terms of industrial development, the State, as a trustee for the people, should have a substantial share through public corporations; decent wage standards should also be established; and rights given for trade union organisations and consultation with the workers. These rights, and the opportunity for Africans to rise into skilled occupations at the rate for the job, would insure against Africans being regarded merely as a source of cheap labour rather than as real partners. It is then that 'economic development' would begin to make sense to Africans.

The Kariba scheme is one of the greatest in Africa. Its total expected cost is £113,000,000 and the lake created by the dam will stretch 180 miles. The main part of the investment of the Federation is tied up in Kariba and the power it will provide of 7,650 million kilowatts could be the basis for an industrial leap forward in Central Africa. It could in its turn bring great benefits to the 7,500,000 people of Central Africa if they are given an opportunity of sharing the wealth created. Unfortunately, the availability of masses of primitive people gives private developers—and, indeed, the state as well—the chance to obtain labour at less than fair prices. In the very early stages of development when a nation has to make a supreme effort to create the means of communications it may be moral to exploit cheap labour in this way. During the second stages, as the economy expands and secondary industries are set up, it is not only immoral to exploit cheap labour, it is also economically foolhardy. Fair wages to Africans would ensure a bigger market which would stimulate more industry and development. Today in the towns it is virtually impossible for African workers to support their families because of the low wages they receive. The employer cannot demand a high standard of work; he even expects the lower standard. If more Africans were paid according to the value of their work, rather than at the lowest possible rate at which they can be recruited, industrial relations would be much better and the community a more stable one.

There are now signs that the copper companies of Northern Rhodesia are trying to reverse their previous policy of buying African labour at the cheapest possible rate. There is a great deal of good sense and honest realism among the managerial element of the copper companies. They have seen the long term sense of having contented African workers rather than short term cheap labour. But the change of policy has been left so late that the vested interests of white workers may prove to be an obstacle. Fortunately some European workers are in favour of African advancement, as I was to find out when I reached the Copperbelt.

I wanted to visit the Kariba Dam to see the conditions of work and also to see the re-settlement of the people who had to move from their traditional homes because of the new Kariba lake. But I could not see the workmen as the area had been declared 'closed' when the strike took place and the Federal troops were flown in. Official statements had tried to give the impression that the 'trouble makers' were Nyasa employees who were linked with the Nyasaland African Congress but all evidence showed that the dispute was an industrial one. Eventually the Italian contractors increased the Africans' wage rates and the work went on, but by then the leaders were intimidated and effective trade unionism had been made impossible. Although the area was officially 'closed' I saw the dam, but not through permission from the Federal Government who had made the order.

I drove from Lusaka with a Colonial Government officer who was a keen intelligent man and obviously sincere in his basically pro-African outlook. It was refreshing to be with the Colonial Office again after a week in the hive of white settler hypocrisy in Southern Rhodesia. From the main road we turned down one which went through hitherto completely undeveloped scrubland and forest. We met the local District Officer, transferred to his Land Rover and drove towards Kariba. When we reached the barrier which said, ominously, 'No Unauthorised Person Allowed Beyond This Point', the District Officer showed his pass to the guard and gave some excuse to enable the Colonial Office and me to go through as well. Suddenly we saw the dam itself, rising like a magnificent monument from its bed in the great Zambezi. Only Italian workers were about as all the Africans were on strike.

I was very interested in the plight of the 29,000 Valley Tonga people who were moved before their homes were swallowed up by the rising waters of the Zambezi. Many of them could not believe that the river would rise as far as the villages where they had spent all their lives and had stubbornly refused to move. In one village the men were so angry that they attacked the District Officer with spears. When the askaris shot back several of them were killed. The villagers moved to the new sites prepared for them. I went with the DO concerned to see the people in their re-settlement areas. This time there was no armed guard.

The track along which we travelled was perilous even for a Land Rover. Every few miles we came to a pool of mud which would have been as slippery as butter to the wheels of an ordinary car. In several places the vehicle turned into the rough grass towering over us, making a new track as it crashed through. The first village we reached had ten or twelve rondavel huts and some emaciated cattle attended by young boys who were either naked or dressed in filthy khaki shorts. We spoke to some of the men through an interpreter; they were sullen and resentful at first, until they realised that we were there to see their conditions of life. They told us about the death of many of their children through malnutrition and dysentry. There had been an epidemic. Food was very limited until a new harvest. The Government had provided maize meal to help them over the period but there was not much else to go with it. As we talked people were staring at us list-lessly—it was obvious that they were not getting enough to eat. I asked the District Officer about the dysentry and he said it was because the people would not learn how to dig latrines. They have no idea of hygiene, he said. 'Even if we dig the latrines for them we cannot make them use them. These people are the most primitive in Rhodesia, and it is hard to teach them anything.'

I looked into one of the huts. It had a dark, dank interior and the sole possession of that family was a cooking pot. A small child was running about with smiling eyes, but had a big round belly and gingerish hair—both signs of Kwashiorkor. Some of the other children who came to stare at us had sores around their eyes and sores on their legs. The nearest dispensary was ten miles away.

We drove on through the bush and passed a reservoir which the District Officer had encouraged the people to build by a bore-hole. Women came from miles around to get clean water and to wash their clothes. No one can ever over-estimate the importance of water in Africa. The two greatest gifts of the Government in rural areas are first a bore-hole and, second, a school. A few miles away we found a school. It was a primitive mud building and the only school equipment, besides a few crude benches, was a blackboard. The teacher was not from the village. He belonged to another tribe and had been sent to the area by Lusaka. This more advanced African was undertaking a pioneering job among the primitives, but for him it was a rewarding one. The children were eager to learn and surprisingly quick-witted. I looked at the notebook of one round-eyed child to check her arithmetic. I have seen worse in London primary schools. The children came outside to an improvised playing field to show us a dance before we left. They sang melodiously in a circle, while each took a turn to stand in the middle and dance and sing a verse. Despite the depressing environment those children were very lively. I came away from the resettlement area feeling that we owed much more to the Valley Tonga than they had been given. They had been given cash compensation, unlike the Batonka who had been moved on the south side of the river in Southern Rhodesia, and with that they had bought some cloth and, perhaps, some cattle. But more and better food to build up their strength before their own harvests arrived would have been a good policy. It should also have been possible in an undeveloped area to have organised a more ambitious farming development. The migration of a people is an opportunity to begin a transformation of their lives.

If the new land had been prepared well in advance of their own resettlement, and with the co-operation of an advance party, it is unlikely that the Government would have faced the tribe's opposition to the move from their old valley land. The resentment which has followed could also have been avoided. Having thought all that I still had to recognise, with gratitude, the hard work of the colonial officials in the field who so often have to undertake their task with inadequate resources and little real drive from the top.

On the road back we passed several thundering great concrete lorries used for transporting the cement from Lusaka to the Dam site. Africans were allowed to drive those lorries, which indeed was a feat along those roads. Considering the state of the roads the accidents were few but when crossing a bridge over a deep ravine we saw the spot where a lorry had crashed the week before.

When I went to the other end of Northern Rhodesia, near the Belgian Congo, I saw a vastly different aspect of African life. The copper miners are worlds apart from the primitive Tonga along the Zambezi. The bleak, barren area has been transformed into thriving communities since copper was discovered in 1923. Complete company towns have been built. The companies and the Chamber of Mines rule on the Copperbelt. Copper has also transformed the economy of

Rhodesia. It is by far the most important economic asset of the Federation, as copper makes up 50 per cent of its exports. Copper is the main reason why Southern Rhodesia wanted Federation in 1952. Its own economy, which is based on tobacco and gold, was not strong enough to bear the cost of the development which it wanted to pursue, both in Southern Rhodesia itself and at Kariba. It saw the chance of sharing the copper wealth of Northern Rhodesia within a Federation.

A third of the total taxation raised in the Federation, and a quarter of the national income, comes from copper. Copper is extracted from the bowels of the earth by white and black miners and I wanted to know how much they received for their part in this great enterprise. I found some interesting facts.

The total gross value of copper in 1957 was £89,500,000. Taxation for the territorial and Federal Governments took £30,500,000 and the amount the 46,000 workers received was £21,000,000. Even after running expenses, depreciation, and capital costs are paid for it is obvious that the profits are considerable. Royalties paid to the British South Africa Company alone amounted to £8,800,000; although half of these went in taxation, there must be many who feel, like Sir Roy Welensky, that they have been an unnecessary burden on Northern Rhodesia. It had been agreed that they should come to an end in 1986.

A closer examination of the wages costs reveals that the 7,200 European employees in that year received total earnings of £13,785,000, an average of £1,899 each, while the 38,700 Africans received £7,341,000 (including cost of food provided), which is an average of £189 each. Again, the average European wage is ten times that of the African.

The white miners live in comfortable company houses, which are heavily subsidised; the black miners have smaller company houses, which are, however, of a reasonably good standard. Off duty there is practically no mixing between the races.

On the Copperbelt not all the African children can get to school. Once an experiment was made with compulsory education but the rush of children was so great that the facilities could not be provided without great expense, and this the Government would not afford.

I went to a teacher's training college where refresher courses were being given to the key men in Northern Rhodesia. They were the men who will teach on the Copperbelt but also go out to the little schools in the remote countryside such as the one I had seen in the Zambezi valley. The Principal, a white man, was enthusiastic and earnest, putting all his energy into his job. He walked me from class to class, introducing me to the student teachers. At his request I talked to each class for a few minutes; the Principal then asked for questions. They were not slow in coming.

'What are you in the British Parliament doing about Federation? Do you realise that here in Northern Rhodesia we do not want it?'

Other questions were about scholarships. Their great ambition was to spend at least a year in Britain—for them it is the seal on a man's career.

At tea I met the college staff, which included an American on a Fulbright grant, a South African negro, three or four English teachers —all mixing quite chummily in the staff room. The Principal was a dedicated man. 'My students are first class people,' he said. 'Give them a chance and they will change this country. It is only a question of time.' He begged for more facilities. 'We have to run these colleges on very small budgets, while money is poured into the beer halls.'

I strolled with him to his house and he told me of an experience which had shaken him to the core. His son had gone to the local European children's school, as there was no inter-racial school for him to attend, and on the day before had come home full of excitement. There had been talk at school about trouble in Nyasaland and the state of emergency in Southern Rhodesia. 'Say, dad,' the boy had said, 'did you know we are going to have a war with the munts?'

There are white men like that Principal who are trying to bridge the gap between the Africans and Europeans. They are the men of vision in Central Africa and I was fortunate to meet a few of them. The Principal of the Hodgson Technical College at Lusaka, for instance, who is helping to train hundreds of boys to be craftsmen, bricklayers, motor mechanics and engineers. He and his staff are doing a good job. Even more important is the task which Jack Purvis, the mineworkers' leader, has set himself. He is as much a Rhodesian as Welensky, whom he knows well from early union days. As an official of the European Mineworkers Union Purvis has been struggling to make and keep friendly relations with the African miners. Purvis hopes that a new, happy co-operation can be built up between Africans and Europeans. As part of his effort to reach an understanding he established a joint committee upon which both the African Mineworkers Union and the European Mineworkers Union are represented.

After I had taken a trip 6,000 feet below the earth to see a copper mine at work (an excellent way to clear my mind, although it was physically exhausting), I sat and talked with the committee for several hours. It was one of the most exhilarating experiences I have ever

had in Africa. The committee did not attempt to achieve a great deal
at that meeting, but the manner in which the members approached
their common problems and common objectives was most refreshing.
Against the background of bitterness and hatred built up by both
extremist white settlers and black extremists, that committee was
creating something honest and good in human relationships. The
miners were talking together as men and not as white men or black
men. In the chair was Lawrence Katilunu, President of the African
Mineworkers Union, and around the table sat seven or eight members
of the European executive and six or seven members of the African
executive. 'We want no colour bar on the mines,' they all agreed.
'On the surface, for social reasons, it may be necessary, but down
there we work shoulder to shoulder and one man's life may depend
on another. We can recognise no colour distinction between miners,'
said a white man.

But it has not always been like that. Only a few years ago white and
black fought over trivial incidents. Some European workers abused
the Africans and the Africans in their turn made things difficult for
the Europeans. Now the feeling of enmity is being replaced by co-
operation.

The European Executive members said that they were anxious that
Africans should have a chance to take on skilled jobs at the rate for
the job and not at cut rates, which would undermine African and
white workers alike. Within several companies they had made representations about this because the firms were trying to cut the rates.
In another company a Coloured track layer who worked as hard as
any white man, and as well, was refused the European rate. The white
workers went to the management and asked for his rate to be increased
to equal theirs, and agreed that he should be admitted to their Union.
The management refused.

A very forceful white miner called Ash, who came from South Africa,
said, 'We know that our future is tied up with Africans. The companies would like to keep us apart and play one side off against the
other—we don't want any truck with that.'

Africans and white settlers, for once, found themselves in complete
agreement.

16

Strong Arm Politics

—————

I was in Northern Rhodesia a few weeks before the territorial election was due to be held. It was being fought on one of the most fraudulent constitutions ever designed. All the Africans to whom I spoke, with the exception, that is, of two African candidates put up by the UFP, considered it to be a fake. Those two were elected, but by European votes. Other Africans called them stooges, which is quite understandable in view of the fact that only a handful of Africans could ever bring themselves to vote for the UFP. The few Africans who were on the electoral roll would rather vote for the reactionary Dominion Party than support the Welensky party.

I had tea with Mr Chileshe, a former Member of the Legislative Council who was running again as an independent, and in his house I met a number of school-teachers at Northern Rhodesia's one and only African secondary school. They all agreed that the constitution was dishonest, but they agreed to vote to obtain from it what advantage they could. Mr Chileshe, however, stood little chance. He had been an effective and excellent Member but as so few seats were allocated to Africans elected by Africans, and as the common roll qualifications were so high, he was, in fact, being gently eased out of constitutional politics.

Elections in Northern Rhodesia are really only a happy hunting ground for the white settlers; Europeans have a better chance of being elected to the Legislature than in any other country. With a total white population less than that of a single typical constituency in Britain, there are no less than fourteen seats specifically reserved for Europeans, not counting the seats they also have in the Federal Assembly. The Africans have only eight Members and two of those are elected by white votes. With 75,000 Europeans and 2,500,000 Africans the proportions mean one Member for 5,350 Europeans and one Member for 300,000 Africans. It could hardly be called democratic and the Africans I spoke to were not very pleased.

In Central Africa it is not unusual for strange constitutions to be imposed in the interests of maintaining the rule of a minority. The Federal Constitution itself is such a structure, but in Northern Rhodesia special efforts were made to give the illusion that Africans were actually participating. It was the hope of the local white politicians, in particular Mr John Roberts, the territorial leader of the UFP and shadow of Sir Roy, thus to have a case for breaking the Protectorate away from the watchful eye of the Colonial Office in Whitehall.

But the constitution was made so unbearably complicated and unfair that no one in his right senses would believe that Africans had any real share of the power. The qualifications for the ordinary roll (set at £720 annual income or £480 plus primary education or £300 plus four years' secondary education), allowed only 796 Africans on to the roll. But as there were 22,592 non-Africans the African votes had little influence on the results in the twelve ordinary constituencies.

A special roll was also established, open to those with £150 a year or £120 plus two years secondary education. The Colonial Secretary, in a White Paper published in September 1958, five months before the elections, estimated that 24,648 special voters would be enrolled; in the event there were only 6,846 or just over a quarter of his figure. To make sure, however, that not too many Africans would get on this roll it was decided that the qualifications should be progressively raised over ten years, eventually reaching the ordinary voters' scale.

Anyway, only six seats were allocated to 'special voters', and to make matters worse each candidate for those seats had to obtain a certificate of approval from at least two-thirds of the Chiefs in his constituency before he could stand. Some special constituencies were five hundred miles across and candidates spent all their time visiting Chiefs.

Even putting together the ordinary and special votes, the number of Europeans on both rolls was 1 in 3, but the number of Africans only 1 in 300.

The African National Congress decided to participate in the elections although they objected to the constitution. Their only candidate was Harry Nkumbula, the President General, who stood in one of the six 'special' seats for Africans and was elected by 572 votes to 71. Congress also gave support to Mr Katilungu, standing as an independent in the Copperbelt 'African Reserved' seat; he also had the support of the Dominion Party. It was a strange alliance brought about by a hope of defeating the UFP African candidate. But Mr Musumbula was elected, with 4,451 votes, almost every one European; he has since become one of the 'African' Ministers in the Government.

I met Nkumbula soon after he returned to Lusaka after having ridden 200 miles round his vast constituency on a bicycle collecting the Chiefs' signatures. He was a very bitter man, angry with the Colonial Secretary for imposing an undemocratic constitution and angry also with Kenneth Kaunda who had split the movement and formed the Zambia Congress. Kaunda was busy persuading potential voters to boycott the election.

Some say that the split occurred because the teetotal, non-smoking Kenneth Kaunda, who had been Nkumbula's energetic General Secretary, had objections to Nkumbula's drinking habits and his love of the high life. Others thought it was because Nkumbula co-operated too much with the Europeans and was too fond of talking to Harry Franklin, one of the liberal settlers. Whatever the reasons, the split was a real one; the National Congress broke from top to bottom, with Kaunda taking off the young militants and Harry Nkumbula keeping some solid support in the rural areas and on the Copperbelt.

The Governor, Sir Arthur Benson, was not afraid to take sides in this dispute between the Africans. He came out openly for 'our Harry', as he called him, and Zambia he stigmatised over the radio as being 'Chicago type gangsters'. The Zambia leaders were arrested and rusticated before the elections took place. The Governor's broadcast contained a number of inaccuracies, including one so obvious that it had to be corrected. So anxious was the Governor to rush through his measures that there was not time to print the Official Gazette on the correct date, and a firm of Lusaka lawyers had been anxious to prove that because of this the whole action was illegal. But no Government has been brought down by a slip in the dateline, although it is a very tempting idea.

A few days before they were rusticated I went to see the Zambia leaders at a little house which they had turned into an office in the African housing area in Lusaka. They were the first to tell me of the arrest of the officials and some 500 members of the Southern Rhodesian African Congress about which they had heard on the radio. This news was not a complete surprise to me, for the leaders themselves had warned me that they feared the Government would take some action against them because of their own success, but I was shocked that Southern Rhodesia could take the action without having any kind of excuse for such repression.

As I sat in that little house with the Zambia leaders they felt the net drawing around them too. They took pains to emphasise that although they were opposed to the elections because the constitution was so hopelessly biased against Africans, they were not intending to use violence on election day. 'The Government keeps saying that we are planning to use violence and we keep issuing denials,' they said. 'Congress under Nkumbula has also been spreading these rumours about our planning violence, but it is all part of a trick to stop us getting the support which the people would give to us.'

When I thought about the Zambia leaders, (Kenneth Kaunda, by the way, whom I knew personally from meetings in London and for whom I had a great respect, was not among them and was on safari), I felt that the remarks made by Sir Andrew Cohen in his lectures in the United States were particularly apt. He said about our attitude to African nationalists, 'We should treat them neither as saints nor as agitators, but as individuals with whom we should make every effort to establish human contact. We should not be disappointed when a nationalist turns out to be less than perfect. We tend to hold nationalists to European standards. We should recognise that as people they are not essentially different from the rest of us.'

Nkumbula has since used the Legislative Council as a sounding board for opposing Federation and as a forum for his demands for a democratic constitution for Northern Rhodesia.

Many of the 75,000 Europeans in Northern Rhodesia are not settlers; they go in to work on the Copperbelt for only a few years to make an income, and then return to Johannesburg with their families. And yet, through the UFP, they are demanding the ending of the Protectorate status in favour of white political domination. It would be a blunder of the first order for more power to be transferred to Northern Rhodesia's Legislature before the indigenous people are participating effectively. It must be recognised openly and frankly that in Northern Rhodesia, as in Nyasaland, the Belgian Congo, Tanganyika and Uganda, the Africans will eventually be running the country. The white politicians cannot expect to deny the facts of history merely because the settlers number 3 per cent of the population against 1 per cent elsewhere. Already, Ministers have been appointed from the UFP, but they cannot be compared in ability and experience with the Colonial Office officials whom they are replacing. The Colonial Government is put in an impossible position by this unhealthy compromise with white settler-dom. I was told by people in the territory who should know the truth, that the really able white men are refusing to have anything to do with politics, dominated as it is by the Welensky party.

The policy of appointing Ministers from the elected Members is a valuable one in a country, such as Tanganyika, where the party has the genuine support of the governed. But in Northern Rhodesia the policy of making Ministers out of the UFP Members can only have the effect of inflaming African opinion against the Government and making it almost impossible for Colonial Office rule to be effectively administered. The position has not been improved by appointing a Southern Rhodesian, who has his roots in the Federation, as the new Governor. As the Protector of 2,000,000 Africans the United Kingdom Government must be able to discharge its responsibilities through the Colonial Office structure until such time as the Africans have a genuine share in the legislative process. Any other policy comes perilously near to repeating the disastrous mistake of the 1923 transfer of power to the 35,000 white settlers of Southern Rhodesia who had been clamouring to cut the apron strings tying them to Britain. Today's trouble in Central Africa follows from that mistake. If the white settlers in Southern Rhodesia had not been given entrenched political power, the Africans in Northern Rhodesia and Nyasaland would never have been so opposed to closer association and Federation would have been achieved peaceably under the Colonial Office. Mr Lennox-Boyd, without the problem of a white minority, succeeded in Nigeria.

In Central Africa I met many long-serving Colonial civil servants. They were men who had sacrificed their lives for comparatively small rewards, working with the Africans in remote districts. Of all the Europeans in Central Africa their voices on Federation should be respected, for they are in a position to know what is best for the two Protectorates. They have no political axe to grind, their interest is the long-term welfare of the people, which should be the concern of Great Britain too, and yet these are the men who, along with the Africans themselves, appear to have been consulted least about the Federation. When senior officials met in London early in 1951 to consider the scheme for Federation little account seems to have been taken of the feelings of the men in the field. Sir Andrew Cohen and Mr Gorell Barnes, who drew up the Federal scheme, were working from theory rather than intimate first-hand experience.

Later that year Mr James Griffiths, the Labour Colonial Secretary of State, refused to push forward the scheme because he and the Labour Government considered there were not sufficient safeguards for Africans. As is well known, when the Conservatives won the 1951 Election they immediately took steps to push Federation through, against the opposition of the overwhelming mass of African opinion. The Federal constitution, born as it was of compromise and political chicanery, became a thoroughly unsatisfactory instrument for administering Central Africa. Yet the more the Conservative Government realised the folly of its measures the more determined it became to push Federation through.

Lord Home, as Secretary of State for Commonwealth Relations on one of his visits to Northern Rhodesia, told the civil servants in the field, who had never been consulted anyway, that they should go out to the Africans and tell them that Federation was there to stay and that it was in the Africans' best interests.

They replied, 'The Africans won't believe us. They know differently.'

'Oh,' replied the noble Lord, 'why don't you tell them about the economic benefits of Federation?'

This has become a standing joke among civil servants in Northern Rhodesia. 'Tell the Africans about the economic value of Federation!'

They replied that the Africans know that the economic foundation of the Federation is in Northern Rhodesia itself and that millions of pounds from copper has gone to subsidise the other two countries. The Africans know that if there had been no Federation there could have been more schools, more hospitals, and more development to their benefit in Northern Rhodesia itself.

I was overwhelmed with invitations from white politicians. I met more European than African politicians: the whites were at cocktail parties, the blacks were out campaigning. When the Dominion Party on the Copperbelt heard that I had been to a party sponsored by the UFP, they rushed in with their own invitation. But the Dominion Party in Northern Rhodesia stands no chance of making an impact whilst the white electors are so impressed with the personality of Welensky. They like Welensky's tough, blunt manner. When it becomes apparent that even he cannot achieve independence from Britain without concessions to democracy which would give the Africans political power, then Welensky's star will begin to wane.

The Africans loathe him. To them he is the arch-enemy determined to foist white minority rule on the black majority. Such is their enmity that those who were electors voted for the Dominion Party candidates where there was no other choice. The *Central African Examiner* estimates that of the 7,617 Africans who were qualified as voters probably not more than 400 voted for UFP candidates. Ironically, the spokesman of the Dominion Party, which openly advocates white domination, owes his election to African votes. Dr Gert Smith, in the Southern Constituency, had 609 votes against Mr Beckett of the UFP with 604. There are twenty-two African votes there; undoubtedly they swung the election against the UFP in that constituency.

There are just a few Africans who have decided to throw in their lot with the European Parties. Some of them genuinely feel that it is hopeless for the Africans to struggle against the white settlers and that the sooner they make their peace the better. Quite a number, on the other hand, are co-operating for what they can get for themselves. There have been several notorious examples of Africans hawking themselves, alternately, to the Dominion Party and the UFP as candidate in the hope of being elected to a comfortable income on European votes. Others have agreed to work with the European parties out of disgruntlement with Harry Nkumbula or the other African political leaders. They felt this was one way in which they could get their own back on them. But the number of Africans co-operating in any of these categories in Northern Rhodesia is under a hundred. They cannot claim any following on the part of the African people, but for the time being they serve a very useful purpose for Welensky. He points to them as an example of 'partnership' in practice. I met several of the 'partners'. They did not make an impressive showing. I was introduced to two who were standing in the election by Mr Malcomson, one of the extrovert characters of the UFP, and now a Minister for Local Government. He dealt with them as if they were prize guinea-pigs and prompted them every time I addressed a question in their direction. I was left with the feeling that they did not have minds of their own. Judging from the number of African votes they collected apparently the rich Africans who had the vote had the same opinion.

I also had tea with Mr Godwin Lewanika at his home. He is a leading member of the Barotse tribe whose King, it is said, sold the mineral rights of the land on which the copper companies later developed the mines and where they have extracted as much as £100,000,000 of copper in one year. The King's name was Lewanika, the payment received, £850. Mr Godwin Lewanika, who claims to be his son, is now a Member of the Federal Assembly for the UFP and a member of the African Affairs Board.

The Central Africa Party of Sir John Moffat and Mr Garfield Todd has collected more African support than the UFP and the Dominion Party combined and it is much nearer to being a genuine non-racial Party. But it will not break the support the nationalists receive. In Tanganyika and even in the Belgian Congo Africans are coming into their own. Northern Rhodesia cannot fail to be influenced by events over the border. The Africans' slogan of 'one man, one vote' is not likely to lose its appeal, and in saying that they refuse to be called 'extremists'.

As Kenneth Kaunda said, 'To say we were shouting "Africa is for Africans alone" is distorting the truth. What we have said and shall continue to say—rustications or no rustications, prisons or no prisons—is that the MAJORITY MUST RULE. In the same way as the English rule England, the French rule France, Japanese rule Japan, Indians rule India, Africans MUST RULE Africa. But this is far from saying "Africa is for Africans alone". After all, one finds thousands of other people in Britain and these other countries mentioned above but the rule is in the hands of the majority, and quite naturally the minority groups have little or nothing to fear. Thus do we find relations between the British and the Indians in India on one side and between the British and Ghanaians in Ghana on the other far better than they were before national independence and self-determination in those two countries. I repeat, race relations there are normal and natural because of MAJORITY RULE!'

Kaunda and Mumukayumba Sipalo, who were President and Secretary of the Zambia Congress, were imprisoned for sedition in March 1959, and their Congress was banned. Their followers, however, soon formed another movement—the United National Independence Party (UNIP)—and organised a congress to coincide with the date in January 1960 when their leaders were due to be released. More will be heard from this Party; African nationalists are not easily curbed.

17

One More Prohibited Immigrant

When I reached Northern Rhodesia during the last week of February 1959, both the African National Congress of Harry Nkumbula and the Zambia Congress asked me to speak at their meetings. I declined the invitations, as I did not want to become embroiled in the campaign for the territorial elections which was already under way. But while I was following a programme of visits and interviews officially arranged by the Northern Rhodesian Government, the Rhodesian Press, controlled by the Argus Group in Johannesburg, were whipping up a campaign against me. In every paper and on almost every page they printed bitter attacks from various settler sources.

It seemed that in addressing two meetings of Africans in Southern Rhodesia I had committed a most heinous crime. I have since reflected that Vice-President Nixon said many more daring things about freedom to the Russians when he was visiting the Union of Soviet Socialist Republics than I said to Africans living in the British colony of Southern Rhodesia. It is a sign of the settler political psycho-neurosis that so many Europeans in Southern Rhodesia were so absolutely outraged when I spoke to Africans about human rights.

After the vituperative campaign in the newspapers most people forgot what the meetings were about and the general impression was created that I had 'gone to the munts and inflamed them against the Europeans'. Nothing could have been further from the truth. Stirring up trouble between races is certainly not one of my political ambitions and the specific object of my speeches was to preach friendship and understanding for the white settlers and to advocate the rejection of violence as a political weapon.

I was told, by Mr Chad Chipunza, one of the African Federal Members of Parliament for the UFP, after the meeting I had addressed in the African township of Highfield, that the translation by George Nyandoro had been quite accurate; others said that my advice had been effective. Within the Congress ranks there were a few supporters who favoured using violence but this attitude had no hold on the organisation and had even less appeal after I had spoken.

Quite apart from the need to have contact with visitors from outside, I felt that people in Southern Rhodesia are entitled to know what a large section of British opinion thinks about the future of Central Africa. It is a sorry commentary on the insecurity of the white settlers that they should have reacted so violently when I attempted to break down the barriers of misunderstanding. Their nerves have become frayed as a result of living in a society where false values have gradually eroded human ideals; most of them want to regard their lives as quite normal and decent but deep in their subconscious is the realisation that their treatment of the African is wrong and shameful. Generations of Christian teaching and a century of liberal political thought still have an influence on them, but their settler personalities struggle against it. They fight against the influence because it conflicts with the structure of white privilege and power which they have carved out for themselves, and in doing so they have become almost schizophrenic.

But I was not without my defenders. One white MP told me that my remarks had been excellent, and other Europeans told me privately that they approved. Some of them said it was very difficult to state basic truths in Central Africa as too many years of double talk and double think had made it almost impossible for people to understand simple concepts. One leading journalist in Salisbury, Clyde Sanger, who was then with the *Central African Examiner*, wrote to the *Rhodesia Herald* in answer to their editorial which called me a 'pedlar of mischief':

'Sir,

'To suggest that Mr Stonehouse's behaviour at Highfield was that of a "pedlar of mischief" who spoke "fiery words" to "inflame his listeners" is nonsense—and dangerous nonsense, because the thousands of Natives who heard him and then read your misinterpretation will be further alienated.

'Your editorial comment was presumably based on a single sentence from Mr Stonehouse's speech—"Hold your heads high, and behave as if the country belonged to you"—the remark which so angered Mr Winston Field.

'I was present at the meeting and I would like to put his remark back in its context for you.

'The burden of Mr Stonehouse's speech was that the British Labour Party had won for the working man his rights after a century's struggle, and was therefore concerned that other peoples should win also their rights to human standards of living; the next Labour Government was pledged to put £160,000,000 towards fighting ignorance and poverty in the colonies every year, but Congress and other nationalist organisations would forfeit the sympathy of the Labour Party if they used violence—and over and over again with considerable courage he condemned the use of violence.

RIGHT AND WRONG

'Then he went on: "So you must work for your rights in peace and then you will be much more likely to have the rest of the world behind you. Your slogan should be: 'Work hard, educate yourselves, and organise.' Use the right way, and you will win. If you use the wrong way you will be giving the most powerful weapons to those people who do not want to achieve the same things as you do. I ask you to have pride in your country. Hold your heads high and behave as though the country belonged to you. If you behave in a way that you are ashamed of, you cannot be surprised if people who are now your friends do become ashamed of you."

'Are those "fiery words" calculated to "inflame"? Was Mr Stonehouse peddling mischief?

'HAG-RIDDEN'

'Even taken out of context, the phrase "Hold your heads high and behave as if the country belonged to you" should be unobjectionable to anyone not hag-ridden with racial fears. For Mr Field to say that this phrase "was inciting people to civil disobedience" is pathetic: for you to endorse Mr Field's demand that Mr Stonehouse be banned is an admission that you do not subscribe to the principles of partnership.

'Mr Field complains that Mr Stonehouse "should show such gross irresponsibility and direct interference in our affairs as to address a meeting in Salisbury of the African National Congress". May I suggest that some of our MPs should interfere enough in their own affairs to make a speech in a Native township? I would hope that their speeches had as good effect in counselling patience and non-violence as Mr Stonehouse's did.' CLYDE SANGER.

Salisbury.

In spite of Mr Sanger's eye-witness account a section of the Europeans was determined to make a victim of me. Many of them, including apparently the Federal Government itself, had a League of Empire Loyalists outlook. They considered that the Europeans had a right to run the Federation without any interference from Britain, and a visiting MP, particularly Labour, is an affront to their doctrine. Because of the pusillanimous political leaders and the lack of political education, most Europeans have no understanding of the status of the Federation. They think that it already has all the powers to run its own affairs, whereas, of course, it is a Federation only in the loose sense of the word. The two Northern Protectorates continue to be under the direct supervision of the British Colonial Secretary, who appoints the two Governors, who are fully responsible for law and order. Constitutional questions for both these territories and also for the Federation itself are matters for the United Kingdom Parliament.

It is true that for the experimental stage from 1953 to 1960 some responsibilities were transferred to the Federal Government, to give it something to experiment with. The drafters of the first Constitution made a silly blunder when they included immigration among them. Although the Governors of the two Protectorates were left fully responsible for African education, police, security, and other essential matters affecting the territories, it was made possible for the Federal Government to interfere in the recruitment of personnel to do just those jobs within the Protectorates.

We do not know exactly how many people have been made Prohibited Immigrants by the Federal Government as many of them do not want the fact known, but the list available publicly is already formidable. Mr Albert Lewis, for instance, was appointed by the European Mineworkers Union of the Copperbelt to be its General Secretary after he had been a prominent trade unionist in Britain, working on the staff of the Trades Union Congress. Notwithstanding protests from the TUC he is a Prohibited Immigrant still. The Rev. Tom Colvin, missionary for the Church of Scotland, was prevented from returning to his work in Nyasaland. The long list includes other clergymen, including Michael Scott, and journalists such as Basil Davidson of the *Daily Mirror* and Miss Rosalynde Ainsley of *Africa South*. Former colonial civil servants who are *persona non grata* with Sir Roy Welensky are also banned. Commander Thomas Fox Pitt, who served with distinction in the Royal Navy and who was a Provincial Commissioner in Northern Rhodesia, where he served in the Colonial Service for most of his life, was prevented from making a visit to see friends. Appropriately enough he is Secretary of the Anti-Slavery Society.

The campaign building up against me was designed to force the Federal Government to use the immigration powers against a British Member of Parliament as a supreme boost to the jaded settler ego. It

was seen as one way of insulting the British Parliament whose 'interference' they despised. The Press played its part with gusto and it
found many titbits to quote. On the Copperbelt a Mr Len Catchpole, a
former mayor of Ndola, cabled Mr Gaitskell:

'URGE IMMEDIATE RECALL STONEHOUSE FROM FEDERATION HE IS
INFLAMING A CRITICAL SITUATION'

Mr Catchpole commented: 'I have always said—even when Barbara
Castle was here— that these irresponsible people should be declared
Prohibited Immigrants.'

A Mr T. A. Moore of Umtali in Southern Rhodesia sent a telegram to
Catchpole which read:

'SUGGEST PETITION JUDGE IN CHAMBERS ORDER RESTRAINING STONE-
HOUSE MAKING FURTHER PROVOCATIVE SPEECHES ON GROUNDS OF
ENDANGERING YOUR AND FAMILY'S SAFETY AND JEOPARDISING FINAN-
CIAL INVESTMENTS'

The campaign was not without its lighter moments; the following
fascinating item also appeared in the local press:

'NAMES CAN BE MISLEADING'

'KITWE, Tuesday.—What's in a name?

'Threatening to change theirs to "Featherstonehaugh"—pronounced
"Frenshaw"—is Kitwe's Stonehouse family, who have been plagued
since early this morning by phone calls from people asking whether
they were any relation to Labour MP, Mr John Stonehouse.

"There is absolutely no connection—and, what is more, we were
Conservatives in Britain," declared harassed Mrs Jane Stonehouse, who
works in the mine personnel department (and whose initials are the
same—J. T.—as the Member's).

'Her husband, Robert, employed by the Rhodesia Congo Border
Power Corporation, is the only Stonehouse on the Copperbelt.'

When I arrived at Ndola by air I found that a reception party had
been arranged for me by Len Catchpole, whose previous exploits had
included a beer drinking contest with an elephant. According to the
Copperbelt newspaper 500 Europeans turned up at the airport to
protest at my arrival, but I was told by the police that the actual number
was much less than half of this and that almost all of them were
bystanders who had gone there in the early evening to see what the
famous Mr Catchpole was up to. The Copperbelt has, after all, very
few amusements. The police told me too that the crowd at the airport
included the General Manager of a leading Company, a Magistrate, and
many other prominent citizens, and they certainly did not turn up to

make trouble. The police, however, took no chances and whisked me away from the airport by a little-used back road.

Meanwhile questions were asked in the Southern Rhodesian Parliament, and Sir Edgar Whitehead, the Prime Minister, said he had referred the matter to Sir Roy Welensky for urgent attention.

I went on with my tour. There were a lot of people to meet and a lot of places to visit. Despite the artificial row fomented in the Press I found everyone I met charming and friendly. The white politicians went to some trouble to arrange cocktail parties for me so that I could meet more of their supporters and they all told me not to take the Press seriously. 'They have to do this sort of thing to sell the newspapers.' The Government in Northern Rhodesia, who were my hosts, did not seem in the least perturbed. Every day I saw Government officials and none expressed any misgivings about my continuing my Northern Rhodesian engagements. They also knew that I was travelling on to Nyasaland to investigate the situation there and I had made no secret of the fact that I had an invitation to stay with Dr Hastings Banda as well as with the Governor of Nyasaland.

There had been a number of incidents in Nyasaland arising out of illegal meetings and some stones had been thrown at European cars. I felt it incumbent on me in my capacity as a Member of Parliament to see and judge the situation at first hand. The Federal Government thought otherwise and decided, in some haste, to add me to their long list of Prohibited Immigrants. It did not even have the courtesy to consult either of the Governors who were my hosts. It so happened that Sir Arthur Benson, the Governor of Northern Rhodesia, was in Salisbury giving a lecture; when he heard about the Federal decision he immediately protested to Sir Roy Welensky. His protests were ignored and the Federal Government did not advise the Governor of the steps they intended to take. Unknown to the Northern Rhodesian Government or any of its officials, Mr Jack Wood, the Principal Immigration Officer of the Federal Government, was flown from Salisbury to the Copperbelt to serve an order upon me.

I was staying at a Government rest centre in Kitwe on the Copperbelt, only a few miles from the Belgian Congo, and during my stay I was busy making many visits. The District Commissioner, a hardworking, efficient fellow, shepherded me between appointments, whisking me from the executives of the Chamber of Mines in their palatial offices to the more humble rooms of the trade unionists, and then on to the Mindola Mine. There he handed me over to the safekeeping of a giant Afrikaner mine manager, who helped me into a pair of white overalls and white helmet and took me down the fifty-miles-an-hour lift into the bowels of the earth. I returned to have lunch and to talk with the Labour Officer and his wife in a sparsely but comfortably furnished bungalow.

'Our labour problems on the Copperbelt are sorting themselves out,' said the keen Labour Officer, 'but my God it has been a headache. It is getting easier now the Africans stay here for a career, rather than return to the Reserves after a short contract.'

In the evening the DC left me at the rest centre, where I found that more Europeans had been asking to see me. It was a little ironic that at the time the newspapers were letting off steam about the uselessness of a fact-finding tour by a Member of Parliament, so many of their readers were taking advantage of my visit. On that evening I found a group of young men in their middle twenties who had been waiting at the centre for quite a long time. Because they were white, rather high-spirited, and spoke with South African accents the warden had warned the DC, who rushed to the spot, thinking that I was in danger of being abducted. By the time he arrived, however, I had left quite willingly with them. I had never taken the wild threats seriously, but the DC, I suppose, thought he had to take no chances.

At the home of the South Africans I sat and discussed Africa with them late into the night. They were teachers at the local schools and they introduced me to several friends, including a Public Works Supervisor in his early fifties who had been in Rhodesia for a quarter of a century.

'You know, Mr Stonehouse,' he said, 'you mustn't judge all the whites simply by what you read in the newspapers. We are not all as bad as the loudmouthed people who like to make trouble. You must realise that we look upon Africa as our home and we want to find a way of living here with the Africans, but we want to get on with them as friends. That master race stuff does not appeal to us.'

The young South Africans had moved into Rhodesia because they hated the Afrikaner policies in the Union. 'That is plumb madness, down there,' one of them said. 'At least we have some chance of avoiding it here in Rhodesia.'

Just before midnight we parted the best of friends, but as they drove me back to the rest centre they warned me that earlier in the evening they had noticed two suspicious looking characters asking for me. They advised me to avoid them as they looked the types who might be out to make trouble and as it was the end of an eighteen-hour day of talking and touring I agreed that sleep would be preferable to more conversations. As we approached the centre the South Africans said, 'Yes, they are still there, they are waiting in a car. If you go in the front way they will see you, but we can drop you round the back entrance and you can hop into your room. If you don't turn on the light, they won't know you've returned.' I slipped into my room as they suggested and soon sank into a deep delicious sleep.

It did not last long. I was woken by some sharp raps on the door. I looked at my watch. I had only been asleep for half an hour.

'Who is it?' I said, 'Can't you come back in the morning?'

'Open up,' said a deep voice, 'This is the Chief Federal Immigration officer.'

I opened the door, slipping a dressing-gown over my pyjamas, and climbed back into bed, asking the two men to sit down in the two easy chairs.

'Well, what is it?' I said.

The burly man, who did all the talking, handed me a visiting card, from which I gathered that he was Mr Jack Wood of Salisbury, Southern Rhodesia. His colleague, who said only about two words during the whole night, was also introduced as a Federal Officer.

'We have come from Salisbury on behalf of the Federal Minister for Home Affairs to advise you to leave Rhodesia within the next twenty-four hours, for your own good. You should not visit Nyasaland.'

He then read out an official statement to me and I wrote it down as I sat up in bed. It said that as the Federal Government could not guarantee my safety and as my intended visit to Nyasaland would be likely to provoke unrest with possible danger to life and property, I should make immediate arrangements to leave the Federation.

'That is perfectly ridiculous,' I replied. 'I am on a tour arranged by the Northern Rhodesian Government and they have expressed no concern. Have you consulted them?'

'There is no need for the Federal Government to consult them.'

'And, as for my visit to Nyasaland, I have an invitation to stay with the Governor there and he has not withdrawn it. Have you asked him about this?'

'No, this is a Federal Government request.'

'Well,' I said, 'I cannot accept the advice of the Federal Government when the Governors of both territories are quite happy about my visits; they are responsible for the police and it is their advice I should prefer to follow.'

Wood became quite angry. 'Well, what are you going to do about it?' he snapped. 'You will have to give us your reply.'

'I am not giving you a reply now, in the middle of the night.' I said. 'I intend to consult the Governor first. You will have to wait until tomorrow.'

'Well, then,' he replied brusquely, 'I have no alternative but to read an Order that I have here declaring you to be a Prohibited Immigrant.'

It was obvious that the Governor counted for nothing to those two Federal officers, who acted throughout with a brash self-assertion. None of the Northern Rhodesian Government officers knew about Wood's mission. As the District Commissioner was responsible for my movements I dressed and took Wood and his colleague to the DC's house to read over to him the Federal Government statement. When Wood confirmed my account of our conversation as accurate we asked the two Federal officers to withdraw into another room while the DC and I talked about the consequences of their action. The DC, in his dressing-gown but with not a hair out of place, was astounded. 'Earlier in the evening,' he said, 'I heard that there might be some trouble from some young South Africans at the rest centre, but I never thought anything like this would happen.'

I explained to the DC that as a British Member of Parliament in a Protectorate responsible to the United Kingdom's Secretary of State I could not accept the authority of the Federal Government to order me out of the territory.

'If the Governor gave me this order I would, of course, accept it,' I explained, 'as his actions can be questioned in the House of Commons.'

'I quite see that,' replied the DC.

'Do you think the Governor knows about this?'

'I have no idea.'

'Surely, if he had known you would have been advised?'

'I should have thought so.'

We sipped cold beer from the refrigerator while we ruminated on this Gilbertian situation. But as there was little that could be done until the morning we all went back to our beds. Before I left the DC said, 'We will, of course, go on with your tour tomorrow. We have a lot of people lined up for you to see.' It did not look as though the DC was taking the Federal order very seriously.

Sure enough the next morning he called for me at the appointed time. But first, he telephoned to the Provincial Commissioner and told him about the events of the night before. The PC was equally astounded and promised to inform the Governor. I sent cables describing the circumstances and explaining my attitude to Mr Butler, Home Secretary and Acting Prime Minister (Mr Macmillan was then in Russia), Mr

N

Lennox-Boyd, the Colonial Secretary, and the Labour Party leaders.

I went on with the programme as previously arranged by the DC and I finished my day by having dinner with a white dental surgeon who supported Welensky.

On the following morning I drove in a Government car to Ndola, where the PC invited me to stay in his large, comfortable house and give me the services of his Public Relations Officer, a cheerful ex-newspaperman with a handlebar moustache, who turned out to be a very pleasant companion. The Government officers were all surprised about the Prohibition Order. One of them said that Welensky had always fought the Colonial Office in his climb up the political ladder, 'but we never thought he would go as far as this.' There was no love lost between Welensky and the Colonial Office officials in Northern Rhodesia; they regarded him as an upstart politician and he regarded them as bureaucrats from Whitehall.

With the PRO I went to Luanshya to meet some local politicians and made a tour of the copper company town, and I realised on the way that we were being followed. I pointed out the green car I suspected, about a hundred yards behind, to the PRO and he said breezily, 'Don't worry about that, they're friends. The Special Branch are watching to see that the Federal Immigration Officers don't attempt anything.'

I was beginning to get used to these cloak and dagger exploits between the Federal and the territorial governments.

That evening at the PC's house, I met the editor of the *Northern News*, a very frank and friendly man. After I had issued a statement to the effect that I could not recognise the authority of the Federal Government's order over a British Member of Parliament in a territory responsible to Britain, Sir Malcolm Barrow, the Federal Home Minister, issued a retort that he would see that the order was enforced. By this time more than twenty-four hours had elapsed since the notice had expired but no action had been taken against me.

Next morning's *Northern News* had an editorial which was the most reasonable I read in Rhodesia. 'Twenty-four hours after being ordered to leave the Federation, Mr John Stonehouse, the British Labour MP, was sleeping soundly in his bed in Ndola.

'He had no intention of obeying the order from Salisbury, and no one had attempted to enforce it. There was no indication that the Northern Rhodesian Government was moving in the matter—on the contrary, Mr Stonehouse was still officially the guest of the Northern Rhodesian Government, and a Colonial Office statement said: "He will complete his tour of Northern Rhodesia." Not, it should be noted, his planned tour of Nyasaland. Whether that will take place remains to be seen.

'But from Salisbury came an angry warning from Sir Malcolm Barrow: "If Mr Stonehouse carries out his threat to flout the law, the consequences will be entirely of his own making."

'The position is a confused one, but two points are clear. The first is made by Mr Stonehouse himself—that the police in Northern Rhodesia are responsible for his safety here, not the Federal Government, and no one here appears in the least worried. Why, therefore, this concern on the part of the Federal Government?

'The second is the clear indication that the Federal Government on the one hand (or at least Sir Malcolm Barrow) and the Northern Rhodesia Government on the other (with the support of the Colonial office) are in disagreement. No doubt Mr Stonehouse would accept from Sir Arthur Benson an order to go, for he would be able to challenge such an order in the House of Commons, but it has not been forth-coming. In the Commons, Mr Stonehouse cannot question the pro-priety of the Federal decision.

'This open conflict between Governments is the most deplorable feature of an unhappy incident, of which a great deal more will certainly be heard.

'At least let us be clear that the police are not involved. They will carry out any lawful order. The dispute is at a much higher level.'

The Provincial Commissioner and I talked for a long time about Federation and its consequences and I gathered that he would like to say more about his attitude than he was allowed to do. When he discussed whether I should travel on to Nyasaland he thought I should go.

Next day I flew from Ndola to Lusaka and at the airport only one man was offensive. He came up to me and shouted, 'Bloody white kaffir, why don't you go home to your black mammy?'

At Lusaka airport a black Humber Super Snipe was drawn up on the tarmac and a smart aide-de-camp, dressed in a well-cut lounge suit, ushered me to it. 'We are a little late for lunch, the others may have started, but the Governor is expecting you,' he said. The sentry saluted as we entered the portals of Government House. At the lunch table were five guests, including an ex-director of Hoovers and an ex-MP, both on flying tours with their wives. There were also two young aides-de-camp—young men not long out of University.

During the afternoon I saw several Departmental Heads and, in the early evening, had a cocktail party given for me by the Speaker of the

Legislative Council, to which Ministers and Members were invited but which several Welensky supporters boycotted. Later at a press conference a reporter from Salisbury warned me that the Federal Immigration officers might attempt to arrest me during the night. He invited me to spend the night in his room at the Ridgeway hotel to avoid them.

Back at Government House I discussed the ridiculous position with the Governor. I said I would accept instructions either from him or the Colonial Secretary as these actions could be questioned later, but could not accept the jurisdiction of the Federal Government. The Governor was angry with the Federal authorities as his protests had been of no avail. The order put him in a very awkward position as legally the Federal Government were responsible for immigration control. The Governor showed me a message from the Colonial Secretary which 'advised' me to return to Britain. I said, 'But I cannot accept *advice* like this. It would be tantamount to accepting the authority of the Federal Government. At this stage the Colonial Secretary or yourself must give me instructions, which, of course, I would accept.'

The Governor would not give instructions, but begged me to accept the advice of the Colonial Secretary, promising to provide an aircraft to fly me to Salisbury to make connection there with a London-bound 'plane. I said I could not accept these facilities as I felt it was my duty to travel on to Nyasaland. That evening I had spoken on the telephone to the *Daily Herald* correspondent in Blantyre who advised me that Sir Robert Armitage at an afternoon press conference had said he had no objection to my going to Nyasaland and that 'full official facilities' would be provided for me.

'In those circumstances,' I told the Governor, 'I shall keep to my earlier plans and catch the 'plane tomorrow morning.'

He then said that the consequences would be my own responsibility as my Northern Rhodesian tour would come to an end the following morning. He added, 'My police are completely loyal to me, but I cannot ask them to defy the legal authority of the Federal Government. If I do, that will be a powerful argument for the Federal Prime Minister in his attempts to obtain control of the police, which I have resisted. We are now in a very delicate stage in our relationships with the Federal Government and we don't want to upset them.'

The Governor also told me that following pressure from Sir Roy, Lord Perth, the Minister of State for the Colonies, had cancelled his visit to Nyasaland.

With the Governor's approval I put through a radio-telephone call to the House of Commons and told Mrs Barbara Castle briefly what had happened and that I proposed travelling on to Nyasaland, unless the Party advised otherwise. She asked me to ring back and I booked another call for 10 o'clock to Mr Gaitskell. Waiting for the call to come through I talked to Sir Arthur Benson and his Chief Secretary, Evelyn Hone (now Sir Evelyn and Governor). At 10 o'clock the call had not come through and it transpired that the radio link through Salisbury closed down at 8 o'clock and that the Johannesburg radio link closed at 10 o'clock. With the Governor's authority South Africa eventually agreed to call out the engineers and re-connect the radio link. As by midnight the call had still not been connected I asked the exchange to put it through to the Ridgeway Hotel.

The Governor saw me to the entrance of Government House and we parted friends, although we had both been placed by the Federal Government in an impossible position. For his part the Governor had loyalties to the Colonial Office but his powers were inhibited by the Federal structure, whereas my loyalties were to the U.K. Parliament. Our common interests did not end in Rhodesia; he had lived as a boy in Wednesbury when his father was the vicar of Moxley Parish Church, and I had become the MP for his home-town.

David Patterson, the reporter from Salisbury, was waiting for me at the Ridgeway Hotel, and in his room I took the call to Mr Gaitskell in London. The radio link was not too satisfactory but, for the first time, I heard that a debate about my Prohibition had been arranged for the following day; he asked me whether I would be able to get back for the debate. I replied that I would try to get to Nyasaland and if that failed I would endeavour to return for the debate. It was then 1 o'clock in the morning, Rhodesian time, and 11 p.m. in Britain.

I had a fitful sleep for a few hours, not knowing whether in the morning I would be able to continue my tour to Nyasaland, but as the Governor there had not contacted me I assumed that I was expected. The same aircraft which left Lusaka at 7 a.m. for Blantyre actually flew on to Salisbury on a scheduled service. I knew that if it was impossible for me to stay in Nyasaland I would be able to travel on after the stop at Blantyre and make a connection at Salisbury airport with the London-bound Britannia. As this was due to arrive in London at about 3 p.m. I would be able to rush from London airport to the House of Commons just in time for the debate.

18

Deportee

ON March 3, 1959, the state of emergency was declared in Nyasaland. At 5.30 a.m., on that same morning, just as the first light was seeping through the window, the porter-cum-hotel-telephone-operator called us with tea. He knew how important it was for me to get to Lusaka Airport by 6.30—half an hour before the plane for Blantyre was scheduled to leave. We had asked him to book a car and he said that he had done this and that it would arrive at 6 o'clock.

I hastily dressed and shaved and by five to six we were waiting in the hallway of the Ridgeway Hotel for the hired car to arrive. When it did not come Patterson said that perhaps the company had been warned by the Federal officers not to send a car to the hotel. It would suit them fine, we thought, if I missed the 'plane and was left stranded at the hotel. And as that morning there was no airport bus by 6.15 we began to get worried. We walked outside but no car or bus was in sight. In the car park sat a man in the front seat of a car trying to look as though he were reading a newspaper.

Just as we were getting desperate we heard the sound of a car; turning into the drive of the hotel was the Government Humber. The African chauffeur was smiling broadly and jumped out to open the door for us. This was the same driver I had used the previous day and who had helped me to move my things to the hotel, and he had apparently overheard our discussion about the next morning's programme. Either he had turned up on his own initiative, or the Governor had instructed him.

We drove quickly to the airport, arriving at 6.25 a.m. to find a welcoming party there in the persons of the Chief Federal Immigration Officer and another tough looking gentleman. Wood looked even more worried than at our midnight encounter three days before.

I took my suitcase directly to the Departure counter where it was weighed; I was handed a boarding pass for the aircraft by the receptionist, who acted as though everything was in order. I turned to wait

in the lounge for the half an hour before the scheduled departure for
Nyasaland; apparently I was the only passenger. Wood and his
associate, a ferocious looking character at close quarters, then
approached me and said, 'You are not to get on that aircraft. We for-
bid you to go to Nyasaland.'

I ignored them and noticed two European police inspectors standing
in the corner of the airport lounge. There was no one else there except
the receptionist and the reporter. Wood then came nearer and literally
breathed down my neck and his assistant moved up alongside me.

'We are warning you, Mr Stonehouse, you cannot take that aeroplane. A state of emergency has been declared in Nyasaland and your
'plane has been cancelled.'

I turned to the receptionist to ask for confirmation and for details
of other travel available. She shrugged her shoulders as though she did
not want to be involved and then went away. This was the first I had
heard of the state of emergency in Nyasaland. The last information I
had received by telephone from Blantyre the night before was to the
effect that at a Press conference the Governor had said that he saw no
reason for a state of emergency to be declared. I was very surprised at
this sudden change of policy, but Wood gave me no time to consider
its implications; he was already shouting at me, 'An aircraft has been
arranged to fly you immediately to Dar es Salaam.'

I replied that in view of the changed circumstances I must consult
the Governor.

'No,' said Wood, 'You must come along with us. We are going out
to the tarmac to put you on that aircraft.'

'But I want to consult the Governor,' I said again.

They made no reply to this but took hold of my arms and attempted
to hustle me along the corridor towards the tarmac. I called to the police
officers, 'Please intervene, I wish to consult the Governor, who is
responsible for law and order in this territory.'

The police saw that I was being manhandled but they did nothing
except look unhappily helpless, as I tried to free my arms from the grip
of Wood on one side and his Assistant on the other. All this time David
Patterson was making notes on the back of an envelope and I called
out to him, 'Please note that I am not allowed to consult the
Governor.'

This seemed to make Wood and the other man even more angry
and, puffing and blowing like old bulls, they dragged me along the
corridor. By this time some other newspaper men had arrived and it
was apparent that any further resistance would be quite pointless, as

well as undignified, so I walked out to the tarmac with the two Federal officers.

In the struggle I had lost a button, so Wood gave me a sixpenny piece and said, 'This is by way of compensation. Now you cannot sue me for assault.'

The aircraft, a four-seater Piper Apache, was being prepared, and I was now told that the other officer, a Mr Wicks, was to accompany me all the way to Dar es Salaam. I climbed into the aircraft next to the pilot and Wicks sat behind me. With his close-cropped hair and square head he was one of the toughest looking characters I have ever had to spend a day with. He was an Afrikaner by birth and had made a name for himself as a rugger forward.

Within minutes after the take-off Lusaka disappeared from sight, its Government House, its clusters of official buildings becoming insignificant against the vastness of the surrounding country. As we swung towards the north-east the pilot, a cheery friendly fellow, struck up a conversation just as though we were on a typical safari trip, as on any other day of the week.

Our first hop was 400 miles to a place called Kasama in the north-eastern corner of the territory. We flew over miles of empty land, occasionally broken by cultivated patches where we could see groups of huts, and now and then we could see a stretch of road.

We flew into some ominous looking clouds and the earth below was blotted out; at one moment we were flying as through thick fog and in another we were looking at the billowing clouds stretching on all sides of our tiny aircraft, overtowering us and making us feel even more insignificant. There was no way to avoid the storm, we were right in the thick of it. In minutes it lashed at us, the hail clattering on the cockpit until it seemed it would break under the force; the little craft was shuddering under the shocks.

According to the altimeter we were gaining and losing height uncontrollably as we floundered in and out of the air currents, which lifted us 500 ft one minute and forced us down the next as though we were a child's kite. Then the rain and the hail lashed at us again as we flew through another storm cloud; the noise, at times, was deafening and the sky was like a witch's cauldron. I looked at the pilot; he was obviously worried. When eventually we came through that storm I could sense the shadow of blackness behind.

Then the pilot pointed out the great Bangweulu swamps which stretch for a hundred miles and said, 'It wouldn't be too clever if we came down on that lot.'

In such a tiny aircraft it was possible to have a feeling of the enormous size of Africa, lying undeveloped below, waiting for the energy and science of man.

Two hundred miles before we reached Kasama the pilot was already signalling the airport controller. When the reply came through, crackling on the radio, it was comforting to know that even in this remote area we were still in contact. As we circled Kasama air strip a Rhodesian Airforce Dakota came in to land, gliding silvery bright below us. Within fifteen minutes we were down.

'This is becoming quite an air centre,' someone remarked in the makeshift buildings of the airstrip.

As this was my first opportunity to protest to a Northern Rhodesian Government officer about my ejection from the territory, I did so and gave a cable to the perplexed local DC to transmit through the Governor to the Colonial Secretary. The other people on the airstrip, who were Rhodesians and not Colonial Office types, eyed me with curiosity, tinged with suspicion. There was no open hostility but I felt that the campaign in the Rhodesian Press had had its effect in representing me as the ogre of white settlers.

The aircraft was airborne again and I was heartily glad to be flying out of Rhodesia and away from that atmosphere of mistrust and racialism, where the techniques of the police state are all too much in evidence. The white leaders who abuse African nationalists for being selfish power-grabbing politicians (and who may well deserve that description themselves), reflect the politically immature, ill-informed and prejudiced electorate. The settlers are not the open-hearted, pioneering types one would expect to find in a wide open country, because they have failed to tackle the psychological and social problems of adjusting themselves to the millions of Africans in Africa. If they had gone to Canada or to Australia they would be entirely different people. The Rhodesian environment had inhibited them and warped their natural regard for their fellow men, until they almost hate the black men among whom they live. This attitude stems from the earliest pioneering days of Cecil Rhodes when his pioneering columns were recruited on the promises of land and loot. The result today is that most settlers are quite unconcerned with the conditions of the Africans and this attitude has almost become an engrained racial characteristic. For many whites race distinctions are synonomous with class superiority.

I had found that liberal-minded settlers were well aware of the problem and discussed it with great feeling, but there are so few of them in Central Africa and, by themselves, they can hardly turn the scales.

One solution suggested by a United Kingdom representative was that all European settlers who did not want to accept the conditions of living among Africans should be given a one-way ticket to Australia. He thought that a Commonwealth re-settlement scheme would be well worth the expense in the long run and that the relationships between the remaining settlers and the Africans would be immeasurably improved.

The aeroplane was heading eastwards, crossing a two-hundred-mile stretch of land between the tips of Lake Nyasa and Lake Tanganyika. The pilot was concerned that we should not miss Mbeya airstrip; he had never flown to Tanganyika before. On his knee he looked at the route map and for a time I took over the controls. The Poroto mountains were treacherously near Mbeya; we avoided them with the help of radio instructions and landed safely. A reception party were waiting for me, but this was quite unlike the one which saw me off at Lusaka.

'Welcome to Tanganyika,' said the booming, genial PC. 'We were advised that you were coming and we hope you will enjoy your stay here.'

They were also kind to the worried-looking Wicks, who in his haste to become my escort had forgotten to bring his passport. They did not declare him a Prohibited Immigrant and we drank the coffee and ate the sandwiches ordered by radio. Another 400 miles over some of the roughest, wildest country in Africa lay between us and Dar es Salaam; we had no time to waste as we had to land before nightfall. I checked on the possibility of changing the route and heading north towards Nairobi, but that was over 600 miles away and well beyond the capacity of the Piper. I now knew that it would be impossible to make the connection with the London-bound Britannia and that therefore I would miss the Parliamentary debate asked for by the Opposition.

We skirted the mountains of the Southern Highlands, looking down on impenetrable forests before heading east, over the great plain of scrub and bush, empty of people. For hour after hour we saw no roads, no huts, no sign of cultivation. The sun was a yellow ball in the blue afternoon sky and its bright light threw up all the colours of the land below us. If we looked carefully enough we could see the shadow of the 'plane flitting over the ground as graceful as a running gazelle over the hills.

Suddenly Wicks said, 'Look! Animals.' Sure enough in a clearing of the scrub were some little moving specks. 'Elephant,' said the pilot, and he pushed the joystick forward and the aeroplane came down like a swallow. The outlines became clearer, we saw a few trees, then bushes and then elephants, a great herd of fifty, running, frightened by the strange sounds. The pilot, enjoying his exploit, swooped the aeroplane low over the thundering herd and then skimmed over one old tusker apart from the main herd. The pilot drew back the stick and we left the elephants looking like insects crawling on a brown-green carpet below.

After two hours of monotonous barrenness we saw the great Rufiji, cutting through the landscape like a silver sword, some patches of cultivation and a few tracks. Ahead of us, through the haze, was the blue of the Indian Ocean and soon, unexpectedly, we came upon Dar es Salaam and landed.

The humidity hit me like a warm wet towel and my dark lounge suit, donned in the morning for my visit to the colder clime of Nyasaland, was strangely out of place.

The reporters gathered around with their questions and a tall Government officer said, with a chuckle in his voice, 'The Governor invites you to Government House for cocktails, or you can come to lunch tomorrow. While you are in Dar we are putting a car at your disposal.'

I thought, 'How bizarre! Such hospitality from one British Government for the Prohibited Immigrant of another!'

* * * *

On the following day, while I was still in Tanganyika, the debate took place in the House of Commons. From the Opposition Front Bench Mr James Callaghan moved,

'That this House regrets the failure of Her Majesty's Government to protest to the Federal Government of Rhodesia and Nyasaland at their action in designating the honourable Member for Wednesbury a prohibited immigrant; and declares that the entry of a citizen of the United Kingdom into a British Protectorate should not be subject to the veto of the Federal Government of Rhodesia and Nyasaland.'

He said that it was intolerable if Members of Parliament, or indeed Ministers who might be appointed by a future Government, who were not *persona grata* with the Federal authorities had to have their admissibility into British Protectorates determined by the Federal Government.

In fact the situation Mr Callaghan referred to was created by the

Constitution of 1953, under which the Federal Government was given control over immigration in respect of the two Protectorates of Northern Rhodesia and Nyasaland, although almost all the powers in those two territories, including defence and police and all matters directly concerned with African welfare, continued to be exercised by the Governors directly responsible to the British Colonial Secretary and the United Kingdom Parliament. It is therefore within the powers of the Federal Government to prohibit any civil servant or Governor or, indeed, the Colonial Secretary himself. The only British subjects visiting the Protectorates who are specifically excluded from the immigration control of the Federal Ministers in Salisbury are members of the armed forces. So much for the brilliant draughtsmen of the Federal Constitution.

Later in the debate Mr Dingle Foot, the Member for Ipswich, clarified the responsibilities of Members of Parliament, quoting from Blackstone: 'Every Member, though chosen by one particular district, when elected and returned, serves for the whole realm. For the end of his coming hither is not particular, but general; not barely to advantage his constituents, but the *common* wealth.'

He went on to say, 'These definitions of the functions of Members of Parliament are just as valid today as they were three centuries ago, but there is this difference—that nowadays the realm for which we all have the responsibility to serve includes not merely this island but all the territories for which we have legislative responsibility, and for the administration of which Ministers are supposed, however inadequately, to answer.'

Mr Dingle Foot concluded his speech by asking two questions: 'Is it the view of Her Majesty's Government that whether a British Member of Parliament may visit Northern Rhodesia or Nyasaland should depend upon the unfettered discretion of the Federal Government in Salisbury? If this is not their view, what steps do they propose to take to preserve the rights of British Members of Parliament in relation to these territories?' Neither of these questions have yet been answered by the Conservative Government.

At the end of the debate, the Labour Opposition divided the House and were joined in the division lobbies by Mr Grimond and other Liberals.

After spending a week in Tanganyika and Kenya, where I had already made arrangements to visit prison camps, I returned to London on March 12 and on the following day, Friday, I made a personal statement in the Commons. I told the House the actual facts about my visit to Rhodesia and corrected some of the inaccuracies in the speech, a week earlier, of Mr Cuthbert Alport, then the Under Secretary of State for Commonwealth Relations. My account of what really took place has never been disputed.

I may add that I have never been given any adequate reasons by the Federal Government, or indeed anyone else, for the order making me a Prohibited Immigrant, and the order remains in force to this day.

19

Federation—The Open Wound

In the 1920s many attempts were made to secure closer amalgamation of the three central African territories, but they were resisted. The Africans objected to the proposals and most of the white settlers in Southern Rhodesia saw no value in acquiring millions of Africans in countries where there were no economic assets. A Royal Commission under Lord Bledisloe appeared to bury the idea. It reported in 1939 that the small European population of 68,000 was not equipped to take over the government of three territories with an area of 500,000 square miles and an African population of 4,000,000. The idea was abandoned and the Africans and Europeans together went to fight for democracy and freedom.

After the war, interest in federation was revived in Rhodesia. Great emphasis had been put on European immigration into Southern Rhodesia and every year thousands of British immigrants, as well as South Africans, poured into the country. It cost an average of £2,000 a head to settle them and as a result the Southern Rhodesian national debt grew to high proportions. In 1952 it was £132,000,000, and a third of the European population had arrived in the country since 1945. Sir Godfrey Huggins (now Lord Malvern of 'all Africans are liars' fame) had been anxious to press ahead with amalgamation to form a British dominion in the middle of Africa. He also hoped that the other East African territories—Tanganyika, Uganda and Kenya—would eventually join. Amalgamation, however, was out of the question as the Africans were so vehemently opposed to it. The compromise suggested was a form of federation which would link the territories politically and yet give Africans in the two northern Protectorates the semblance of some protection.

When the proposal was put before Mr Arthur Creech Jones, then the Colonial Secretary in the post-war Labour Government, he was not enthusiastic, seeing the disadvantages of trying to marry the concepts of white settlerism of Southern Rhodesia with a gradual evolution towards African participation in the government of the Protectorates. But Creech Jones was under pressure from Sir Andrew Cohen, then head of the Africa department at the Colonial Office, to have an investigation into the scheme, so he allowed discussion among the officials to go ahead.

Meanwhile pressure for Federation was building up among white Rhodesian politicians. They held an unofficial conference in February 1949 at Victoria Falls on the initiative of Welensky, then leader of the European faction in the Northern Rhodesian Legislature. The Labour Government (and the Colonial Secretary notably) were still opposed to a Federation undertaken without African agreement. Creech Jones expressed this on a visit to Northern Rhodesia soon after the Welensky conference and angered settlers when he opposed unlimited European immigration.

Mr Creech Jones lost his seat in the Election in February 1950 and Mr Griffiths became Colonial Secretary. The officials at the Colonial Office, with the bit between their teeth, went ahead with the organisation of the officials' conference which took place in March 1951. It was purely exploratory, but in Labour Party circles there was some concern that Federation was being discussed behind the backs of the Africans. Among those with doubts was Mr John Dugdale, then the Minister of State for Colonial Affairs, and he went to Mr Attlee and threatened to resign. The Prime Minister put his anxieties at rest and told him that on no account could he agree to Federation being imposed against the will of the Africans.

In Central Africa tension among the Africans grew as they realised that their future was being discussed. Whatever the economic advantages of Federation might be in the distant future, the Africans did not want to pay the price of losing Colonial Office rule in the short term and the chance of independence on a democratic basis in the long run. The pressure from Sir Godfrey Huggins as Prime Minister of Southern Rhodesia was considerable and a conference of governments took place at Victoria Falls in September 1951, which Patrick Gordon Walker, the Secretary of State for Commonwealth Relations, and James Griffiths, Colonial Secretary, attended on behalf of the Labour Government. However, as the scheme being discussed did not have sufficient safeguards for Africans, the conference was adjourned without reaching any definite conclusions, and Sir Godfrey returned to Salisbury 'unhappy and frustrated', according to sources close to the Prime Minister.

Mr Gordon Walker and Mr Griffiths returned to Britain to take part in the General Election. Labour lost the election and the chance to establish Central African Federation with African consent. The Conservative Party, which has links with the white settlers and with the companies operating in Central Africa, decided to press ahead with Federation, even against African opposition. (Lord Salisbury, whose family have always had connections with Rhodesia—it was at one time proposed to call it Cecilia after the family name—was then Secretary of State for Commonwealth Relations and is now a Director of the British South Africa Company. Mr Julian Amery was a Director of the same company before he became a Conservative Minister. Colonel Crosthwaite-Eyre, Mr Frederick Bennett, and Sir Victor Raikes are among the other Tory politicians who have business interests in Central Africa.)

Another conference was called in April 1952 in London and this time there were no hesitations. A White Paper was issued to show the determination to forge ahead, despite renewed African objections and a virtual African boycott of the Conference. African faith in Britain received a blow from which it has not yet recovered, for Britain was going back on all its pledges to the British Protected persons who had been under the wing of the Colonial Office for half a century. The Labour Party, consistent with the line it had been taking, demanded adequate safeguards for Africans, and when there were not forthcoming opposed the Federation scheme by dividing the House of Commons.

The Chiefs from Nyasaland, who had come to London, in January 1953, to make their protests against the 'steamrollering' of their country into the Federation, were ignored. They went back disillusioned men and many of them became supporters of the Nyasaland African Congress, then beginning to develop massive support in that hitherto politically tranquil country.

In that year there were only two African Members (increased by one during the year) on the Nyasaland Legislative Council of nineteen Members. The Africans were not elected but nominated by the Governor from names submitted by the African Protectorate Council. All the other Members, excepting one Asian, were Europeans, of whom no less than five were 'unofficial' Europeans representing local white residents and business interests. The European population at that time was only 5,000 against 2,500,000 Africans; it is no wonder that the Africans were alarmed by the approval given to Federation by the rubber-stamp Legislative Council on which they had no effective representation.

The Congress pressed for reforms but the only concession they received was an increase in the size of the Legislative Council to twenty-two Members, of whom five were Africans, elected, for the first time, by the African Provincial Councils. The election took place on March 16, 1956 and five Congress supporters, including the forceful Mr Chipembere (then twenty-five years of age) and the able Mr Kanyama Chiume (an ex-student of Makerere College, then aged twenty-six) were elected. The three retiring 'nominated' African Members were heavily defeated and a Mr Matinga, who supported Federation, received only one vote.

From that date the successful five kept up a vigorous campaign against Federation (Chipembere once called it 'a European benefit club') and made the Legislative Council debates a rallying centre of the opposition although, of course, they were always automatically outvoted.

During the debates on Federation in the House of Commons the Conservatives had referred to the African Affairs Board, which had powers to refer legislation which it deemed discriminatory against Africans to the United Kingdom Government. The inclusion of this Board in the Federal constitution raised a storm of protest among the settlers in Southern Rhodesia, who believed that they had the divine right to rule and opposed any interference by the U.K. Parliament. Sir Godfrey Huggins realised that if their opposition built up he would not get a favourable vote in the Referendum which had to take place among the Southern Rhodesian electors. (No one considered consulting the Southern Rhodesian Africans, who were disregarded.) The African Affairs Board was then whittled down to be but a sub-Committee of the Federal Assembly, rather than an independent body directly representing African interests. In 1957 the African Affairs Board objected to the Federal Constitution Amendment Bill on the grounds that it was putting the Africans in a worse position and asked that the United Kingdom should use its powers to prevent the legislation from being implemented. This advice was rejected by the Conservative Government, and again the Labour Party divided the House of Commons on the issue.

The African Affairs Board, which had been called the safeguard of African interests, was now considered by the Africans to be absolutely useless. The final nail in the coffin of its effectiveness was hammered in two years later when the UFP obtained a majority of representatives on the Board. The African Affairs Board was thus rendered completely impotent, for the majority of members could not condemn legislation passed by their own party in the Federal Assembly.

o

In 1957 Sir Roy Welensky, on one of his many visits to London, squeezed another concession from the British Government. It was agreed that no legislation affecting the Federation would be introduced in the United Kingdom Parliament without the prior approval of the Federal Government. He also persuaded the British Government to agree that the review of the Federal Constitution which was due to take place between seven and nine years after Federation came into being, should be held at the earliest possible date, that is October 1960. Welensky was making it clear that he wanted Dominion status at the earliest possible moment. The Labour Party, through its spokesmen in the House, rejected these agreements with Welensky since they transgressed the spirit of the Federal Constitution, which assumed no amendments until a full review of the working of the Federation had taken place. In the Preamble of the Constitution the Africans are given an assurance that Dominion status would not be granted until the prior approval of the Africans in the two Protectorates had been obtained, but most Africans despaired of this safeguard, fearing that it would be as worthless as the other.

Their question, 'How is the Preamble to be interpreted?' has yet to be answered. Will it be by Referendum of the whole population? If so, there would undoubtedly be a decisive majority against the Federation. Or will it be by a vote in the Legislative Councils? As the African representatives are in a minority in both, this could hardly be looked upon as representing African opinion. The Africans fear that this is the way which will be chosen, so setting the seal upon the fraudulent contract which has brought them into a Federation with Southern Rhodesia against their will. The opinion in the Labour Party throughout all these manoeuvres gradually hardened, until in March 1957 a statement was issued which went further than anything Labour had said before in public. It called for:

(*a*) an unequivocal statement that the objective of the Federation is complete democracy and equal rights for every citizen;
(*b*) the revision of the Federal franchise to ensure genuine African representation in the Federal Parliament;
(*c*) the rapid elimination of racial discrimination in both social relations and industry;
(*d*) the extension to other levels of education of the inter-racial policy now being developed so encouragingly at University level.

It added that the attitude of the Labour Party to the 1960 talks would be decided by the progress made in those matters and continued: 'The

Labour Party regards itself as completely bound by the Preamble to the Constitution, which declares that the people of Northern Rhodesia and Nyasaland should continue to enjoy separate government under the special protection of Her Majesty for as long as their respective peoples so desire. Labour believes there should be a review of the powers of the Federal and territorial governments so that the position of the protectorates is safeguarded. We reaffirm the pledge that dominion status shall not be conceded until all the inhabitants of the Federation have expressed a desire for it through the exercise of full and equal democratic rights. In order to enable African views to be more effectively expressed at this Conference and as a step towards full democracy, the Labour Party believes that Africans in Northern Rhodesia and Nyasaland must now be given opportunities for much greater participation in their governments. To this end it urges immediate constitutional reforms to ensure a majority of elected Africans in the Nyasaland Legislative Council and the appointment of African Ministers equal in number to those of other races. In Northern Rhodesia there should be parity of representations between Africans and other races in both the Legislative and Executive Councils. Labour also believes that the franchise in both territories should be broadened immediately as an instalment of progress towards a common roll and full adult suffrage.'

Throughout 1958 the opposition to Federation grew among the Africans. In Nyasaland the feeling grew to such a pitch that they sent urgent pleas to Dr Hastings Kamuzu Banda to return to his country to lead the campaign against Federation. Banda was an almost legendary figure to the Nyasas. He had very humble beginnings; as a boy he had walked from his home, working his way, to South Africa, where he struggled to keep alive while he studied. Then he went to the United States, where he obtained a degree in history and political science at the University of Chicago and then a medical degree.

He went to Edinburgh where he finished his medical training. There he took an interest in church matters as well as medicine and, although then still under thirty, became an elder of the Church of Scotland. Then from 1937 he practised medicine—from all accounts very conscientiously—in Liverpool, Tynemouth and Brondesbury, North West London, from 1945 to 1953.

Banda never lost interest in Nyasaland and its problems and, in London, acted as a spokesman for Nyasaland Africans. In January 1953 he helped the Chiefs to present their petition against Federation to the Colonial Secretary for transmission to the Queen. He was asked to return to Nyasaland but he was reluctant to do so until the Africans had had an opportunity to accept Federation; he did not want to stimulate opposition to it. So he went to Ghana and set up another medical practice, but such was the pressure from Nyasaland that he eventually agreed to return to lead the Congress.

I chaired a meeting for Banda in the Grand Committee Room at the House of Commons just before he returned to Nyasaland, and at the meeting he vigorously expressed his hopes and anxieties. He is a dynamic, forceful personality and he knows what he wants and will go for it with a single-minded determination. The demands of Congress, which he supported, were for an enlarged Legislative Council with thirty-two African Members elected on universal adult suffrage, two ex-officio Members (Attorney General and Financial Secretary) and six seats for non-Africans also elected on universal adult suffrage, which would mean that they would have the support and approval of Africans.

The Executive Council (or Cabinet) of Nyasaland has never had an African Member; Congress demanded that besides the Governor and the two officials it should include the leader of the majority Party and five to nine Members appointed on his advice. If conceded, these demands would have allowed home rule for Nyasaland, subject only to the Governor's veto, and would have given Africans some confidence in Federation.

The tempo of the Congress campaign increased after Banda's return. Although he was the President General, he played no part in the day-to-day organisation of its activities and limited himself to making policy speeches. It was left to his executive to run Congress, and this they did very effectively.

Until 1958 there had been no regular contact between the Congresses of the three Central African territories, but pressures from within and without were bringing them closer together. Besides the informal contacts between the members and officials of the Congress, two bodies were set up to co-ordinate their campaigns and to keep them in touch with the African movement in other countries. PAFMECA, (Pan African Movement of East and Central Africa), was the inspiration of Tom Mboya and Julius Nyerere. Both leaders were anxious that political developments in their own countries should not be held back because of conditions elsewhere. Nyerere feared that what happened in Tanganyika could be dictated more by Colonial Office concern for the after effects in Kenya than by genuine interest in the affairs of the territory. Both leaders knew that events in Central Africa could have serious repercussions on political progress in East Africa. They feared that if Africans in the two Protectorates of Northern Rhodesia and Nyasaland could be denied political rights in the interests of keeping the white settlers happy, the same argument could be applied in Kenya, which has almost the same sized European population as Northern Rhodesia. They knew that the latter-day empire builders like Lord Malvern had more than once expressed a wish that the Central African Federation should be extended to East Africa as a whole. They were also well aware that diehard whites in Kenya were anxious to call on Sir Roy Welensky for assistance to prevent Kenya succumbing to a black democracy. The greatest influence on these African leaders, persuading them to take a far wider interest in affairs beyond their own countries, was the force of pan-Africanism, increasing like a flood since Ghana obtained independence.

The All-Africa Conference in December 1958 in Accra was the climax, and Tom Mboya as the Chairman of the Conference became the symbol of the young emergent African. Delegates attended from the independent African countries, Ghana, Guinea, Ethiopia and British, French, Belgian, and even Portuguese colonies, which had long kept their subjects cut off from outside influence. There were big delegations from other countries outside Africa as well, the biggest one of all from the United States of America, carrying a greeting from Vice-President Nixon. But the Conference organisers left the visitors to the plenary sessions; the work was done in private committees. Will Griffiths, MP, and Bob Edwards, MP, attended as observers from Britain and on behalf of the Movement for Colonial Freedom. Kwame Nkrumah, the Prime Minister of Ghana, gave the Conference his greetings in the manner of an elder statesman and the message went out to the whole continent.

The resolution which has excited most attention was the result of a compromise between the Africans from south of the Sahara and the Algerians. The Algerians wanted recognition of their war against the French, they wanted violence to be one of the weapons used by subject peoples to achieve independence from colonialism, but the black Africans wanted non-violence and the policies of Ghandi. The Algerians, however, were insistent and eventually, after hours of discussion and private meetings in the hotel rooms of Accra, a compromise resolution was worked out which was agreed to by both sides. It gave recognition to those subject to military repression to use force in retaliation. It satisfied the Algerians and did not violate the Africans' principles.

Sir Roy Welensky has been most critical of the Accra Conference; it has been his favourite theme (apart from the wickedness of the Labour Party) at the settler political rallies. He blamed the Russians for inciting a campaign of subversion. In fact the Russians had little influence, and much less than they would have liked. The Africans, showing acute diplomacy, are determined not to become pawns in the cold war between East and West. They are grateful for the interest from the Americans and the Russians, but not anxious to accept dictates from either side. It is a most foolhardy policy to confuse African nationalism with communism. The nationalists are asking for nothing more than the rights enshrined in the Atlantic Charter. Accusing them of being communists will only help what little communist influence there is in Africa to expand and extend. It is indeed most unlikely that Africans who have struggled against foreign domination should want to put themselves into the arms of another foreign power.

At Accra attempts were made to heal the breach between Harry Nkumbula and Kenneth Kuanda, but in the event no repair was possible. If anything, the split was worse after Accra than before, and Harry came under attack from Africans outside Northern Rhodesia for being a collaborationist. In turn he had some harsh things to say about other movements and some pretty bitter comments about Dr Hastings Banda. But no one can deny that Hastings Banda has had more support in Nyasaland than Nkumbula has had in Northern Rhodesia. The report of the Devlin Commission confirms that thousands flocked to his meetings and that he was universally respected among Africans.

In Nyasaland the Nyasas had been expecting constitutional reforms to be announced. The Government and the Colonial Secretary had promised that these would be announced towards the end of August 1958—but they were still not available even by the end of that year. Banda was a tough negotiator, but, as he revealed in a letter to James Callaghan, MP, he would have been prepared to compromise. The Africans' main interest was to ensure an African majority in the Legislative Council before the constitutional talks in October 1960. They feared that without that majority decisions would be taken in the Legislative Council approving Nyasaland's inclusion in the Federation.

Early in 1959 the constitutional proposals had still not been made and the Congress decided to hot up their campaign against the Government. A series of meetings were called for the week-end of January 24 and 25 and to these meetings all the chairmen and secretaries of the Congress branches were summoned. As the meeting was overcrowded on the Saturday, and there was no other hall available in Blantyre, it was agreed that the next day the meeting should continue at a well-known meeting place a few miles out of Blantyre and just off the main road. It was there on January 25, under the gum trees, that an historic meeting took place. It became the subject of Government despatches, of a White Paper, and eventually a Commission of Enquiry headed by a judge and, inevitably, a debate in Parliament.

The meeting was mainly an organisational one and for that reason Dr Banda did not attend. The people who attended the meeting on January 25 were sworn to secrecy as it was the intention of the Congress leaders to start a passive resistance campaign, but as is usual at such gatherings, many other proposals were put forward, some in the general discussion and others probably in small groups. No one was allowed to take notes, although the officials were expected to report back to each of their branches. The discussions were conducted in two vernacular languages, but mainly in Chinyanja. One of the reasons Dr Banda did not attend these sessions was the fact that he could not understand the language and needed an interpreter.

One Congress man who was unable to understand what was going on was attending the meeting as official photographer. Thomas Karua had returned only a year before from Tanganyika, where he had lived most of his life, and was employed by Congress to take a film of the meeting. He also operated the Congress tape recording equipment and the microphone system. Although Karua was not a very important man in the Congress set up he later became a key witness for the Devlin Commission. Nothing much was known about the proceedings of the meeting on January 25 for several weeks, but when an official announcement was made it was a political blockbuster.

On Tuesday March 3 the state of emergency was declared in Nyasaland and Congress leaders by the hundreds were rounded up in the early hours of the morning, including Dr Hastings Banda dressed only in his pyjamas. Many of them were put on aeroplanes at Chileka airport and flown, handcuffed, to Southern Rhodesia.

That afternoon in the House of Commons Mr Lennox-Boyd made a dramatic announcement. After question time he sought the permission of the Speaker to announce to the House the Nyasaland state of emergency and said:

'. . . the situation continued to be so dangerous and there was such clear indication of the intention of the Congress to stir up further disturbances, involving widespread violence and murder of European,

Asian and moderate African leaders, that the Governor was compelled this morning to declare a state of emergency.'

Later that evening in the debate which was urgently called by the Opposition, he is recorded in Hansard as saying:

'As I said earlier today, some days ago information came to the notice of the Government of Nyasaland which was of a very serious kind. I have seen this information. I am not in a position to disclose it—(Hon. Members: 'Oh.')—nor its source. Nor would any responsible Minister do so, nor any right hon. Member opposite who has ever held high office. I commend that thought to the hon. Member for Cardiff, South-East, who has not as yet had that particular privilege. That information made it clear that plans had been made by Congress to carry out widespread violence and murder of Europeans, Asians and moderate African leaders; that, in fact, a massacre was being planned.'

His Under Secretary, Mr Amery, talked of a 'blood bath' and referred to Mau Mau in Kenya. Strangely enough, the Governor in Nyasaland made no announcement about a 'massacre' in his broadcast, nor in his circulars to District Officers, or the Chiefs, until several days later. Why the Colonial Secretary felt it necessary to announce a 'massacre' in Parliament when it had not yet been verified is a mystery which has not yet been solved. British public opinion was sceptical, but the Government turned down the Opposition demand for a Parliamentary Commission to Nyasaland to investigate the situation at first hand. Instead, a few weeks later, they announced the Commission of Enquiry which would be semi-judicial, composed of eminent men who were Conservatives, under Mr Justice Devlin.

Politicians and public alike awaited the Devlin Commission's report with an expectancy seldom exceeded; fifty MPs queued at the Vote Office for copies on the publication day in July 1959 and thousands of copies were sold to the public within hours.

While the Devlin Commission was writing its report the controversy about Federation still went on. Nyasaland Chiefs who were not members of Congress spoke and wrote against it. Sir Roy Welensky said that more had been done in the five-and-a-half years of Federation than was done in the previous sixty years of British rule in Nyasaland. In a reference to the Commission, he welcomed the investigations and said: 'I have no doubt that any report the Commission may make will serve to convince the ostriches and the cloud dwellers that the facts had better be faced now, rather than later. . . . Whatever facts the Commission may decide to publish as a result of its enquiry into the disturbances in Nyasaland, there are facts which are already common knowledge but which require restating because they have been mis-understood in the minds of some—and clear thinking is particularly important at this time when we are approaching the 1960 constitutional review.'

When the report arrived in Salisbury Sir Roy must have had the shock of his life, for it said that Nyasaland was a police state. (It had not been asked to comment about Southern Rhodesia.) On the first page of the Report, the Commission clearly says:

'The protection of privacy, essential to the Government, was needed just as much by many of the individuals who gave evidence before us. Nyasaland is—no doubt only temporarily—a police state, where it is not safe for anyone to express approval of the policies of the Congress party, to which before March 3, 1959 the vast majority of politically-minded Africans belonged, and where it is unwise to express any but the most restrained criticism of government policy.'

The Commission described the Africans' opposition to Federation and their answer to the case for 'economic advantages':

'They want above all else self-government for the black people in Nyasaland such as they have seen happening in other parts of Africa. They think that under the British Government they may eventually get it and that under Federation they never will. They do not seriously address their minds to the economic problems which will arise if Nyasaland leaves the Federation; they have not thought out financial plans for making ends meet without the £3,000,000 that comes from Federation. All that will provide for itself when the time comes; and anyway poverty is better than slavery.'

The Commission then told the Nyasaland Government and Welensky where they were wrong:

'The Government's view is that these nationalist aspirations are the thoughts of only a small minority of political Africans, mainly of self-seekers who think that their prospects of office will be worse under Federation; and that the great majority of the people are indifferent to the issue. We have not found this to be so. In the first place we do not think that all the Congress leaders have more than the usual share of personal ambition; they are first and foremost fervent African nationalists. Secondly, the issue touches, or appears to touch the African, whether he is educated or uneducated, on a point where he is particularly sensitive. For the educated African, that point is the feeling that he is looked on as an inferior being and treated at best as a second-class citizen. The partly educated, who have been to Southern Rhodesia and to the Union of South Africa as labourers in the way we have described, dislike the ways and attitudes which they have seen there. For the completely uneducated, it is fear for his land. The land for him is his means of subsistence and his constant suspicion is that in some way or another the settler would like to take it away from him. Federation means the domination of Southern Rhodesia; the domination of Southern Rhodesia means the domination of the settler; the domination of the settler means the perpetuation of racial inferiority and of the threat to the Africans' land; that is the argument. We have heard intelligent criticisms of Southern Rhodesian policies towards the African.'

To those who had refused to recognise the antagonism to Federation it said:

'. . . it was generally acknowledged that the opposition to Federation was there, that it was deeply rooted and almost universally held. We found it to be so. Even among the chiefs, many of whom are loyal to the Government and dislike Congress methods, we have not heard of a single one who is in favour of Federation. Witness after witness appeared before us for the sole purpose of stating that the cause of all the troubles we were investigating was Federation.'

Then, referring to the dilemma of the Africans, it said:

'The Government says that it cannot and will not go back upon Federation; it treats the question as one that is no longer open. Congress on the other hand believes that in its opposition to Federation it is supported by the whole of African opinion. The frustration which Congress felt is due to the fact that on this issue chiefly, but on all other issues as well, there is no way in which constitutionally it can make its views effective. In the Legislative Council it is of course constantly outvoted.'

The Commission found that 'violent action was to be adopted as a policy, that breaches of the law were to be committed and that attempts by the Government to enforce it were to be resisted with violence.' It also found that there was talk of beating and killing Europeans, but not of cold-blooded assassination or massacre, and said, 'we do not think that there is anything that can be called a plot nor, except in a very loose sense of the word, a plan. Branches were encouraged to resist the enforcement of the law and ways were suggested; but we do not think that anything more detailed than that was planned.' It therefore 'rejected the evidence, such as it is, for the murder plot' and also said that Dr Banda would never have approved a policy of murder and 'would have intervened decisively if he had thought that it was so much as being discussed.'

The Commission criticised the Nyasaland Government for the use of illegal force in making arrests and commented, rather caustically, that it was outside its province to discuss 'whether sound administrative reasons can justify breaches of the law' on the part of the Government.

Reading the 140-page Report it is difficult to find favourable comments on the actions of the Nyasaland Government; such a Report from an officially-appointed Commission is without precedent. The unfavourable findings were rejected by the Conservative Government, and Mr Lennox-Boyd in the debate on July 28 in the House of Commons could quote from only one paragraph, the 166th, out of a total of 186, to support his attitude. That paragraph had recorded that the Congress had discussed and adopted a policy of violence. But also in the debate Mr Bevan pointed out that 'discussions about violence and threats of violence have come from the very persons to whom the Government propose to entrust the Nyasas'. Lord Malvern, speaking in the Federal Assembly in September 1956, said: 'We have complete control over our own Defence Forces. I only hope we shall not have to use them as the North American Colonies had to use theirs, because we are dealing with a stupid Government in the United Kingdom.'

Bevan referred also to Sir Roy Welensky, who said in 1957: 'We go forward to the Conference Table in 1960 firmly believing that the achievements of the Federation fully justify the granting of independence. Should we fail to convince Her Majesty's Government of the justice of that, this will be the time to take stock and decide what other action is necessary. I, personally, would never be prepared to accept that the Rhodesians have less guts than the American Colonists had.'

Bevan challenged the Colonial Secretary to mention 'anything that Dr Banda has said which is more provocative than that'.

After he had given evidence, Karua, one of the key witnesses to the Commission, had flown back to England to tell a fantastic story. He said that soon after he arrived in Khami prison, Bulawayo, the Nyasaland Special Branch officers asked him to make a statement confirming the 'massacre plot' story. At first he refused, but later agreed to do it after he had spoken to his fellow detainees, who told him that he was the only one who could do what the police asked and get out of Nyasaland, via Tanganyika, as he held a Tanganyikan passport. According to Karua, after he had done what the police wanted he was flown back to Blantyre and signed a statement confirming that the massacre plot had been arranged at the meeting on January 25, although, he

says, it was well known to the police that he did not understand the vernacular languages in which the meetings had taken place. He told them
that if there had been a murder plot he would certainly have been told
about it by some of the Congress officials. His story was carefully
checked by the Government officers, who also set up a model court so
that Karua could practise giving evidence. He then went before the
Devlin Commission and told them his faked story, watched by the
Government Law Officer who guided him through his evidence.

When the Devlin Commission returned to Nyasaland they asked to
see Karua again and it was then that one of the Commissioners, Mr
Williams, suspected that Karua was telling lies. After this Karua, who
had been paid by the police and kept in police accommodation during
this period, had fares paid for his wife, newly-born child and himself, to
fly to Tanganyika. When he arrived there he went to Julius Nyerere
and obtained help to fly to London, where again he appeared before the
Devlin Commission and changed his previous story completely,
admitting that it was a pack of lies.

Although Karua was not the principal witness of the Government he
was the main corroborator of the chief informer. The Commission, in a
masterly understatement, call him an unreliable witness, but the
Government has not yet accounted for the way Karua was used by
them as a main witness.

Also attending the meeting on January 25 was George Nyandoro
from Southern Rhodesia, following up the policy of close co-ordination
between the two movements. At the Executive meeting which followed
the meeting I addressed in Bulawayo, George gave a report of the
Nyasaland meeting, but his report contained no reference to violence
and no reference to any murder plans. When the official announcements
were made describing the Nyasaland Congress's plans for violence and
discussing the so-called murder plot, George's colleagues in the
leadership of the Southern Rhodesia Congress were as surprised as
anyone else. They were angry too, because they thought that George
had been misleading them and keeping information back which he
should have told them at their own meeting.

By this time they were all in Khami prison themselves, having been
arrested in the Southern Rhodesian state of emergency. When detainees
began arriving from Blantyre they saw their chance to get at the truth.
They found out which of the Nyasas had attended the meeting on
January 25 and conducted their own 'Devlin' enquiry within the prison,
for they had to convince themselves that George had not been lying
and that the Nyasaland Congress had not broken the Accra resolution

of non-violence. Their investigations were thorough and eventually they convinced themselves that George had given them a full report and that there was no murder plot.

Meanwhile, in the House of Commons, Mr Macmillan announced on 21 July 1959 the setting up of a Commission which would have the following terms of reference:

'In the light of the information provided by the Committee of Officials and of any additional information the Commission may require, to advise the five Governments, in preparation for the 1960 review, on the constitutional programme and framework best suited to the achievement of the objects contained in the Constitution of 1953, including the Preamble.'

The structure of the Commission, with only six Members (and all Privy Councillors) from the UK Parliament but thirteen chosen by the Central African Governments, gave no confidence to the Africans. Lord Monckton was appointed Chairman, but most Africans decided to boycott it although they were quite prepared to co-operate with a genuine Parliamentary Commission. The Labour Party also refused to nominate members as the Commission had to work within the 'framework' of Federation and the secession of Nyasaland could not even be considered. Both the Africans and the Labour Party justifiably suspected Welensky's influence on the Macmillan Government. Sir Roy had made no bones about his dislike of interfering British Parliamentarians. He said he was not prepared to be put on trial and when Lord Home had flown out to consult him about the idea of the Commission he had made clear that it could be appointed only if there were representatives on it appointed by the Governments of Central Africa and if its terms of reference did not put the Federation's future in jeopardy. The composition was heavily weighted in favour of Government nominees, who would support Federation, and even the five African members could not be considered representative. Mr Gaitskell, in one of his best speeches in the Commons, said that they would be regarded by their fellow Africans as 'stooges' and Mr Callaghan said that they would be known as 'quislings'.

Certainly this reflects the attitude of Nyasa Africans, who remain intensely suspicious of the Government; anyone who co-operates with it is regarded as a traitor. When Chipembere and Chiume were expelled from the Legislative Council for their Congress activities the Governor announced that not only would they be replaced but that there would be an additional two Africans, as though this was an example of great reform. The Africans were not impressed as the new Members were to be *appointed* by the Governor himself rather than elected; in fact the Governor found it very difficult to find nominees and two in the first list resigned very soon after their appointment.

Soon after his release, in August 1959, from the Southern Rhodesian gaol where he had been imprisoned for five months, Mr Orton Chirwa —Nyasaland's only African barrister—formed the Malawi Congress Party, with virtually the same objects as the banned Congress; within a few weeks it had a paid-up membership of fifteen thousand.

If Mr Iain Macleod, the Colonial Secretary, wants a peaceful solution to Nyasaland he will give Malawi more consideration than his predecessor gave to Congress, and, if he is wise, he will allow Dr Banda to return from prison to lead it. Banda has become a symbol to Nyasaland, and as long as he is a martyr the Government will be unable to obtain the co-operation of the Africans.

*   *   *   *

In Southern Rhodesia Sir Edgar Whitehead had not bothered to announce massacre plots to justify the rounding up of hundreds of Africans and he needed only to give vague justifications to his tame Parliament to have them unanimously accepted. The arrest of the Congress members took place only three days after I had flown out of Salisbury and waved goodbye to Paul, Robert and George. Thousands of police and Rhodesian Regiment troops were put on to the job of detaining men, women and children.

Patrick Matimba, who was living in the town of Salisbury with his Dutch wife, had special attention. No less than nine policemen, including two Europeans, knocked him up at 3 o'clock in the morning. When he asked for explanations none were given. He thought at first that he would be spending only a night for interrogation and then would be allowed to return home, but his detention lasted five months. In the end he was released only on condition that he left Rhodesia with his family to live in Holland.

Paul Mushonga's wife and child were also put into prison and were not released until nine months later.

Sir Edgar Whitehead announced to the Southern Rhodesian Parliament that he intended to take permanent powers to control subversion in the territory. When the bills were published they raised a storm of protests from University lecturers at Salisbury University, from the Church authorities, and even a few squeaks from the Dominion Party, making a strange alliance in opposition. The bills were only slightly amended and their repressive character remained. Under the Unlawful

Organisations Act of 1959, all the African political parties were banned, including, ironically enough, the Northern Rhodesian African National Congress whose leader, Harry Nkumbula, is a Member of the Legislative Council and was 'our Harry' to Sir Arthur Benson. But if Nkumbula steps over the border into Southern Rhodesia he will be arrested immediately or deported.

One of the advantages of Federation is supposed to be freedom of movement, but this privilege is not extended to those African politicians who have not been arrested and is withheld from an increasing number of visitors from overseas. Under the Unlawful Organisations Act it is an offence to wear any badge or to shout any slogan associated with a proscribed movement. Strictly speaking, anyone shouting 'Freedom' is committing an offence, and the famous Moral Re-Armament film of that name and the expensive brochure which describes it should logically be banned in Southern Rhodesia.

It is also assumed in the Act that any person attending a meeting of a proscribed organisation is a member of it and will be charged unless he can prove otherwise. This provision must make it very difficult for African police informers; what protection can they now have if in the course of their duties they attend proscribed meetings?

The Native Affairs Amendment Act imposes severe penalties on Africans living in the Reserves. No one is allowed to hold a meeting of more than twelve people without special permission from the Native Affairs Commissioner, unless he is a Federal Member of Parliament. It is therefore impossible for an African to have normal social relationships with a group of friends. Any African 'insolent' to a European officer is also guilty of an offence punishable by a £50 fine (which is more than a year's income to most Africans) or six months in jail. If Mr Justice Devlin and his colleagues can describe Nyasaland as a 'police state', one wonders what description they would accord Southern Rhodesia. Others have called Southern Rhodesia 'fascist' and 'Hitler-like'.

The other Act in this notorious trio, the Preventive Detention Act, is a measure which clothes ruthless repression with Parliamentary legality. Under it any person can be detained for up to five years without trial. An appeal can be made to a tribunal but notwithstanding anything which this Government-appointed tribunal might report, the Government's decision is final.

Under the 1923 Southern Rhodesian Constitution the United Kingdom Government has the power, through the Governor, to control this legislation, particularly discriminatory clauses. The relevant parts of the Constitution, The Royal Letters Patent 1923, are worth quoting.

'28. Unless he shall have previously obtained Our instructions upon such Law through a Secretary of State, or unless such Law shall contain a clause suspending the operation thereof until the signification in the Colony of Our pleasure thereupon, the Governor shall reserve—

(*a*) any Law, save in respect of the supply of arms, ammunition or liquor to natives, whereby natives may be subject or made liable to any conditions, disabilities or restrictions to which persons of European descent are not also subjected or made liable;

(*b*) any Law which may repeal, alter or amend, or is in any way repugnant to or inconsistent with such provisions of these Our Letters Patent, as may under these Our Letters Patent be repealed or altered by the Legislature.

'30. No Law passed by the Legislature shall take effect until either the Governor shall have assented thereto in Our name and on Our behalf, and shall have signed the same in token of such assent, or until We shall have given Our assent thereto by Our Order in Our Privy Council.

'31. It shall be lawful for Us, Our heirs and successors, to disallow any Law within one year from the date of the Governor's assent thereto, and such disallowance, on being made known by the Governor by Speech or Message to the Legislative Council and the Legislative Assembly, or by Proclamation in the *Gazette* shall annul the Law from the day when the disallowance is so made known.'

This power has never been exercised, but as Mr Cuthbert Alport, who became Conservative Minister of State for Commonwealth Relations, says in his book, *Hope in Africa*: 'Many people assume that it has therefore ceased to be effective. This is not true. Any laws passed by the Southern Rhodesian Parliament, falling under Sections 28 and 40 of the Letters Patent, are in fact referred to the Secretary of State for Commonwealth Affairs and have, under Governments of various political complexions since 1937, been approved by him.'

It has been a convention for the UK Government to be advised of legislation in advance, and on some occasions amendments have been suggested before the bills were published, but for the repressive and other recent Acts this procedure was not followed. Nevertheless, it was possible for the UK Government to intervene and it was asked to do so by 120 Labour and Liberal Members of Parliament who wanted the repressive Acts annulled. The Government, however, refused to intervene and by its collusion has condoned fascist legislation in a British Colony.

20

1960 and After

THE Conference, in 1960, on the future of the Federation will be concerned with more than structure of government, systems of franchise, or other aspects of constitutional manipulation. It will charter the lives and hopes of nearly eight million people; and its decisions will be of immense significance to the rest of Africa. On the west coast Africans with their newly-won independence are watching closely what happens in Central Africa and the leaders of African countries with a longer history of independence are also concerned. Even Haille Selassie has made a forthright declaration in his African Freedom Day message:

'The tide which is sweeping Africa today cannot be stayed. No power on earth is great enough to halt or reverse the trend. Its march is as relentless and inexorable as the passage of time. The day is long overdue for a change of attitude on the part of those nations which have heretofore sought to hinder or impede this movement or which have been content in the past to remain passive in the face of the impassioned cries for freedom, for justice, for the right to stand with their fellow men as equals among equals, which have gone up from this Continent.'

Or, as President Tubman of Liberia put it, 'You cannot sit on the momentum of freedom.'

Africans will not be party to the illogicality of allowing Nigerians on the West and Somalis on the East independence in 1960 whilst in Central Africa their black brothers are held back. The pressure of the white settlers in Central Africa to achieve dominion status has confirmed the suspicions of Africans. When Sir Roy Welensky declared that in the event of trouble with the Labour Party he would 'go it alone', Africans were saying, 'Could there be a worse example of irresponsibility and lawlessness? Who is threatening violence now?' Welensky knew that the responsibility for legislating for the future of the Federation belongs to the United Kingdom Parliament, and, however much the white element may think it has a right to rule in

Central Africa, the British public and their elected representatives have to think of far wider considerations than the interests of only a minority of the Central African population.

The total of white settlers, 280,000, is less than 4 per cent of the population of the Federation, but their importance in the territories is, of course, far greater than their numbers signify. Practically all industry and commerce is European-owned and controlled and there are hundreds of technicians and engineers who are, at the moment, indispensable. But this does not, in the twentieth century, give them any right to political privilege. Indeed, it could be argued that particularly *because* Africans are poorer, less well-educated, and desperately in need of help, they are entitled to have a share in the political direction of the countries in which they live. They need the vote more than the Europeans, who have economic assets and technical skills at their disposal. The African workers on the Kariba dam site who went on strike with the slogan 'We will not die for fourpence an hour' would never have had Federal troops flown into the area to intimidate them if they had been voters.

Government can never succeed in altruism unless that altruism corresponds to that of the electorate. Missionaries and teachers need it, but politicians depend on votes and if the votes are mainly those of a privileged section any altruism which existed in the heart of the politician withers away as a plant in the waterless desert. There is nothing to feed it, and altruistic politicians are dismissed, like Garfield Todd, to wander in the wilderness, hawking political ideals to audiences who are largely voteless.

When the white politicians of Central Africa like Welensky and Whitehead, who aspire to lead an independent dominion, boast about their 'interest' in Africans and their anxiety to achieve something they call 'partnership' they should remember that most people in and out of Africa are less gullible than they think. The platitudes of these politicians taste like stale cakes which have developed mildew underneath—they may look all right from a distance but when you pick them up they crumble with their rottenness. 'Partnership' does not exist in Central Africa and is never likely to exist until the colour bar in public places is removed, the colour bar in industrial employment is removed, racial segregation on the land is removed, and when every adult in Central Africa has the dignity of using a vote to elect representatives to speak on his or her behalf.

When Sir Roy asks for dominion status he is asking Britain to cut from her protection five million Africans in the two Protectorates.

Informed world opinion will ask, 'What have the Africans done to deserve that banishment from the protection of the British crown?' Until recently, the Nyasaland Africans, a hard-working people in an impoverished country, have been tranquil, passive, and happy—except for a short period of violence during the first world war. Thousands of them have gone hundreds of miles to work in factories and in the mines, helping to increase the wealth of the European companies and getting very little in return. Thousands also have served loyally in the armies in two world wars and those who have served with them give them much credit for their courage and steadfastness. The recent troubles in Nyasaland, during which not a single European was killed, were due to an unrelenting opposition to the enforced Federation of their country with the Rhodesias. The masses are not interested in the economic arguments for Federation. They suspect that most of the economic advantages from development will flow to the white settlers and to the white investors anyway. They are probably right. The figures for the copper mines in Northern Rhodesia and for manufacturing industries in the Federation as a whole certainly confirm many suspicions, and so do the actual details of wages paid. The average income in industry is £1,136 per annum for Europeans and only £73 per annum for Africans. Moreover, this does not take into account the poverty of the peasants.

The Nyasas admit that thousands of their people have to travel to the two Rhodesias to seek work, but thousands of them go to the Union of South Africa too. Would that be an argument for federating Nyasaland with the Union of South Africa? Southern Rhodesia also has an influx of African labour from the Portuguese colonies of Mozambique and Angola. Is that an argument for federating these two colonies with Rhodesia? It is said that Nyasaland, through Federation, has obtained subsidies to enable more schools to be opened and health facilities to be extended. Against that, because health is a Federal responsibility and many of those working in the Nyasaland Health Department, both African and European, have refused to become Federal civil servants, there has been a loss on that side as, in large numbers, they have left the service altogether.

Where does the subsidy of £4,000,000—£5,000,000 a year come from? It comes largely from the taxation obtained from the copper exploitation in Northern Rhodesia, where thousands of Nyasas work at low wages, and are making their contribution in that way to the subsidy to their own country. It is the height of hypocrisy for the Federal Government to take money from one British Protectorate, pay it to another, and then claim all the credit. But when seen against the needs of a poor country like Nyasaland the subsidy itself is quite inadequate. It is only 5 per cent of what is paid to the Sheik of Kuwait by Britain for oil. It is small in comparison with the amounts that the industrialised West, through the Special United Nations Fund for Economic Development (SUNFED), the Colonial Development and Welfare Scheme, and other agencies, should be channelling into Nyasaland. If the subsidy paid by Rhodesia, through Federation, to Nyasaland is ever cut because that country is allowed to secede, there should be at least a dozen other ways which could, together, provide even more than that amount to assist the impoverished Nyasa people.

The real arguments for including Nyasaland in the Federation have never been economic, they have been political. Nyasaland was brought into the Federal scheme because the white settlers of Southern Rhodesia could never countenance an independent black Ghana so near to their borders. Besides, they wanted some insulation against the rising tide of nationalism in Tanganyika and further north. But now the tide is nearer than they think; it is rising high in the Belgian Congo, where the Africans are preparing for democratic self-determination. There are even rumblings in the two Portuguese colonies, poised either side of the Rhodesias like two great volcanoes and likely to erupt within the next decade.

There are certainly few geographical reasons for the Federation between Nyasaland and Rhodesia. The common frontier is in a very remote area and there is no physical link between Nyasaland and Southern Rhodesia. There is not even a reliable all-weather road to connect Northern Rhodesia and Nyasaland, and there is no railway link. When aircraft fly from Salisbury or Bulawayo to Blantyre they fly for miles over Mozambique. It is only an accident of European history that Nyasaland is now connected with the Rhodesias. For the Africans it would be much more logical to be linked to Tanganyika, or perhaps, eventually, to an African Mozambique. Already, Julius Nyerere has said that Tanganyika Africans would be willing to have Nyasaland linked with them; although they are both poor countries this would be a far happier relationship than a shot-gun marriage with Rhodesia.

'Ah, but,' say the pundits, 'if Nyasaland is allowed to secede, then the Africans of Northern Rhodesia will demand the same privilege.' Why not? If the Africans in Northern Rhodesia don't want to be linked with Southern Rhodesia why should they be made to do so? The economic argument will not work in this case since the Northern

Rhodesian economy, with its copper, is strong enough to stand on its own. It will become even stronger as the copper companies undertake their imaginative scheme to develop the Kafue flats, which will, if fully successful, produce agricultural products worth £100,000,000 a year. This, added to the £100,000,000 worth of copper, will give Northern Rhodesia an economic strength equalled by few African territories. If the Africans in Northern Rhodesia prefer a Federation with Nyasaland and Tanganyika, which some day may extend to include Kenya and Uganda, why should they be denied it?

'Oh, but the Federation has lasted too long to be broken up': this will be the last but one ditch of the defenders. 'Think of the Kariba Scheme, in which Federation has become so much involved; think of the Rhodesian Railways, now a Federal responsibility; how are these things going to be unscrambled?' So the argument will run. But it should not be beyond the wit of man to evolve a structure of economic co-operation between the territories as may be necessary to support Kariba and suchlike, without outright political Federation, just as it has been possible in Europe to achieve economic co-ordination without the sacrifice of political sovereignty.

But we have reached the last ditch and the last shots are still to be fired by the advocates of Central African Federation. Out come the crocodile tears of the professional altruists. The final heartrending appeal they will make will not be about economic co-ordination or political federation, or complicated things like that; they will put their hands on their hearts and say, 'Why don't you think of the poor African in Southern Rhodesia? If you leave Southern Rhodesia isolated like a political adolescent searching for a home she will have to look towards the South—and there lurks the horror of Afrikanerdom and "apartheid".'

But Southern Rhodesian whites will not be forced to choose absorption into South Africa if the links north of the Zambezi have been cut. In the first place the white Southern Rhodesians, who are mainly British, will not want to be linked with the Boer south. In the second place the Boers won't want them. They have trouble enough dealing with 9,000,000 Africans in their own boundaries and in South-West Africa and will not want to take on another 2,000,000. In the third place, the Africans in Southern Rhodesia would not be much worse off, if at all, in the Union of South Africa than they are now. They have 'apartheid' in land already. All of them, except a handful, are denied the vote—it will be no change for them to be voteless. And to all intents and purposes, the colour bar is the same.

Of all the Africans I met in Southern Rhodesia only two or three thought that the Federation was worth while as a way of stopping their absorption into South Africa. The others said it made no difference to them whether they were linked with South Africa or linked with the Federation or remained as Southern Rhodesia, as all were equally abhorrent if the African did not have the vote. They said, indeed, that Africans south of the Zambezi would be most unlikely to achieve the human rights and the vote to which they aspired unless Africans in the two Protectorates won the campaign for these aims in their own countries.

Fourthly, Britain decides what happens to the Southern Rhodesian Constitution as Southern Rhodesia is still a colony, subject for constitutional change to legislation in the United Kingdom Parliament. In short, she could not, except unconstitutionally, join the Union of South Africa without Britain's permission.

Sir Roy Welensky, despite all the arguments against Federation in its present form, continues in his latest speeches to demand Dominion status from the Constitutional Conference. But if Dominion status is granted before the Africans have an entrenched stake in the political field as voters, the damage to race relations would be incalculable; the Federation would follow the example of the Union of South Africa and what African rights there are would be whittled away by the increasing influence of settlers whose conception of white security only makes sense in terms of complete domination over blacks. As it is, the white politicians by their bluff talk have alienated black opinion almost beyond redemption. If the white settlers in Central Africa are sincere about wanting 'partnership' with the Africans, and if they really want Federation to continue and to be a success, they could give some practical demonstration of their sincerity.

They could, for instance, propose an adaptation of the scheme which has proved so successful in Tanganyika in helping to solve the problems of a multi-racial country. They could propose, as an interim measure, a Federal Assembly of sixty with, say, twenty-eight African Members, twenty-eight European Members, and four for other communities, elected on a common roll with a reasonable franchise qualification—like the £150 per annum income in Tanganyika— selected in twenty-eight constituencies with each elector using two votes, one for a European candidate and one for an African candidate. In the four constituencies where another minority was resident, they would use three votes, the third being for an Asian.

This system would ensure a fair cross-voting and a more than generous representation for Europeans in the Federal Assembly. There could then be a trial period of between three and five years, during which time the Africans in the two Protectorates could be given confidence in the idea of Federation by realising that African electors were playing a part in determining policy. During that time the Federal powers over immigration and health should be transferred back to the Protectorates and this would also capture the goodwill of Africans. Europeans might well wake up one glorious morning and find that instead of having to bludgeon millions of recalcitrant Africans into Federation they would have hopeful, happy and eager 'partners' in an enterprise of building up a genuine non-racial democracy.

This kind of policy is immeasurably more in the interests of the white settler families in Central Africa than the rushed, rash actions of Welensky or the foolish talk by Lord Malvern of military action, which would be as abortive as Dr Jameson's raid on the Transvaal. Their interests, individually, are every bit as important as the interests of the individual African family and their future in Central Africa could be a creative, purposeful one. But it certainly cannot be happy if the African masses all around them have to be goaded into submission. A new dynamism is needed in Central Africa if the white settlers are to live out their lives in peace and happiness and it must be a dynamism directed towards non-racial democracy and genuine partnership.

If, because of the narrow, parochial-minded policies which have been perpetrated by some white politicians over the last few decades, the average white Rhodesian is unable to grasp the need for the new dynamism, then the U.K., as the protecting power, has a duty to provide it in the interests of the two races and of all the individual families concerned. The task of Britain in these circumstances is the most difficult one it has to pursue, among all the retreats from colonialism in which it has been engaged since the war; most difficult because in other territories like India, Burma, Ceylon and Ghana representative institutions were in existence when the transfer of power took place. In Malaya the task was more complicated because of the different races living in the peninsula, but even there the experiment has succeeded because Chinese and Indians, along with the Malayans, have been given equal political rights and a successful inter-racial political alliance has been developed.

In Central Africa, however, the problem is complicated by a factor which has not been present in any other nation granted independence. There is a white settler minority, mainly emanating from

Great Britain, with entrenched interests in the territory. The problem is difficult, but Britain cannot shirk it; and it is not solved by listening only to the persuasive arguments of the whites. The problem can only be solved if new ideas can sweep away the shibboleths of the past. If Federation breaks up because the white settlers will not accept a sane alternative to the maelstrom of conflicts which now exists then they have only themselves to blame. The Africans are not against Federation on principle and their leaders are intelligent enough to understand that association between countries is valuable. At the Accra Conference they approved the idea of federation between African countries and were anxious to stimulate it—but they cannot accept a Federation which leaves the Africans in an inferior position in a country where they comprise 97 per cent of the population.

But, whatever the white settlers may do, in their wisdom or un-wisdom, the responsibility is still with Britain. The facts Britain must judge. They are: firstly, that the overwhelming majority of Africans in Northern Rhodesia and an almost unanimous African population in Nyasaland are opposed to Federation in its present form. Secondly, that even the white minority in Southern Rhodesia is deeply divided about Federation. When the last territorial election took place the Dominion Party candidates, representing a policy opposed to the Welensky concept of Federation, polled more first preference votes than the UFP. The number of Southern Rhodesian electors supporting the UFP policy for Federation is only a minority of the minority.

In these circumstances Britain cannot transfer her responsibilities and, in the interests of future relationships with Africa, should continue to exercise ultimate control in Central Africa until genuinely repre-sentative institutions have been established.

It is commonplace to say Africa is on the march. The pace of change is so great that it is now not a question of *whether* Africans will be running Africa, but *how soon?* The evolution of Africa from the backwardness of the primitive to the scientific civilisation of the twentieth century is taking only decades whereas in Europe it took centuries. It is not for us to say that Africans may be happier in a primitive state, as though Africa were some great garden of Eden, because Africa can no longer be cut off from the world outside; it is being pounded with a barrage of ideas and Africans themselves are eager for the new opportunity.

The political developments are as dramatic as the economic and as important. The African who has been brought up to obey a Chief or a clan head realises that his vote gives him power to dispose of the powerful. He may use his first vote fumblingly, but he soon realises from the lively personalities pleading for his support that his vote is valuable and this produces a change in his own political outlook. Instead of obeying the whim of the ruler he has become an individual in his own right, recognised as such by the community around him and able to begin that process of self education through which everyone passes before he reaches citizenship.

What can we in the west do? This is not the time to sentimentalise about the African as though he is merely the simple savage needing our paternal protection. He is past that. He wants democracy, self respect, and independence from colonialism. He does not want to be exploited as cheap labour, nor to be ruled by a white minority.

We must not expect Africans to pay the price of violence to obtain what they have been taught to expect as their natural rights. Violence will create deep bitterness and hatred between the races and between Africans and will make it easy for African autocracies to seize power. As democracies are more likely to succeed in a relatively tranquil situation we should help Africans to move towards self-determination as smoothly as possible, allowing for the growth of a wide diversity of organisations as well as representative assemblies.

For the minorities of Asians and Europeans it is just as important that this natural evolution towards democracy should take place. They will be safer and happier in a well balanced society where there is government based on consent rather than in one in which they are engaged in a perpetual struggle to keep themselves on top. They must recognise the inevitable in Africa, and we must help them to come to terms with it before time runs out.

Index

Accra Conference, 126, 213-4
Acholi, 67
Aden, 21-2
African Mineworkers Union, 175-6
African Affairs Board, 209
African Daily News, 151, 165
Aguthi Detention Camp, 131, 133
Ainsley, Rosalynde, 188
Albert, Lake, 65
Alport, Cuthbert, MP, 205, 224
Amery, Julian, MP, 208, 216
Amin, Mr, 125
Arabia, 22
Armitage, Sir Robert, 196
Ash, Mr, 176
Asians in Uganda, 90-4
Asian Association (Tanganyika), 136, 141
Attlee, Mr, 15
Atura, 65
Auschwitz, 115

Baganda, 37-41
Bamangwato, 25
Banda, Dr Hastings Kamuzu, 190, 211-2, 218-9, 222
Barnes, Gorell, 181
Baring, Sir Evelyn, 131
Barrow, Sir Malcolm, 194-5
Basude, Leonard, 90
Bataka Party, 41
Batonka, 173
Bebetiti, Miss, 138
Bechuanaland, 25
Beckett, Mr, 182
Belgian Congo, 60, 68
Belsen, 115
Bennett, Mr, 140
Bennett, F., MP, 208
Benson, Sir Arthur, 190, 195, 197, 223
Bevan, Aneurin, MP, 219

Binaisa, Godfrey, 14
Bomani, Paul, 137
Boswell, Mr, 129
Bledisloe Commission, 206
Blundell, Michael, 130
Briggs, Group Captain, 130
British East Africa Company, 38
Broken Hill, 150
Brockway, Fenner, MP, 5, 15, 19, 42, 87
Brown, K. E., 145
Buchenwald, 115
Buganda, 37, 38-41, 49
Bukoba Co-operative Union, 137
Bulawayo, 150, 162-3
Bundibugyo, 99
Bunsen, Bernhard de, 60
Bunyoro, 39, 64
Burma Market, 28, 29
Burton, 15
Busoga, 79
Butler, R. A., MP, 193
Bwete, Eriza, 43

Callaghan, James, MP, 203, 214
Cameron, Mr, 129
Campbell, Alexander, 108
Capital Club, 148
Capricorn Africa Society, 148
Carter Commission, 145
Castle, Barbara, MP, 168, 196
Catchpole, Len, 189
Cazziol, Dr R., 63, 81, 83-4
Central Africa Party, 154
Central African Examiner, 186
Central African Federation: *see* Federation of Rhodesia and Nyasaland
Central African Post, 150
Chamber of Mines, 173, 190
Chamberlain Government, 134

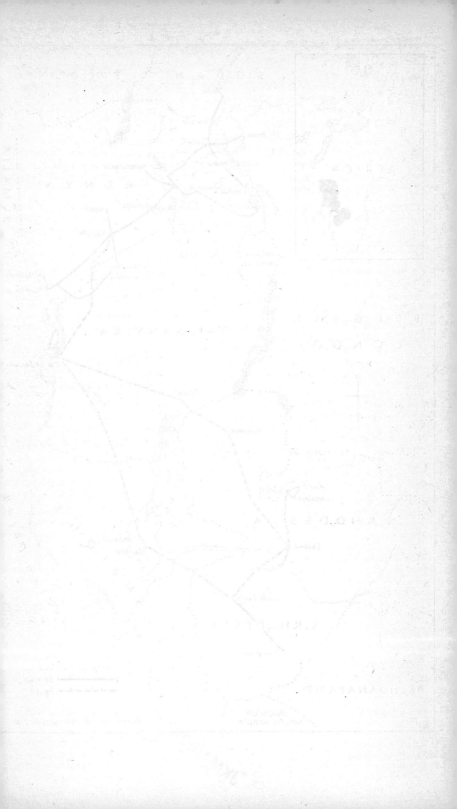